WALL
STREET
JOURNAL
BOOKS

A HEART,
A CROSS,
AND A FLAG

AMERICA TODAY

Peggy Noonan

A WALL STREET JOURNAL BOOK
Published by Free Press
New York   London   Toronto   Sydney   Singapore

WALL
STREET
JOURNAL
BOOKS

A WALL STREET JOURNAL BOOK
Published by Free Press
Rockefeller Center
1230 Avenue of the Americas
New York, NY 10020

For information regarding special discounts for bulk purchases,
please contact Simon & Schuster Special Sales:
1-800-456-6798 or business@simonandschuster.com.

DESIGNED BY KRIS TOBIASSEN

Manufactured in the United States of America

1 3 5 7 9 10 8 6 4 2

Library of Congress Cataloging-in-Publication Data
Noonan, Peggy, date.
A heart, a cross & a flag : America today / Peggy Noonan.
p. cm. — (A Wall Street Journal book)
Collection of articles published in the Wall Street Journal from Sept. 2001 to Sept. 2002.
1. United States—Politics and government—2001– 2. September 11 Terrorist Attacks,
2001—Influence. 3. National characteristics, American. 4. United States—Social
conditions—1980– 5. War on Terrorism, 2001– I. Title: Heart, a cross, and a flag.
II. Title. III. Series.

E903 .N66 2003

973.931—dc21   2003048336

ISBN 0-7432-5005-2

These articles were previously published individually in *The Wall Street Journal.*

For the ones who ran into the fire

Contents

Preface

This is a book about love. That's an odd thing to say about a collection that spans 9/11/01 to 9/11/02, and that centers on the attacks on America. But the primary emotion I felt in those days was a love, or a tender sense of appreciation, for everyone who played a part in the drama—the dead, the survivors, the firefighters and the heroes on the planes, the families left behind and their shaken neighbors down the block. For us. September 11 changed everyone, and for me, among the changes was one that had a professional impact. It liberated me to include in my work what I felt but had not always expressed: the idea that people are precious, that they're beautiful and deserving of honor and respect. And the knowledge that we are all brothers and sisters together, whatever our circumstances. Before 9/11, I held these convictions but they did not always seem pertinent, or appropriate, to what I was writing. But after 9/11, I felt free to say what I thought and let it frame my work, and even become an engine for that work.

I think that I have this in common with a lot of people. People always say we became better, more appreciative as a people after 9/11, especially New Yorkers. But I think the event simply left a lot of people feeling freer to be who they were, as if, in Os Guinness's phrase, tragedy cracked our hearts wide open and forced the beauty out.

· · ·

I call this book *A Heart, a Cross, and a Flag* because those were the things that rose from the rubble. The heart stands for those who were brave for others, and for the greater fellow feeling among our citizens that followed the collapse of the Towers and the bombing of the Pentagon. The cross stands for a rediscovered respect and gratitude for religious faith. The flag was the renewal of American patriotism that followed the terrible day. The heart and the cross on the cover were given to me by an iron worker named Larry Keating who ran, without orders or clearance, to the fallen towers early in the afternoon of 9/11, and was the last worker to leave when the takedown and cleanup were over, ten months later. The burn marks and the stress marks where the thick steel bent tell you where they are from. Larry was a reader of these pieces, and when he heard from a mutual friend that I was pouring coffee one night near Ground Zero he found me and handed me an old, beat-up paper bag. Inside were the heart and the cross. He had cut them from Tower Two.

The heart, the cross and the flag rose from the rubble and filled the clouds over the Trade Center, the Pentagon, and a blank Pennsylvania field. They rose with the smoke and entered the air all around us.

I haven't changed a word. These pieces were written on the run, starting the day the Towers were hit and continuing for fifty of the next fifty-two weeks. They are imperfect. But it seemed to me when I reread them that their flaws—of tone, language, and emphasis among other things—were true to the event, that they reflected the jaggedness of the time, and the fears and emotions it engendered. It just felt right to print them as they ran.

A number of thoughts and observations in this book became Officially Accepted Truths of the event and its aftermath, and were, to the best of my knowledge, said here for the first time. "God Is Back" spoke of the resurgence of religious feeling on the mean streets, "Welcome Back, Duke" celebrated the return of a certain kind of manhood, and "Courage Under Fire" attempted to make New York's firemen more nationally celebrated and understood. I feared early on that what they did was not getting serious enough attention in the country.

·   ·   ·

September 11 was also to an extraordinary degree a changer of individuals. For so many people it was a moment in which the points of their lives came together and made their importance clear. For others it was a kind of reckoning.

A lot of lives changed. I'm still seeing them change. You probably are too.

September 11 is a terrible story and a beautiful story. I'll never get over it and I'm glad I won't. This is a book for those who feel the same.

1

What I Saw at the Devastation

This, for me, is the unforgettable image of the day: the fine gray ash that covered everything downtown, all the people and buildings and cars; the ash that flew into the air in the explosions and the burning and that settled over half the city. It was just like Pompeii, which also was taken by surprise and also was left covered top to bottom with ash, fine gray ash.

This is what everyone in New York says, sooner or later, when they talk about what happened: "It was such a beautiful day. It was the most beautiful day of the year." It was. Clear stunning cloudless skies, warm but not hot, a breeze. It was so clear that everyone in town and Jersey and the outer boroughs—everyone could see the huge, thick plumes and clouds of black and gray smoke. Everyone could see what happened.

And when it began, everyone was doing something innocent. It was morning in New York in the fall and workers were getting coffee and parents were taking their children to school.

And yet: For all the horror we are lucky. If you are reading these words you are among the beneficiaries of great good fortune. Those of us who were not in the World Trade Center or the Pentagon or nearby, those of us who were not among the terrified victims on the planes, those were not heroic firemen and tough cops—on a local TV show last night the reporter Dick Oliver was asked how it was that so many firemen died, couldn't they have escaped, and he said, with a rough voice that had love in it, "Firemen

1

don't run out of buildings. Firemen run into buildings"—are blessed indeed.

And not only because we are alive. We are lucky because for some reason—for some reason, and we don't even know what it was—the terrorists didn't use a small nuclear weapon floated into New York on a barge in the East River. We are lucky that this didn't turn nuclear, chemical or biological. It could have, and I thought the next time the bad guys hit it would have. Instead they used more "conventional" weapons, fuel-heavy airliners and suicide bombers. And so the number of dead will be in the thousands or tens of thousands and not millions or tens of millions.

We have been spared. And now, chastened and shaken, we are given another chance, maybe the last chance, to commit ourselves seriously and at some cost to protecting our country.

People were saying "This is like Pearl Harbor," but it wasn't Pearl Harbor. Our fleet wasn't taken out; we weren't attacked by a nation whose planes had clear markings; we lost 10,000 or 20,000 people, and they were civilians. If it has to be a movie, yesterday really to most of us in New York was *Titanic*. It was the end of a world, the drowning of illusions as brave men and women held hands and jumped; it was, I hope, the end of the assumptions that ease and plenty will continue forever, that we rich and powerful folk will be kept safe by our status, wealth and luck; it was the end of a culture of indifference to our nation's safety. Those Twin Towers, those hard and steely symbols of the towering city: they were the ship that God himself couldn't sink.

I was, like most of New York, very afraid. My sense from the beginning was: This isn't going to be over for a while. My son, fourteen, had just begun at a new high school in Brooklyn, just a stone's throw across the river from the World Trade Center. He'd left for the subway at 7:30. At 8:45 as I watched TV I saw the first explosion, and the breathtaking telephone report of a terrified man who had seen, he said, a big plane fly straight into one of the towers. "Oh my God," he said over and over, and it was like hearing the first report of the *Hindenburg*. I was still watching when something—I thought it was a helicopter—hit the second tower and it blew. And then minutes later the Pentagon.

Phones went down. I could not reach my son or his school. He's new there—no friends yet, no teachers he felt close to. And Manhattan was cordoned off; no one could get in. Should I go, try to walk to Brooklyn, try to get across the bridge? But what if he calls? If I don't answer he'll think I was hurt.

But the Internet did not go down, and I was comforted by instant messages from friends reporting in, e-mails from friends with information— the phones were down but the Net stayed up, and I kept it on all day. I thought a network or newspaper would be hit—the bad guys had targeted the great symbols of American power, the wealth of Wall Street, the military might of Washington. Now I thought: They will hit their much hated media. I sent an e to a friend at a newsmagazine: You guys may get hit, go home. I e'd word to my praying friends: Pray for the children at my son's school. They e'd back: Pray for my aunt at her school.

I waited by the phone, by the computer, hoping for word. The phone would ring and go dead, or I'd pick it up and get a busy signal.

I ran out, got cash at the bank, walked to Ninety-second Street and saw, with awe, that the clouds of smoke were visible all the way up here, five miles away. Trucks unloading food at restaurants and grocery stores were double- and triple-parked, their cab doors open, radios blaring. The Church of the Heavenly Rest, an Episcopal church in the neighborhood, immediately taped flyers to utility poles: "On this tragic day, come and pray."

Three hours later, at noon, my son got through. They had heard the explosions; the head of the high school had come in and said, "Please, peacefully, follow me downstairs." Most everyone was calm and purposeful; they gathered downstairs and listened to a radio. My son had a long line of kids behind him wanting to call home and he couldn't speak long. "I'm safe," he said. "We're all completely safe."

I told him the attacks seemed over—he covered the phone and yelled to the line, "My mother says the attacks seem to be over." I said it had all ended, he said, "She says it has ended." In times of crisis every American becomes an anchorman.

He told me with the offhand gallantry of a fourteen-year-old boy, "It looks like I'll be sleeping in Brooklyn tonight." The school took him and all the children who couldn't get home in, cared for them and sent them to the homes of teachers who lived nearby. My son was with a gaggle of boys at the French teacher's house. He had seen people sobbing on the subway in Brooklyn.

I walked over toward church after noon, and now the scene was silent and jarring. The sidewalks and gutters were jammed with an army of expressionless marchers going from downtown to uptown, silently trudging through the trafficless city.

Midday mass was pretty full, and people seemed stricken. I saw a neighbor I'd been trying to reach. "We're all fine," she said.

"Did a rat stand on its hind legs this morning?" I asked.

"No, and if it had, I would have run to your house to tell you."

Like so many in New York, she has feared a catastrophic terrorist event for years, the type from which you have to flee, quickly. Years ago she told me that she saw a rat in her neighborhood, and he had risen on his haunches and then scrambled away. For no reason she could remember, she said a prayer at that moment: "Dear Lord, if the big terrible thing is ever coming, will you warn me by having a rat rise like that?" She often prays this. I was very glad she had not seen the rat.

I walked by a local school yard. On the steps, a group of young tough kids who are often there playing a boom box. They have the look, the manner, of danger, and everyone says drugs are sold there. Yesterday they were on the steps, boom box blaring, only this time it was news reports telling us what was happening. The well-suited men and women marching by would stop and listen to the news, and then nod with thanks and leave. I listened for ten minutes and when I left I said "Thank you, gentlemen," and they smiled and said "Welcome." They were offering a public service.

In the afternoon I went to the home of a friend in midtown—again stunning silence, and the streets now empty of people and traffic. On the way home, in the early evening, I went to get on a bus, and as I went to put my fare card in, the driver said softly, "Free rides today."

The bus was jammed, and people had what Tom Wolfe calls "information compulsion": Everyone was talking about where they'd been, what they'd seen, "I was in the Trade Center at eight A.M. and left fifteen minutes later."

A funny moment: A seat opened up and we disagreed over who should get it. "Oh I don't need it." "No, I'm getting off in a minute." The courtesy made us all laugh. An elderly Englishwoman in a seat chatted with a young girl standing nearby. As the young girl left, she turned and said, "I'm so sorry you're seeing the city like this." The Englishwoman shook her head and put out her hands as if to say: *No, I am seeing the best.*

As I watched television I became aware, as everyone I've spoken to has mentioned along the way, that the great leaders in our time of trauma were the reporters and anchors and producers of the networks and news stations. What cool and fabulous work from Peter Jennings, Dan Rather and Tom Brokaw, what stunning work from Brit Hume and Aaron Brown, Katie Couric and Diane Sawyer, and the cameramen who took stupendous and dangerous pictures, and the guests like Richard Holbrooke and Norman Schwarzkopf and Tom Clancy, who added knowledge and context and well-grounded viewpoints. They all did that knowing it was dangerous where they were, knowing it could get worse, that the weapons or targets could change. They stood their ground and did their jobs.

Those anchors and reporters, they led us Tuesday, with cool and warmth, with intelligence and deep professionalism. And every one of them must have known he, or she, was one way or another in harm's way. These men and women of the media should all get a mass Medal of Freedom the next time it's given. They really helped our country.

The night of the attack my son got through to me again, and he told me more of what he'd seen and then he told me, just before he rang off, of the amazing thing he'd seen. At dusk, as the sun was going down over the city, he looked over at Manhattan. The rays of the sun hit the smoke and debris floating in the air, hit it strong and at an angle, and it all reflected on the water of the river and the light it produced was beautiful. "It looked golden," he said. "It was all the color of gold."

Even in horror there is beauty to be seen, even in trauma there is strength to be gained, and at the heart of every defeat is the seed of a future victory. After the *Titanic* sank, they reformed international maritime law, mandating enough lifeboats for passengers and constant radio contact.

And that is what we must do now, that is where the golden lining can be:

We must admit that we have ignored the obvious, face the terrible things that can happen, decide to protect ourselves with everything from an enhanced intelligence system to a broad and sturdy civil-defense system, with every kind of defense that can be imagined by man, from vaccines to a missile defense.

For the next time, and there will of course be a next time, the attack likely won't be "conventional."

2

There Is No Time,
There Will Be Time

TUESDAY, SEPTEMBER 18, 2001

(Editor's note: In the summer of 1998 Ms. Noonan wrote this essay for the magazine Forbes ASAP. *It was published in the November 30, 1998, issue, devoted to the subject of time—how we experience time, how modern men and women relate to it in ways that might be different from our predecessors. Ms. Noonan has received many requests for reprints since the events in New York the past week. She loves* Forbes ASAP *too but thought most of her readers were more likely to find it here.)*

I suppose it is commonplace to say it, but it's true: There is no such thing as time. The past is gone and no longer exists, the future is an assumption that has not yet come, all you have is the moment—this one—but it too has passed . . . just now. The moment we are having is an awfully good one, though. History has handed us one of the easiest rides in all the story of man. It has handed us a wave of wealth so broad and deep that it would be almost disorienting if we thought about it a lot, which we don't.

But: We know such comfort! We sleep on beds that are soft and supporting, eat food that is both good and plentiful. We touch small levers and heat our homes to exactly the degree we desire; the pores of our bare arms are open and relaxed as we read the *Times* in our T-shirts, while two feet away, on the other side of the plate glass window, a blizzard rages. We turn

7

levers and get clean water, push a button for hot coffee, open doors and get ice cream, take short car trips to places where planes wait before whisking us across continents as we nap. It is all so fantastically fine.

Lately this leaves me uneasy. Does it you? Do you wonder how and why exactly we have it so different, so nice compared to thousands of years of peasants eating rocks? Is it possible that we, the people of the world, are being given a last great gift before everything changes? To me it feels like a gift. Only three generations ago, my family had to sweat in the sun to pull food from the ground.

Another thing. The marvels that are part of our everyday lives—computers, machines that can look into your body and see everything but your soul—are so astounding that most of us who use them don't really understand exactly what they're doing or how they do it. This too is strange. The day the wheel was invented, the crowd watching understood immediately what it was and how it worked. But I cannot explain with any true command how the MRI that finds a tumor works. Or how, for that matter, the fax works. We would feel amazement, or even, again, a mild disorientation, if we were busy feeling and thinking long thoughts instead of doing—planning the next meeting, appointment, consultation, presentation, vacation. We are too busy doing these things to take time to see, feel, parse and explain amazement.

Which gets me to time.

We have no time! Is it that way for you? Everyone seems so busy. Once, a few years ago, I sat on the Spanish Steps in Rome. Suddenly I realized that everyone, all the people going up and down the steps, was hurrying along on his or her way somewhere. I thought, *Everyone is doing something.* On the streets of Manhattan, they hurry along and I think, *Everyone is busy.* I don't think I've seen anyone amble, except at a summer place, in a long time. I am thinking here of a man I saw four years ago at a little pier in Martha's Vineyard. He had plaid shorts and white legs, and he was walking sort of stiffly, jerkily. Maybe he had mild Parkinson's, but I think: *Maybe he's just arrived and trying to get out of his sprint and into a stroll.*

All our splendor, our comfort, takes time to pay for. And affluence wants to increase; it carries within it an unspoken command: More! Affluence is like nature, which always moves toward new life. Nature does its job; affluence enlists *us* to do it. We hear the command for "More!" with immigrant ears that also hear "Do better!" or old American ears that hear, "Sutter is rich, there's gold in them hills, onward to California!" We carry California within us; that is what it is to be human, and American.

So we work. The more you have, the more you need, the more you work and plan. This is odd in part because of all the spare time we should have. We don't, after all, have to haul water from the crick. We don't have to kill an antelope for dinner. I can microwave a Lean Cuisine in four minutes and eat it in five. I should have a lot of extra time—more, say, than a cave-woman. And yet I feel I do not. And I think: That cavewoman watching the antelope turn on the spit, she was probably happily daydreaming about how shadows played on the walls of her cave. She had time.

It's not just work. We all know the applications of Parkinson's Law, that work expands to fill the time allotted to complete it. This isn't new. But this is: So many of us feel we have no time to cook and serve a lovely three-course dinner, to write the long, thoughtful letter, to ever so patiently tutor the child. But other generations, not so long ago, did. And we have more timesaving devices than they did.

We invented new technologies so that work could be done more efficiently, more quickly. We wished it done more quickly so we could have more leisure time. (Wasn't that the plan? Or was it to increase our productivity?)

But we have less leisure time, it seems, because these technologies encroach on our leisure time.

You can be beeped on safari! Be faxed while riding an elephant and receive e-mail while being menaced by a tiger. And if you can be beeped on safari, you will be beeped on safari. This gives you less time to enjoy being away from the demands of time.

Twenty years ago when I was starting out at CBS on the radio desk, we would try each day to track down our roving foreign correspondents and get them to file on the phone for our morning news broadcasts. I would go to the daily log to see who was where. And not infrequently it would say that Smith, in Beirut, is "out of pocket," i.e., unreachable, unfindable for a few days. The official implication was that Smith was out in the field traveling with the guerrillas. But I thought it was code for "Smith is drunk," or "Smith is on deep background with a really cute source." I'd think, Oh, to be an out-of-pocket correspondent on the loose in Cairo, Jerusalem, Paris—what a thing.

But now there is no "out of pocket." Now everyone can be reached and found, anywhere, anytime. Now there is no hiding place. We are "in the pocket."

What are we in the pocket of? An illusion, perhaps, or rather many illusions: that we must know the latest, that we must have a say, that we are players, are needed, that the next score will change things, that through work we can quench our thirst, that, as they said in the sign over the entrance of Auschwitz, "Work Brings Freedom," that we must bow to "More!" and pay homage to California. I live a life of only average intensity, and yet by 9 P.M. I am quite stupid, struck dumb with stimuli fatigue. I am tired from ten hours of the unconscious strain of planning, meeting, talking, thinking. If you clench your fist for ten hours and then let go, your hand will jerk and tremble. My brain trembles.

I sit on the couch at night with my son. He watches TV as I read the *National Enquirer* and the *Star*. This is wicked of me, I know, but the *Enquirer* and the *Star* have almost more pictures than words; there are bright pictures of movie stars, of television anchors, of the woman who almost choked to death when, in a state of morning confusion, she accidentally put spermicidal jelly on her toast. These stories are just right for the mind that wants to be diverted by something that makes no demands.

I have time at nine. But I am so flat-lined that I find it very hard to make the heartening phone call to the nephew, to write the long letter. Often I feel guilty and treat myself with Häagen-Dazs therapy. I will join a gym if I get time.

When a man can work while at home, he will work while at home. When a man works at home, the wall between workplace and living place, between colleague and family, is lowered or removed. Does family life spill over into work life? No. Work life spills over into family life. You do not wind up taking your son for a walk at work, you wind up teleconferencing during softball practice. This is not progress. It is not more time but less. Maybe our kids will remember us as there but not there, physically present but carrying the faces of men and women who are strategizing the sale.

I often think how much I'd like to have a horse. Not that I ride, but I often think I'd like to learn. But if I had a horse, I would be making room

for the one hour a day in which I would ride. I would be losing hours seeing to Flicka's feeding and housing and cleaning and loving and overall
well-being. This would cost money. I would have to work hard to get it. I
would have less time.

Who could do this? The rich. The rich have time because they buy
it. They buy the grooms and stable keepers and accountants and bill pay-
ers and negotiators for the price of oats. Do they enjoy it? Do they think, *It's
great to be rich, I get to ride a horse*? Oh, I hope so! If you can buy time, you
should buy it. This year I am going to work very hard to get some.

II

During the summer, when you were a kid, your dad worked a few towns
away and left at 8:30; Mom stayed home smoking and talking and ironing.
You biked to the local school yard for summer activities—twirling, lanyard
making, dodgeball—until afternoon. Then you'd go home and play in the
street. At 5:30 Dad was home and at 6 there was dinner—meat loaf,
mashed potatoes and canned corn. Then TV and lights out.

Now it's more like this: Dad goes to work at 6:15, to the city, where he
is an executive; Mom goes to work at the bank where she's a vice president,
but not before giving the sitter the keys and bundling the kids into the car
to go to, respectively, soccer camp, arts camp, Chinese lessons, therapy, the
swim meet, computer camp, a birthday party, a play date. Then home for
an impromptu barbecue of turkey burgers and a salad with fresh Parmesan
cheese followed by summer homework, Nintendo and TV—the kids lying
splayed on the couch, dead eyed, like denizens of a Chinese opium den—
followed by "Hi, Mom," "Hi, Dad," and bed.

Life is so much more interesting now! It's not boring, like 1957. There
are things to do: The culture is broader, more sophisticated; there's more
wit and creativity to be witnessed and enjoyed. Moms, kids and dads have
more options, more possibilities. This is good. The bad news is that our
options leave us exhausted when we pursue them and embarrassed when we
don't.

Good news: Mothers do not become secret Valium addicts out of bore-
dom and loneliness, as they did thirty and forty years ago. And Dad's con-

versation is more interesting than his father's. He knows how Michael Jordan acted on the Nike shoot, and tells us. The other night Dad worked late and then they all went to a celebratory dinner at Rao's where they sat in a booth next to Warren Beatty, who was discussing with his publicist the media campaign for *Bulworth*. Beatty looked great, had a certain watchful dignity, ordered the vodka penne.

Bad news: Mom hasn't noticed but she's half mad from stress. Her face is older than her mother's, less innocent, because she has burned through her facial subcutaneous fat and because she unconsciously holds her jaw muscles in a tense way. But it's okay because the collagen, the Botox, the Retin-A and alpha hydroxy, and a better diet than her mother's (Grandma lived on starch, it was the all-carbo diet) leave her looking more . . . fit. She does not have her mother's soft, maternal weight. The kids do not feel a pillowy yielding when they hug her; they feel muscles and smell Chanel body moisturizer. When Mother makes fund-raising calls for the school, she does not know it but she barks: "Yeah, this is Claire Marietta on the cookie drive we need your cookies tomorrow at three in the gym if you're late the office is open till four or you can write a check for twelve dollars any questions call me." Click.

Mom never wanted to be Barbara Billingsley. Mom got her wish.

III

What will happen? How will the future play out?

Well, we're going to get more time. But it's not pretty how it will happen, so if you're in a good mood, stop reading here and go hug the kids and relax and have a drink and a nice pointless conversation with your spouse.

Here goes: It has been said that when an idea's time has come a lot of people are likely to get it at the same time. In the same way, when something begins to flicker out there in the cosmos a number of people, a small group at first, begin to pick up the signals. They start to see what's coming.

Our entertainment industry, interestingly enough, has plucked something from the unconscious of a small collective. For about thirty years now, but accelerating quickly this decade, the industry has been telling us about The Big Terrible Thing. Space aliens come and scare us, nuts with nukes try to blow us up.

This is not new: In the 1950s Michael Rennie came from space to tell us in *The Day the Earth Stood Still* that if we don't become more peaceful our planet will be obliterated. But now in movies the monsters aren't coming close, they're hitting us directly. Meteors the size of Texas come down and take out the eastern seaboard, volcanoes swallow Los Angeles, Martians blow up the White House. The biggest-grosser of all time was about the end of a world, the catastrophic sinking of an unsinkable entity.

Something's up. And deep down, where the body meets the soul, we are fearful. We fear, down so deep it hasn't even risen to the point of articulation, that with all our comforts and amusements, with all our toys and bells and whistles . . . we wonder if what we really have is . . . a first-class stateroom on the *Titanic*. Everything's wonderful, but a world is ending and we sense it.

I don't mean: "Uh-oh, there's a depression coming," I mean: We live in a world of three billion men and hundreds of thousands of nuclear bombs, missiles, warheads. It's a world of extraordinary germs that can be harnessed and used to kill whole populations, a world of extraordinary chemicals that can be harnessed and used to do the same. Three billion men, and it takes only half a dozen bright and evil ones to harness and deploy.

What are the odds it will happen? Put it another way: What are the odds it will not? Low. Nonexistent, I think.

When you consider who is gifted and crazed with rage . . . when you think of the terrorist places and the terrorist countries . . . who do they hate most? The Great Satan, the United States. What is its most important place? Some would say Washington. I would say the great city of the United States is the great city of the world, the dense ten-mile-long island called Manhattan, where the economic and media power of the nation resides, the city that is the psychological center of our modernity, our hedonism, our creativity, our hard-shouldered hipness, our unthinking arrogance.

If someone does the big, terrible thing to New York or Washington, there will be a lot of chaos and a lot of lines going down, a lot of damage and a lot of things won't be working so well anymore. And thus a lot more . . . time. Something tells me we won't be teleconferencing and faxing about the Ford account for a while.

The psychic blow—and that is what it will be as people absorb it, a blow, an insult that reorders and changes—will shift our perspective and priorities, dramatically, and for longer than a while. Something tells me more of us will be praying, and hard, one side benefit of which is that there is sometimes a quality of stopped time when you pray. You get outside time.

Maybe, of course, I'm wrong. But I think of the time I poured out my fears to a former high official of the United States government. This was a few years ago. His face turned grim. I apologized for being morbid. He said no, he thinks the same thing. He thinks it will happen in the next year and a half. I was surprised, and more surprised when he said that an acquaintance, a former arms expert for another country, thinks it will happen in a matter of months.

So now I have frightened you. But we must not sit around and be depressed. "Don't cry," Jimmy Cagney once said. "There's enough water in the goulash already."

We must take the time to do some things. We must press government officials to face the big, terrible thing. They know it could happen tomorrow; they just haven't focused on it because there's no Armageddon constituency. We should press for more from our foreign intelligence and our defense systems, and press local, state and federal leaders to become more serious about civil defense and emergency management.

The other thing we must do is the most important.

I once talked to a man who had a friend who'd done something that took his breath away. She was single, middle-aged and middle class, and wanted to find a child to love. She searched the orphanages of South America and took the child who was in the most trouble, sick and emotionally unwell. She took the little girl home and loved her hard, and in time the little girl grew and became strong, became in fact the kind of person who could and did help others. Twelve years later, at the girl's high school graduation, she won the award for best all-around student. She played the piano for the recessional. Now she's at college.

The man's eyes grew moist. He had just been to the graduation. "These are the things that stay God's hand," he told me. I didn't know what that meant. He explained: These are the things that keep God from letting us kill us all.

So be good. Do good. Stay his hand. And pray. When the Virgin Mary makes her visitations—she's never made so many in all of recorded history as she has in this century—she says: Pray! Pray unceasingly!

I myself don't, but I think about it a lot and sometimes pray when I think. But you don't have to be Catholic to take this advice.

Pray. Unceasingly. Take the time.

3

God Is Back

God is back. He's bursting out all over. It's a beautiful thing to see.

Random data to support the assertion:

In the past seventeen days, since the big terrible thing, our country has, unconsciously but quite clearly, chosen a new national anthem. It is "God Bless America," the song everyone sang in the days after the blasts to show they loved their country. It's what they sang on television, it's what kids sang in school, it's what families sang in New York at 7 P.M. the Friday after the atrocity when we all went outside with our candles and stood together in little groups in front of big apartment buildings. A friend of mine told me you could hear it on Park Avenue from uptown to downtown, the soft choruses wafting from block to block.

You know why I think everyone went to Irving Berlin's old song, without really thinking, as their anthem for our country? Because of the first word.

I find myself thinking in mystical terms of President Bush's speech to Congress and the country, and I know from conversations with many people that I am not alone.

It seemed to me a God-touched moment and a God-touched speech, by which I mean, in part, that little miracles surrounded it. A president and staff who had no time to produce something fine and lasting, produced it. A president who at his strongest moments had betrayed a certain "I'm

16

kinda surprised to be here" vibration had metamorphosed into a gentleman of cool command—the kind of command you sense in a man who understands he ought to be there, should be leading, can trust his own judgment and rely on you to respect it. A great but wounded country heard exactly what it needed to pick itself up, dust itself off and start all over again.

Mr. Bush had a new weight, a new gravity, a new physical and moral comfort. You could see it. A man who had never been able to read from a TelePrompTer before used the TelePrompTer like a seasoned pro, which is to say like a man who didn't need one. Mr. Bush found his voice, just at the moment when people tend to lose theirs. He didn't rely on bromides or high flights or boilerplate; he gave it to you plain and hard with the common words of a common man. He said, "We will not tire, we will not falter, we will not fail." He said, "They will hand over the terrorists or they will share in their fate." He said, "These demands are not open to negotiation or discussion."

He talked just like George W. Bush.

He found himself amid the rubble.

He talked of prayer like a man who'd been praying, and who understood that tens of millions of Americans and others throughout the world were his powerful prayer warriors. They prayed the right thing would be said and done. It was. And now we feel we have what we needed, hoped we'd have, weren't sure we had: A true commander in chief.

All of this is quite wonderful, a tribute to President Bush and the men and women who work so hard for him. But he, and they, could not have produced that great night alone, and he, and they, would be the first to say it.

In the early days after the blast, I visited several of the memorials that have sprung up around town, in Union Square and in the heart of Greenwich Village. I was struck, at first, by the all the religious imagery, especially traditionally Catholic imagery—mass cards, pictures of the Sacred Heart, little statues of St. Anthony and St. Francis, pictures of the Virgin of Guadalupe, votive candles, prayers written on envelopes and pieces of paper grabbed from a desk.

Then I realized there was so much because so many of the firemen and policemen who died were Catholic—Italian and Irish and Puerto Rican men from Queens and Staten Island, from Jersey and Brooklyn. It was their families and friends who had brought the mass cards and the statues of St. Anthony, by tradition the patron saint of missing things, in those early days, when they were still hoping that someone they loved would emerge from the ruins.

On Sunday I watched Oprah Winfrey at the wonderful Spirit of New York special at Yankee Stadium. She prayed aloud—a lot of people prayed aloud—and Bette Midler made everyone feel better just by singing.

That morning I had gone to our local mosque, the biggest in Manhattan, on East Ninety-sixth Street to show sympathy and regard for people who might be feeling frightened and defensive. I watched as men prayed on their knees facing Mecca.

Then a friend came over and we talked about the speech she was going to make at a memorial for a friend of hers who'd died at Cantor Fitzgerald. He was a friend from her Alcoholics Anonymous group. I asked her what she wanted to say, and she said she wanted to tell the rest of the group that the friend they'd lost had always arrived everywhere early. He was early at AA meetings, and he used to greet the newcomers at the back.

On 9/11 he was early at work. After that he probably got early to heaven, where he was probably greeted himself—by Bill W., the great man who was one of the founders of AA. She wanted everyone to know that their friend and Bill W. probably had a great conversation about how meetings are held these days, and about the importance of having greeters in the back for new arrivals and first-timers.

I wasn't surprised by what she said, not only because I know her faith but because some little taboo or self-editing or reticence has lifted in the past few weeks. People are feeling a little less self-conscious about integrating their actual thoughts about their faith into the actual statements they make to friends and family, to coworkers and colleagues.

That's a great thing. In my little town that's a kind of miracle too.

I was thinking the other day: In 1964, *Time* magazine famously headlined "God Is Dead." I hope now, at the very highest reaches of that great magazine, they do a cover that says "God Is Back."

4

Courage Under Fire

FRIDAY, OCTOBER 5, 2001

Forgive me. I'm going to return to a story that has been well documented the past few weeks, and I ask your indulgence. So much has been happening, there are so many things to say, and yet my mind will not leave one thing: the firemen, and what they did. Although their heroism has been widely celebrated, I don't think we have quite gotten its meaning, or fully apprehended its dimensions. But what they did that day, on 9/11—what the firemen who took those stairs and entered those buildings did—was to enter American history, and Western history. They gave us the kind of story you tell your grandchildren about. I don't think I'll ever get over it, and I don't think my city will either.

What they did is not a part of the story but the heart of the story.

Here in my neighborhood in the East Nineties many of us now know the names of our firemen and the location of our firehouse. We know how many men we lost (eight). We bring food and gifts and checks and books to the firehouse, we sign big valentines of love, and yet of course none of it is enough or will ever be enough.

Every day our two great tabloids list the memorials and wakes and funeral services. They do reports: Yesterday at a fireman's funeral they played "Stairway to Heaven." These were the funerals for yesterday:

- CAPTAIN TERENCE HATTON, of Rescue 1—the elite unit that was among the first at the Towers—at 10 A.M. at St. Patrick's Cathedral on Fifth Avenue.

- LIEUTENANT TIMOTHY HIGGINS of Special Operations at St. Elizabeth Ann Seton Church, on Portion Road in Lake Ronkonkoma, out in Long Island.

- FIREFIGHTER RUBEN CORREA of Engine 74 at Holy Trinity Catholic Church on West Eighty-second Street, in Manhattan.

- FIREFIGHTER DOUGLAS MILLER of Rescue 5, at St. Joseph's Church on Avenue F in Matamoras, Pennsylvania.

- FIREFIGHTER MARK WHITFORD of Engine 23, at St. Mary's Church on Goshen Avenue in Washingtonville, New York.

- FIREFIGHTER NEIL LEAVY of Engine 217 at Our Lady Queen of Peace, on New Dorp Lane in Staten Island.

- FIREFIGHTER JOHN HEFFERNAN of Ladder 11 at St. Camillus Church in Rockaway, Queens.

And every day our tabloids run wallet-size pictures of the firemen, with little capsule bios. Firefighter Stephen Siller of Squad 1, for instance, is survived by wife, Sarah, daughters Katherine, Olivia and Genevieve and sons Jake and Stephen, and by brothers Russell, George and Frank, and sisters Mary, Janice and Virginia.

What the papers are doing—showing you that the fireman had a name and the name had a face and the face had a life—is good. But of course it is not enough, it can never be enough.

We all of course know the central fact: There were two big buildings and there were 5,000-plus people and it was 8:48 in the morning on a brilliant blue day. And then forty-five minutes later the people and the buildings were gone. They just went away. As I write this almost three weeks later, I actually think: That couldn't be true. But it's true. That is pretty much where New Yorkers are in the grieving process: "That couldn't be true. It's true." Five thousand dead! "That couldn't be true. It's true." And more than 300 firemen dead.

Three hundred firemen. This is the part that reorders your mind when you think of it. For most of the 5,000 dead were there—they just happened to *be* there, in the buildings, at their desks or selling coffee or returning e-mail. But the 300 didn't happen to be there, they *went* there. In the now famous phrase, they ran into the burning building and not out of the burning building. They ran up the stairs, not down, they went into it and not out of it. They didn't flee, they charged. It was just before 9 A.M. and the shift was changing, but the outgoing shift raced to the Towers and the incoming shift raced with them. That's one reason so many were there so quickly, and the losses were so heavy. Because no one went home. They all came.

And one after another they slapped on their gear and ran up the stairs. They did this to save lives. Of all the numbers we've learned since 9/11, we don't know and will probably never know how many people that day were saved from the flames and collapse. But the number that has been bandied about is 20,000—20,000 who lived because they thought quickly or were lucky or prayed hard or met up with (were carried by, comforted by, dragged by) a fireman.

I say fireman and not "firefighter." We're all supposed to say firefighter, but they were all men, great men, and *fireman* is a good word. Firemen put out fires and save people, they take people who can't walk and sling them over their shoulders like a sack of potatoes and take them to safety. That's what they do for a living. You think to yourself: Do we pay them enough? You realize: We couldn't possibly pay them enough. And in any case a career like that is not about money.

I'm still not getting to the thing I want to say.

It's that what the New York Fire Department did—what those men did on that brilliant blue day in September—was like D-Day. It was daring and brilliant and brave, and the fact of it—the fact that they did it, charging into harm's way—changed the world we live in. They brought love into a story about hate—for only love will make you enter fire. Talk about your Greatest Generation—the greatest generation is the greatest pieces of any generation, and right now that is: them.

So it was like D-Day, but it was also like the Charge of the Light Brigade. *Into the tower of death strode the three hundred.* And though we continue to need reporters to tell us all the facts, to find out the stories of what the firemen did in those towers, and though reporters have done a wonderful, profoundly appreciative job of that, what we need most now is different.

We need a poet. We need a writer of ballads and song to capture what happened there as the big men in big black rubber coats and big boots and hard, peaked hats lugged fifty and one hundred pounds of gear up into the horror and heat, charging upward, going up so sure, calm and fast—so humorously, some of them, cracking mild jokes—that some of the people on the stairwell next to them, going down, trying to escape, couldn't help but stop and turn and say, "Thank you," and "Be careful, son," and some of them took pictures. I have one. On the day after the horror, when the first photos of what happened inside the towers were posted on the Internet, I went to them. And one was so eloquent—a black-and-white picture that was almost a blur: a big, black-clad back heading upward in the dark, and on his back, in shaky double-vision letters because the person taking the picture was shaking, it said "Byrne."

Just Byrne. But it suggested to me a world. An Irish kid from Brooklyn, where a lot of the Byrnes settled when they arrived in America. Now he lives maybe on Long Island, in Massapequa or Huntington. Maybe third-generation American, maybe in his thirties, grew up in the 1970s when America was getting crazy, but became what his father might have been, maybe was: a fireman. I printed copies of the picture, and my brother found the fireman's face and first name in the paper. His name was Patrick Byrne. He was among the missing. Patrick Byrne was my grandfather's name, and is my cousin's name. I showed it to my son and said, "Never forget this—ever."

The Light Brigade had Tennyson. It was the middle of the Crimean War and the best of the British light cavalry charged on open terrain in the Battle of Balaklava. Of the 600 men who went in, almost half were killed or wounded, and when England's poet laureate, Alfred Lord Tennyson, learned of it, he turned it into one of the most famous poems of a day when poems were famous:

> *Theirs not to make reply,*
> *Theirs not to reason why,*
> *Theirs but to do and die.*
> *Into the valley of death*
> *Rode the six hundred.*
>
> *Cannon to right of them,*
> *Cannon to left of them,*
> *Cannon in front of them*
> *Volley'd and thunder'd.*
> *Stormed at with shot and shell,*
> *Boldly they rode and well,*
> *Into the jaws of death,*
> *Into the mouth of hell*
> *Rode the six hundred.*

I don't think young people are taught that poem anymore; it's martial and patriarchal, and even if it weren't it's cornball. But then, if a Hollywood screenwriter five weeks ago wrote a story in which buildings came down and 300 firemen sacrificed their lives to save others, the men at the studios would say: *Nah, too cornball. That couldn't be true.* But it's true.

Brave men do brave things. After 9/11 a friend of mine said something that startled me with its simple truth. He said, "Everyone died as the person they were." I shook my head. He said, "Everyone died who they *were*. A guy who ran down quicker than everyone and didn't help anyone—that was him. The guy who ran to get the old lady and was hit by debris—that's who he was. They all died who they were."

Who were the firemen? The Christian scholar and author Os Guinness said the other night in Manhattan that horror and tragedy crack open the human heart and force the beauty out. It is in terrible times that people with great goodness inside become most themselves. "The real mystery," he added, "is not the mystery of evil but the mystery of goodness." Maybe it's because of that mystery that firemen themselves usually can't tell you why they do what they do. "It's the job," they say, and it is, and it is more than that. So: The firemen were rough repositories of grace. They were the goodness that comes out when society is cracked open. They were *responsible*. They took responsibility under conditions of chaos. They did their job under heavy fire, stood their ground, claimed new ground, moved forward like soldiers against the enemy. They charged.

There is another great poet and another great charge, Pickett's charge, at Gettysburg. The poet, playwright and historian Stephen Vincent Benét wrote of Pickett and his men in his great poetic epic of the Civil War, "John Brown's Body":

> *There was a death-torn mile of broken ground to cross,*
> *And a low stone wall at the end, and behind it the Second Corps,*
> *And behind that force another, fresh men who had not fought.*
> *They started to cross that ground. The guns began to tear them.*
>
> *From the hills they say that it seemed more like a sea than a wave,*
> *A sea continually torn by stones flung out of the sky,*
> *And yet, as it came, still closing, closing, and rolling on,*
> *As the moving sea closes over the flaws and rips of the tide.*

But the men would not stop:

> *You could mark the path that they took by the dead that they left*
> *   behind, . . .*
> *And yet they came on unceasing, the fifteen thousand no more,*
> *And the blue Virginia flag did not fall, did not fall, did not fall.*

The center line held to the end, he wrote, and didn't break until it wasn't there anymore. The firemen were like that. And like the soldiers of old, from Pickett's men through D-Day, they gave us a moment in history that has left us speechless with gratitude and amazement, and maybe relief, too. *We still make men like that. We're still making their kind. Then that must be who we are.*

We are entering an epic struggle, and the firemen gave us a great gift when they gave us this knowledge that day. They changed a great deal by being who they were.

They deserve a poet, and a poem. At the very least a monument. I enjoy the talk about building it bigger, higher, better and maybe we'll do that. But I'm one of those who thinks: Make it a memory. The pieces of the towers that are left, that still stand, look like pieces of a cathedral. Keep some of it. Make it part of a memorial. And at the center of it—not a part of it but at the heart of it—bronze statues of firemen looking up with awe and resolution at what they faced. And have them grabbing their helmets and gear as if they were running toward it, as if they are running in.

5

Welcome Back, Duke

FRIDAY, OCTOBER 12, 2001

A few weeks ago I wrote a column called "God Is Back," about how, within a day of the events of 9/11, my city was awash in religious imagery—prayer cards, statues of saints. It all culminated, in a way, in the discovery of the steel-girder cross that emerged last week from the wreckage—unbent, unbroken, unmelted, perfectly proportioned and duly blessed by a Catholic friar on the request of the rescue workers, who seemed to see meaning in the cross's existence. So do I.

My son, a teenager, finds this hilarious, as does one of my best friends. They have teased me, to my delight, but I have told them, "Boys, this whole story is about good and evil, about the clash of good and evil." If you are of a certain cast of mind, it is of course meaningful that the face of the Evil One seemed to emerge with a roar from the furnace that was Tower One. You have seen the Associated Press photo, and the photos that followed: the evil face roared out of the building with an ugly howl—and then in a snap of the fingers it lost form and force and disappeared. If you are of a certain cast of mind it is of course meaningful that the cross, which to those of its faith is imperishable, did not disappear. It was not crushed by the millions of tons of concrete that crashed down upon it, did not melt in the furnace. It rose from the rubble, still there, intact.

For the ignorant, the superstitious and me (and maybe you), the face of the Evil One was revealed, and died; for the ignorant, the superstitious and me (and maybe you), the cross survived. This is how God speaks to us. He is saying, "I am." He is saying, "I am here." He is saying, "And the force of all the evil of all the world will not bury me." I believe this quite literally. But then I am experiencing 9/11 not as a political event but as a spiritual event.

And, of course, a cultural one, which gets me to my topic.

It is not only that God is back, but that men are back. A certain style of manliness is once again being honored and celebrated in our country since 9/11. You might say it suddenly emerged from the rubble of the past quarter century, and emerged when a certain kind of man came forth to get our great country out of the fix it was in. I am speaking of masculine men, men who push things and pull things and haul things and build things, men who charge up the stairs in a hundred pounds of gear and tell everyone else where to go to be safe. Men who are welders, who do construction, men who are cops and firemen. They are all of them, one way or another, the men who put the fire out the men who are digging the rubble out and the men who will build whatever takes its place.

And their style is back in style. We are experiencing a new respect for their old-fashioned masculinity, a new respect for physical courage, for strength and for the willingness to use both for the good of others.

You didn't have to be a fireman to be one of the manly men of 9/11. Those businessmen on Flight 93, which was supposed to hit Washington, the businessmen who didn't live by their hands or their backs but who found out what was happening to their country, said good-bye to the people they loved, snapped the cell phone shut and said, "Let's roll." Those were tough men, the ones who forced that plane down in Pennsylvania. They were tough, brave guys.

Let me tell you when I first realized what I'm saying. On Friday, September 14, I went with friends down to the staging area on the West Side Highway where all the trucks filled with guys coming off a twelve-hour shift at Ground Zero would pass by. They were tough, rough men, the grunts of the city—construction workers and electrical workers and cops and emergency medical workers and firemen.

I joined a group that was just standing there as the truck convoys went by. And all we did was cheer. We all wanted to do some kind of volunteer work but there was nothing left to do, so we stood and cheered those who were doing. The trucks would go by and we'd cheer and wave and shout "God bless you!" and "We love you!" We waved flags and signs, clapped and threw kisses, and we meant it: *We loved these men.* And as the workers would go by—they would wave to us from their trucks and buses, and smile and nod—I realized that a lot of them were men who hadn't been applauded since the day they danced to their song with their bride at the wedding.

And suddenly I looked around me at all of us who were cheering. And saw who we were. Investment bankers! Orthodontists! Magazine editors! In my group, a lawyer, a columnist and a writer. We had been the kings and queens of the city, respected professionals in a city that respects its professional class. And this night we were nobody. We were so useless, all we could do was applaud the somebodies, the workers who, unlike us, had not been applauded much in their lives.

And now they were saving our city.

I turned to my friend and said, "I have seen the grunts of New York become kings and queens of the city." I was so moved and, oddly I guess, grateful. Because they'd always been the people who ran the place, who kept it going, they'd just never been given their due. But now—"And the last shall be first"—we were making up for it.

It may seem that I am really talking about class—the professional classes have a new appreciation for the working-class men of Lodi, New Jersey, or Astoria, Queens. But what I'm attempting to talk about is actual manliness, which often seems tied up with class issues, as they say, but isn't always by any means the same thing.

Here's what I'm trying to say: Once about ten years ago there was a story—you might have read it in your local tabloid, or a supermarket tabloid like the *National Enquirer*—about an American man and woman who were on their honeymoon in Australia or New Zealand. They were swimming in the ocean, the water chest-high. From nowhere came a shark. The shark went straight for the woman, opened its jaws. Do you know what the man did? He punched the shark in the head. He punched it and punched it again. He did not do brilliant commentary on the shark, he did not share his sensitive feelings about the shark, he did not make wry observations about the shark, he punched the shark in the head. So the shark let go of his wife and went straight for him. And it killed him. The wife survived to tell the story of what her husband had done. He had tried to deck the shark. I told my friends: That's what a wonderful man is, a man who will try to deck the shark.

I don't know what the guy did for a living, but he had a very old-fashioned sense of what it is to be a man, and I think that sense is coming back into style because of who saved us on 9/11, and that is very good for our country.

Why? Well, manliness wins wars. Strength and guts plus brains and spirit wins wars. But also, you know what follows manliness? The gentleman. The return of manliness will bring a return of gentlemanliness, for a simple reason: masculine men are almost by definition gentlemen. Example: If you're a woman and you go to a faculty meeting at an Ivy League University you'll have to fight with a male intellectual for a chair, but I assure you that if you go to a Knights of Columbus Hall, the men inside (cops, firemen, insurance agents) will rise to offer you a seat. Because they are manly men, and gentlemen.

It is hard to be a man. I am certain of it; to be a man in this world is not easy. I know you are thinking, *But it's not easy to be a woman,* and you are so right. But women get to complain and make others feel bad about their plight. Men have to suck it up. Good men suck it up and remain good-natured, constructive and helpful; less-good men become the kind of men who are spoofed on *The Man Show*—babe-watching, dope-smoking nihilists. (Nihilism is not manly, it is the last refuge of sissies.)

I should discuss how manliness and its brother, gentlemanliness, went out of style. I know, because I was there. In fact, I may have done it. I remember exactly when: It was in the mid-1970s, and I was in my midtwenties, and a big, nice, middle-aged man got up from his seat to help me haul a big piece of luggage into the overhead luggage space on a plane. I was a feminist, and knew our rules and rants. "I can do it myself," I snapped. It was important that he know women are strong. It was even more important, it turns out, that I know I was a jackass, but I didn't. I embarrassed a nice man who was attempting to help a lady. I wasn't lady enough to let him. I bet he never offered to help a lady again. I bet he became an intellectual, or a writer, and not a good man like a fireman or a businessman who says, "Let's roll."

But perhaps it wasn't just me. I was there in America, as a child, when John Wayne was a hero, and a symbol of American manliness. He was strong, and silent. And I was there in America when they killed John Wayne by a thousand cuts. A lot of people killed him—not only feminists but peaceniks, leftists, intellectuals, others. You could even say it was Woody Allen who did it, through laughter and an endearing admission of his own nervousness and fear. He made nervousness and fearfulness the admired style. He made not being able to deck the shark, but doing the funniest commentary on not decking the shark, seem . . . cool.

But when we killed John Wayne, you know who we were left with. We were left with John Wayne's friendly-antagonist sidekick in the old John Ford movies, Barry Fitzgerald. The small, nervous, gossiping neighborhood commentator Barry Fitzgerald, who wanted to talk about everything and do nothing.

This was not progress. It was not improvement.

I missed John Wayne.

But now I think . . . he's back. I think he returned on 9/11. I think he ran up the stairs, threw the kid over his back like a sack of potatoes, came back down and shoveled rubble. I think he's in Afghanistan now, saying, with his slow swagger and simmering silence, "Yer in a whole lotta trouble now, Osama-boy."

I think he's back in style. And none too soon.

Welcome back, Duke.

And once again: Thank you, men of 9/11.

6

Profiles Encouraged

It was September 14 at 9 P.M., and I was on Fifth Avenue, directly across the street from St. Patrick's Cathedral. I was standing, that is, directly in front of the statue of Atlas holding up the world, at the entrance of Rockefeller Center. I was with my fourteen-year-old son. We were waiting for friends who were going to accompany us downtown to see the memorials that had sprung up in Washington Square and other places.

Our friends were a few minutes late. We waited together on the quiet, near-empty street. New York had been attacked only days before, and our city was quiet; people were home. Suddenly to our right, on the sidewalk, we saw two "Mideastern looking men," as we all now say. They were twenty-five or thirty years old, dressed in jeans and windbreakers, and they were doing something odd. They were standing together silently videotaping the outside of St. Pat's, top to bottom. We watched them, trying to put what we were seeing together. Tourists? It was a funny time of day for tourists to be videotaping a landmark—especially when the tourists looked like the guys who'd just a few days before blown up a landmark. We watched them. After a minute or so they finished taping St. Pat's and turned toward where we were. We were about twenty feet away from them, and we eyeballed them hard. They stared back at us in what I thought an aggressive manner: a deadeye stare, cold, no nod, no upturned-chin hello.

They stared at us staring at them for a few seconds, and then they began to videotape Rockefeller Center. We continued watching, and I surveyed the street for a policeman or patrol car. I looked over at the men again. They were watching me. The one with the camera puts it down for a moment. We stared, they stared. And then they left. They walked away and disappeared down a side street.

Let me tell you what I thought. I thought: Those guys are terrorists.

And then I thought: Whoa, wait a minute. I must be experiencing what people experienced after Pearl Harbor, when all of a sudden they'd see a young Asian guy with a camera and get all excited. You can get paranoid. You can get unfair.

I thought: The guys I just saw weren't breaking the law, in any case there are no cops around, and if I drop a dime to overburdened 911—"I saw two Mideastern men taking pictures!"—they'd brush me off.

So I just filed it away, as did my son.

But neither of us could shake it.

Ten days later I am to be a guest on the Oprah show, where we are going to talk about the events of 9/11. A car picks me up in the early afternoon at my apartment to take me to a studio in midtown where I'll talk to Oprah in Chicago. As we drive south down Park Avenue, the driver chats with me, and he seems jumpy. "You bothered like everyone else at what's going on?" I ask.

He says—I paraphrase—"Yeah, I am. I been feeling funny since a thing I saw the other day. I'm standing with a bunch of limos and drivers, we're waiting outside that big building, 520 Madison. And suddenly—we're all hanging around talking—and suddenly we see these two guys, Mideastern guys, in turbans. And they're videotaping 520 Madison Avenue top to bottom. Right in front of us. So we look at them and they look back—and then they keep doing it! So one of our guys starts to walk toward them, and the guys with the camera got outta there quick. And I'm telling you, it gave me the creeps!"

I get to the Oprah studio, do the show, get home, call the FBI tip line. I tell them my name, what I do for a living, say I'm going to tell them something that sounds small but may be big. The FBI tip-line guy is polite, takes notes, thanks me. He asks me to get the limo driver's name, I call around, get the number of his car company. The tip-line guy calls me back, takes the number, thanks me again.

I say, "You guys must be getting fifteen hundred tips an hour." He says yes, but they're all appreciated and if I see any more Mideastern looking men videotaping I should call. I figured: They're busy taking other, more urgent tips, this isn't going anywhere. Then I remembered an FBI agent I'd met in the neighborhood, tried to reach her, couldn't get her at her office or home. I leave messages, hear nothing, figure she's out chasing the bad guys.

Now jump to this past week. Two things happen. My son is surfing Internet chat rooms last Sunday and goes to a conservative site, where he sees an interesting thing. A man or woman has written in to say—again I paraphrase—"The oddest thing happened at work the other day. I work at a petrochemical company, and these two Mideastern looking guys come in and say they want to videotape the inside of the plant for a college course they're taking. They were approached and asked for identification by the manager. They became surly, angry, and left. Later the manager phoned the school they claimed to be students at—and they weren't even registered!"

My son calls to me, we read it and look at each other. I decided to call the FBI again. But the next morning my phone rings and it is the FBI, and it seems to be a real agent, not a telephone answerer. My initial tip-line report has, apparently, trickled up into the "check it out" category. Or maybe they've gotten enough reports like mine that a discernible pattern has emerged. At any rate, the agent asked me to go through my story and the driver's story, and then I threw in the report on the Internet, and he gave me his name and number and asked me to call if I saw anything else.

All this, of course, has me thinking. Maybe it has you thinking, too. I will share some of my thoughts. They are not original or unusual, but I feel they should maybe be said. Again, they are only thoughts and hunches.

I think there are a lot of "sleeper cells"—not a few, as we all hope, but a lot. I think some of them are in Queens and Brooklyn and Manhattan, and in Jersey City and elsewhere in New Jersey. Boston, too. Maybe some are in the capital or Virginia or Maryland. Maybe some of those who delivered anthrax to the U.S. Capitol took a taxi. Maybe on the other hand they took the shuttle from La Guardia. Certainly we know some cell or cells are in Florida.

I think some cell members may not be sure what their next move is.

They're not sure of their next assignment. They haven't been told, or they haven't, perhaps, chosen. I think cell members have been going around taking home movies of potential targets. I suspect they've been downloading them into computers and shooting them off to Osama and his lieutenants in the caves. I suspect they've been building a video library of places they might hit over the next few months and years and decade. And I think once they take one of the targets down they'll happily return to the scene of the crime, take a nice tourist-type videotape of the crater they made—they'll tell the cops they want to record the brave rescue workers—and send it triumphantly home.

That's all based on nothing but hunches.

But there are things we know. As individuals, these men—for they are men, between roughly seventeen and forty-five, which is to say they track in terms of sex and age group American criminals in American jails—are not only "hate filled" and "evil," though they are these things. They are also, obviously, emotionally and intellectually primitive. Their minds, if quick and highly focused, are also limited, stunted. And their young-man's arrogance is both a strength and their potential undoing. (Young male criminals of whatever sort tend to showy arrogance, and it is often their undoing.)

And I think as we attempt to find the bad guys in Afghanistan and elsewhere, we should all be thinking a little more, as citizens, about the search going on here, in America. The people who are trying to kill us with bombs and biological weapons are not from Canada, Chile, China, India, Ireland, Tanzania, Congo, New Zealand or the island of Jamaica.

They are from the Arab Mideast. They are not Israeli.

They are men, and not women.

They are young men. That is, they are not old men, and they are not children.

So: We know the profile of the bad guys.

I think I saw some of them that night across from St. Pat's, and I continue to regret not confronting them, questioning them and, if I had to, tackling them and screaming for help. I could have gotten us all arrested. If they had been innocent tourists I would have apologized, begged their forgiveness and offered to buy them a very nice dinner. If they had not been innocent, I would have helped stop some bad guys.

In the past month I have evolved from polite tip-line caller to watchful potential warrior. And I gather that is going on with pretty much everyone else, and I'm glad of it. I was relieved at the story of the plane passengers a few weeks ago who refused to board if some Mideastern looking guys were allowed to board. I was encouraged just last night when an esteemed journalist told me of a story she'd been told: Two Mideastern looking gentlemen, seated together on a plane, were eyeballed by a U.S. air marshal who was aboard. The air marshal told the men they were not going to sit together on this flight. They protested. The marshal said, move or you're not on this flight. They moved. Plane took off.

Good news: Everything went safely and calmly. Bad news: The two men were probably Ph.D.'s from Yale on their way to a bioethics convention. They made it clear they resented being split up, and I understand their resentment, and would feel real sympathy if they told me about it. You would, too.

But you know what? I think we're in the fight of our lives, and I think we're going to need their patience. And I think those who have not yet developed patience are going to have to grow up and get some.

No one likes "racial profiling," "ethnic profiling," "religious profiling." But I see it this way: If groups of terrorists took out two huge buildings and part of the Pentagon and killed 5,000 people and then decided to unleash anthrax and it emerged that those terrorists were all middle-aged American blond women who tend to dress in blue jeans and T-shirts and like to go by Catholic churches and light candles, I would be deeply upset not only because the terrorists had done what they'd done. I would also be upset because they were just like me! I fit their profile! I look like them! I act like them! Everywhere I went people would notice me and give me hard looks and watch what I was doing. I would feel terrible about this. But you know what else I'd do? I'd suck it up. I'd understand. I wouldn't like it, but I'd get it, and I'd accept it.

Because under very special circumstances—and these are special circumstances—you sometimes have to sacrifice. You have to drop your burly pride a little and try to understand and be accepting and accommodating and generous-spirited.

I think we're going to require a lot of patience from a lot of innocent people. And you know, I don't think that's asking too much. And when it's not given, I think we should recognize that as odd. About as odd as videotaping a great cathedral in the dark.

7

His Delicious,
Mansard-Roofed World

I found the words on a yellow Post-it I'd stuck on the side of the bookcase in my office about a year ago. It had gotten covered up by phone numbers and pictures and doctor's appointment cards, and yesterday, looking for a number, I found it—a piece of yellow paper with the words "His delicious mansard-roofed world." It took me aback. And I remembered what it was.

That night I had been out with friends—it was last fall—and it was fun, and I got home thinking, simply, of something we all should think of more and I don't think of enough: how wonderful it is to be alive, the joy of it, the beauty. And as I thought it—this is the part I remember most sharply—a scene came into my mind of a little French town with cobblestone streets and sharply slanting roofs on eighteenth-century buildings. Which made me think, in turn, in a blink, of New York, and its older architecture uptown and off the park, the old mansions off Fifth Avenue with sloping mansard roofs, and how this is the world we live in.

And I thought at that moment, with those pictures in my head: "His delicious, mansard-roofed world." He being God. I wrote down the words on a Post-it and put it on the bookcase, thinking some day I'd use them in writing about . . . something. Maybe joy. Maybe: us. Or maybe I'd just see them and think: That was a nice moment.

Anyway, the words captured for me a moment of thought.

And last night I found them and thought: *Oh—they speak of a moment in time.*

Yesterday afternoon, I was with a teenage friend, taking a cab down Park Avenue. It was a brilliant day, clear and sparkling, and as the cab turned left at Eighty-sixth Street the sun hit the windows in one of those flashes of bright gold-yellow that can, on certain days or at certain times, pierce your heart. We had been quiet, not talking, on the way to see a friend, when I said, "Do you . . . find yourself thinking at all of the ways in which you might be feeling differently about the future if September 11 had never happened?"

"Oh yes," she said, softly. "Every day."

And she meant it. And neither of us said any more and neither of us had to.

There are a lot of quiet moments going on. Have you noticed? A lot of quiet transformations, a lot of quiet action and quiet conversations. People are realigning themselves. I know people who are undergoing religious conversions, and changes of faith. And people who are holding on in a new way, with a harder grip, to what they already have and believe in.

Some people have quietly come to terms with the most soul-chilling thoughts. A young man I know said to me last week, as we chatted in passing on the street, "I have been thinking about the end of the American empire." And I thought: *Oh my boy, do you know the import, the weight, of the words you are saying?* And then I thought *Yes, he does. He's been thinking, quietly.*

Some people are quietly defining and redefining things. I am one of them. We are trying to define or paint or explain what the Old World was, and what the New World is, and how the break between them—the exact spot where the stick broke, cracked, splintered—could possibly have been an hour in early September.

One thing that passes through our minds is what to call the Old World— "The Lost World," or "The Golden Age," or "Then." We don't have to know yet what to call the New World, and cannot anyway because it hasn't fully revealed itself, and so cannot be named.

But if we can name the Old World, we'll at least know exactly what it is we think we've lost. And this is a funny little problem, because if you go out onto your street right now, if you live anyplace but downtown Manhattan or Arlington, Virginia, the world outside looks exactly—exactly—like the one that existed a year ago. The pumpkins in the stores, the merry kids, the guy who owns the butcher shop outside smoking in his apron. Everything looks the same. Same people, same stores, same houses.

And yet we all feel everything has changed. And we're right.

People say things like, "We have lost a sense of certainty," and I nod, for it is true. But on the other hand, I didn't feel so certain about the future last year. Did you?

People say we have lost the assumption that what we had would continue. Or, this being America, get better.

Certainly people who were carefree have lost their carefreeness. And with no irony I think: *That's a shame.* Carefreeness is good.

Lately when I think of the Old World I think of an insult that I mean as a tribute. It is the phrase *the narcissism of small differences.* In the world that has just passed, careless people—not carefree, careless—spent their time deconstructing the reality of the text, as opposed to reading the book. You could do that then. The world seemed so peaceful that you could actively look for new things to argue about just to keep things lively. You could be on a faculty and argue over where Jane Austen meant to put the comma, or how her landholding father's contextually objective assumptions regarding colonialism impacted her work. You could have real arguments about stupid things. Those were the days! It's great when life is so nice you have to invent arguments.

But the big thing I remember as we approached the end of the Old World, the thing I had been thinking for years and marveled over and also felt mildly anxious about, was this: You could go out and order and eat anything in a restaurant. And I had a sense that this wouldn't last forever, and some day we'd look back on these days fondly.

I would actually think that. It actually seemed to me marvelous that we could order anything we wanted. Raspberries in February! Bookstores, shoe stores, computer stores, food stores. We could order anything. Www-dot-gimme-dot-com.

I think the general feeling was a lovely optimism, which was captured in a great 1980s phrase: "The future's so bright, I gotta wear shades."

This was the thing: abundance. Not only of food but of potential, of hope, of the kid from the project's dream of being the next J. Lo, or West Point cadet, or millionaire. Every middle-class kid in the suburbs thought it absolutely within his grasp to be the next Steven Spielberg or Russell Crowe, or to play Martin Sheen's assistant on *The West Wing*, or run the record industry or direct commercials.

Abundant dreams. There was peace—crime down for the first time in a generation, the world relatively quiet, and in the suburbs they were starting to sleep with the windows open again! And material goods, things from the factory and the farm. As Kevin Spacey says in the commercial for his new movie, "Your produce alone has been worth the trip!" God, it was the age of abundance.

Or maybe just: The Abundance.

I know people who are feeling a sense of betrayal at the big change, as if they thought history were a waiter in a crisp white jacket, and though they ordered two more of the same, instead—instead!—he brought them, on a pretty silver platter, something quite dreadful.

They feel betrayed because they thought what we have been living through the past four decades or so was "life." But it wasn't, it was "super-life."

In the long ribbon of history life has been one long stained and tangled mess, full of famine, horror, war and disease. We must have thought we had it better because man had improved. But man doesn't really "improve," does he? Man is man. Human nature is human nature; the impulse to destroy coexists with the desire to build and create and make better. They've both been with us since the beginning. Man hasn't improved, the weapons have improved.

In the early twentieth century the future was so bright they had to *invent* shades. They had everything—peace, prosperity, medical and scientific break-throughs, political progress, fashion, glamour, harmless tasty scandals. The Gilded Age. And then all of a sudden they were hit by the most terrible war in all of European history, the most terrible plague in all of modern history (the Spanish flu) and on top of it all the most terrible political revolution in the history of man. And that was just the first eighteen years.

People always think good news will continue. I guess it's in our nature to think that whatever is around us while we're here is what will continue until we're not. And then things change, and you're surprised. I guess surprise is in our nature too. And then after the surprise we burrow down into our-selves and pull out what we need to survive, and go on, and endure.

But there's something else, and I am thinking of it.

I knew for many years a handsome and intelligent woman of middle years who had everything anyone could dream of—home, children, good marriage, career, wealth. She was secure. And she and her husband had actually gotten these good things steadily, over twenty-five years of effort, and in that time they had suffered no serious reverses or illnesses, no tragedies or bankruptcies or dark stars. Each year was better than the previous. It was wonderful to see. But as I came to know her I realized that she didn't think she had what she had because she was lucky, or blessed. She thought she had them because she was better. She had lived a responsible, effortful life; of course it had come together. She had what she had because she was good, and prudent.

She deserved it. She was better than the messy people down the block.

She forgot she was lucky and blessed!

You forget you're lucky when your luck is so consistent that it con-founds the very idea of luck. You begin to think your good fortune couldn't be luck, it must have been . . . talent. Or effort. Or superiority.

The consistency of America's luck may have fooled many of us into for-getting we were all lucky to be born here, lucky to be living now, lucky to have hospitals and operas and a film industry and a good electrical system. We were born into it. We were lucky. We were blessed.

We thought we were the heirs of John Adams, Ulysses S. Grant, Thomas Edison, Jonas Salk, Mr. Levitt of Levittown. And we are. But still, every generation ya gotta earn it. It doesn't mean you're better; it means you're lucky, and ya gotta earn it.

How did our luck turn bad, our blessings thin out?

Great books will be written about that. But maybe from this point on we should acknowledge what we quietly know inside: It was a catastrophic systems failure, a catastrophic top-to-bottom failure of the systems on which we rely for safety and peace.

Another way to say it: The people of the West were, the past ten years or so, on an extended pleasure cruise, sailing blithely on smooth waters— but through an iceberg field. We thought those in charge of the ship, commanding it and steering it and seeing to its supplies, would—could—handle any problems. We paid our fare (that is, our taxes) and assumed the crew would keep us safe.

We thought our luck would hold, too.

The people—us, you and me, the sensuous man on the deck—spent a lot of time strolling along wondering, *What shall I pursue today, gold or romance? Romance or gold? I shall ponder this over a good merlot.* We were not serious. We were not morally serious. We were not dark. We banished darkness.

The American people knew, or at least those paying attention knew, that something terrible might happen. But they knew the government had probably done what governments do to protect us. The people did not demand this; the government did not do it. Bad men were allowed in; bad men flourished here, fit right in, planned their deeds. They brought more bad men in after them. They are here among us now; they send anthrax through the mail and watch our reaction, predicating their next move perhaps upon our response.

Our intelligence system failed—but then for a quarter century we had been denying it resources, destroying its authority, dismantling its mystique. Our immigration system failed—but then in many ways it had been encouraged to fail. Our legal system failed. One of our greatest institutions, American journalism, failed. When the editors and publishers of our great magazines and networks want you to worry about something—child safety seats, the impact of air bags, drunken driving, insecticides on apples—they know how to make you worry. They know exactly how to capture your attention. Matthew Shepard and hate crimes, Rodney King and racism: The networks and great newspapers know how to hit Drive and go from zero to the American Consciousness in sixty seconds. And the networks can do it on free airwaves, a gift from our government.

Did the networks and great newspapers make us worry about what we know we should have worried about? No. Did they bang the drums? No. Did they hit this story like they know how to hit a story? No.

In January 2001 the Homeland Security report, which declared flatly that international terrorism would inevitably draw blood on American soil, was unveiled. They called a news conference in a huge Senate office building. Congressmen came, and a senator, Pat Roberts of Kansas. Only a half dozen reporters showed up, and one, from the greatest newspaper in the nation, walked out halfway through. It was boring.

Every magazine and newspaper had, over the past ten years, a front-page story and a cover on the madmen in the world and the weapons they could seize and get and fashion. But they never beat the drum, never insisted that this become a cause.

Why? In part I think for the same reason our political figures didn't do anything. It would have been bad for ratings. *The people don't want serious things at ten o'clock on a Tuesday night, they want Sela Ward falling in love.* I will never, ever forget the important Democrat who told me over lunch why Bill Clinton (president of the United States, January 1993 through January 2001) had never moved and would never move in a serious way to deal with the potential of nuclear and biological terrorism. Because it doesn't show up in the polls, he said. Because it doesn't show up in the focus groups.

It was a catastrophic systems failure, top to bottom. And we all share in it, some more than others.

Except.

Except those who did the remarkable things that day, September 11, 2001—the firemen who charged like the Light Brigade, the businessmen who said, "Let's roll." Which is, in part, why we keep talking about them. To remind ourselves who we are in the midst of the systems failure. They did the right thing just by being what they were, which gave us inspiration just when we needed it most.

And now we have to turn it all around.

Great books, as I said, will be written about these days, and the war on which we are embarked, on how it began and why America slept, and what America did when it awoke. Much awaits to be learned and told.

And what we must do now, in our anger and defensiveness, is support, assist and constructively criticize the systems that so catastrophically failed. For those systems still reign and we still need them. And they are trying to function now, and trying to protect us, with the same sense of loss we all share and the added burden of a mind-bending sense of remorse, frustration, anger and pain.

Where are we right now? We have reached the point in the story where the original trauma is wearing off (except in our dreams, where it's newly inflicted), where expressions of solidarity and patriotism are true but tired, and questions about exactly how well our institutions are handling this—not in the past but right now—are rising. It all began forty-five days ago. We know who did the bombings because they were on the planes, and they left receipts.

But we do not know who their confederates here were, do not know who is spreading the anthrax that has hit Florida, New York and Washington, do not know the dimensions of the threat at home.

Authority figures are doubted. The letter carriers don't trust their superiors to take care of them, and how they feel is legitimate and understandable. The workers in the newsrooms, reassured by the boss that if they were going to get anthrax they would have had it by now, do not trust what they're being told, or the tellers. And that is legitimate and understandable.

We are reading anxious reports. Yesterday I read that the Nuclear Regulatory Commission had admitted it kept nuclear plant vulnerability studies out and about and available for any citizen to see in their libraries. (Q: What were they thinking? A: They weren't thinking; they were feeling, and what they were feeling was lucky.)

More and more one senses we're going to have to be taking as much responsibility for ourselves—and on ourselves—as we can. Doing our own research, taking our own actions, making our own decisions and acting on our own guts.

A week after 9/11, I was on a TV show where I said I'd been thinking about *Mrs. Miniver,* the 1942 movie with Greer Garson as the doughty British matron who saw her family—and thus her country—through the Blitz. I said that we were all going to have to be Mrs. Minivers now; we're going to have to keep the home front going.

I keep waiting for some talk show or news show to do the Mrs. Miniver segment, telling us what to do in case of real and terrible trouble.

And no one is doing it.

So we must all be doing it ourselves. I am researching and talking to experts. Next week I will talk about "How to Be Mr. and Mrs. Miniver"— from how much water to buy to where to put it and how to get everyone in your ambit together. I will share everything I'm told and hear. And let me tell you why I think, in all this mess, we must gather together and talk about how to get through it together, as citizens. *Because our systems are not fully working yet.*

It's a murky time. We're all feeling a little bit lonely, and all of us at one moment or another have the existential willies. Those who have thirteen kids and thirty-four grandchildren are feeling as alone as those who are actually all alone.

We'd all best handle as much as we can ourselves, in and with our own little units.

It may become a terrifically tough time. But we are not alone, as you well know. God loves faith and effort, and he loves love. He will help us get through this, and to enjoy Paris and New York again, and to breathe deep of his delicious, mansard-roofed world. Amen.

8

We're All Soldiers Now

FRIDAY, NOVEMBER 2, 2001

On Halloween I had one of those days that veered from scene to scene. In the morning, in the waiting room of a Manhattan eye doctor's office, I watched and listened as a young secretary who was dressed for the day in a Morticia costume—all in black, white-powdered face, black eye makeup, black pointy witch's hat placed on her desk, white spider-web hose on her legs—called patients and left messages like this: "Mrs. Smith, this is Dr. Jones' office. We referred you to New York Eye and Ear Hospital recently, and so you will have to be tested for anthrax. Please call us."

Near the end of the day I had a long talk with a beloved friend who told me that in her office at a great entertainment magazine in Manhattan the young people who are researchers and editorial assistants—they are called "the kids in the hall"—came in to work dressed for Halloween as characters from recent movies. One young man came in bare-chested, with meticulous tattoos running up and down his arms and across his chest; he had dyed his hair blond and spiked it; he silently walked around the office taking Polaroids of whoever spoke to him and writing on the back what they'd said. He was, that is, the brain-damaged man Guy Pearce played in *Memento*. And he not only won the prize for best costume, he was applauded by everyone at Time Life.

The fabulous wittiness and spirited gaiety of New Yorkers at this time in history can take your breath away. As far as I'm concerned the guy who showed up as Guy Pearce is a national treasure. So are the people with the

46

crazy/funny e-mails about Osama, and the young woman I saw on the street last night in the dark, waiting for a cab to go to a Halloween party. The woman she was with was a fairy princess in pink, with a wand. But the woman who made me laugh was dressed top to bottom in traditional Arab Muslim dress, covered top to bottom in black muslin, veil and all. She was waving her arms and making woo-woo sounds for fun. I just saw her and her friend and started to laugh, and they did too.

Wit and comedy are an expression of the life force, and of life-love. They are an attempt to summon joy. Their practitioners do us a great public service.

The friend who witnessed and applauded "Guy Pearce," and who laughed about it with me like a happy kid, then veered with me to another part of what we're all feeling here in old New York. It is not, as people say, post-traumatic stress disorder. It is post-incident sadness, and there's nothing disordered about it. This is what it's like: The day is going by and everything's fine and you're humming along and doing what you're doing. Then you see something—an image on the TV, someone reporting on the war—and all of a sudden in your head you see the first tower groaning to the ground, and the demonic debris cloud billowing like a natural force, chasing modernity down the street.

We'll all get over it; we are getting over it; but we still get mugged by memories. When I visit Brooklyn someone always says, as we approach the bridge, "That's where the Towers were," and I don't look. I used to, but now I look at the river. I went to a high-rise, looking for a sublet near my son's school, and they said let's go to the top, where the views are. Meaning: where the brilliant Manhattan skyline is, the dream view of all dream views. And I said, without thinking, "I don't want a view." There was silence for a moment. We heard the fax machine whir. Then someone said, "I think we have something on nine."

I have post-incident heartache. Everyone here does. But they also dress up like Guy Pearce, and they also cheer on the Yankees, and they unfurl banners at the House that Ruth Built that say "New York Is Back," and last night they sang "New York, New York" along with the Frank Sinatra recording in the stadium when our team won. They sang loud and straight to the end of the song, even though they're not sure New York is back. It takes a special kind of hardiness to sing like that when you're not sure.

My people are a hardy people, and fabulously vulgar. This morning in the *New York Post* there was an item saying Ground Zero is the new hot spot for meeting guys. And a rental agent told me about a woman who called his office to say she's been commuting downtown for years and, uh, like, who's handling the apartments of all the dead people? He was appalled. Me too. But I also thought: New Yorkers are survivors, and that isn't all bad.

But this is about what's next. I'm going to run long, so park this in your computer if you're busy and come back later.

We continue as a nation on edge. People who live near nuclear reactors are afraid, ditto people in big cities, ditto people near postal depots and people in crop-duster America. That would make just about all of us. (Add now: the entire state of California.) And we know—we have reluctantly perceived—that our stretched and stressed law enforcement and protection and security agencies are working overtime, creatively and against many odds, and still they know essentially nothing. They don't know what will be hit next or how or by whom, they don't know where the anthrax is from or who sent it. The best the government seems able to do is try hard, work hard, and tell a nervous populace to be a little more nervous. One hopes they know much more than they say; one doubts. (And they shouldn't make us more nervous; they should make us more aware, which is not quite the same thing.)

Advice to the administration: Take, as your inspiration for your daily reporting of the situation, the image of George W. Bush on the pitcher's mound at Yankee Stadium. He didn't spin the ball; he threw it straight and down the middle. The competent catcher caught it.

This is what grownups do, and we have proved ourselves the past seven weeks to be a nation of grownups.

We know, for instance, that a nuclear reactor may be hit by the bad men. We wonder: Is every nuclear reactor in the country therefore now being protected by U.S. defense forces on the ground and jets overhead? They should be. And we should be told if it is happening.

A caveat, however. I watched Don Rumsfeld for an hour on TV yesterday. He holds a brisk and direct briefing. It probably took him an hour or so to prepare for it. In all, he probably gives at least three hours a day to one form of the press or another. This keeps our country informed to a degree, but I keep wondering: Could FDR and his cabinet have waged World War II successfully if they'd been spending half their time on the press? Could Lincoln have saved the Union after first Bull Run if he'd spent three hours a day talking to Horace Greeley?

One wonders if this couldn't be more centralized, with one authoritative voice, and everyone else in the government doing what they have to do: find the bad men. (I no longer say bad guys. Guy is too warm, too familiar, too colloquial for the evil ones. So: bad men.)

While the government discovers what is happening with anthrax and other threats, what must the public do?

I think we must repeat history. We must go back to the future. Our country was founded, cleared and hammered together by individuals who did it themselves and together—themselves as autonomous units making the decision to continue pushing west or settle down in eastern Ohio; and together with all the other people who made decisions like theirs. Together they did the house raisings and the barn raisings and started the church that started the first library in the wilderness. The federal government was not, in a daily and present and on-the-ground sense, of much help.

And that's sort of where we are now.

It's back to being pioneer women, hoe in hand; back to being ready to shoo the kids into the cellar beneath the floorboards if the war party comes. And pioneer men working the fields side by side, seeing to the horses and the wheels of the wagons.

So: pioneer women, and men.

Or, as I've said, Mrs. Miniver, our doughty, middle-class, middle-aged Englishwoman keeping the children's dreams alive and chasing Nazis from the kitchen in Blitz-torn England.

How exactly to be a Mrs. Miniver or a pioneer woman? You'd think all the hungry-for-ratings news shows would be doing this story, but they're not. Maybe they think it would look like fear mongering. But it would be received, I think, as helpful. And of course it might help our nation and save lives.

First thing we must do is know this: We are, all of us and each of us, part of the new U.S. defense system. We are all soldiers now. We have been drafted by history. And we must be watchful and protective as soldiers. Second thing: It's good to think locally. Third thing: Carry a camera. Cameras may turn out to be the first and best twenty-first-century homeland defense weapon.

But the point is: We're all in this together and will have to work together, locally and nationally.

"The American people are a huge and sensitive early-warning system," the defense expert Peter Black told me. "We are extraordinarily well-connected citizens." I found Mr. Black on the Internet; he wrote a piece for *Wired* magazine eight years ago that warned of America's vulnerability to various kinds of terrorism, especially of the electrical and infrastructure kind.

"You want to be aware of what potential terrorist targets are, and to do it we have to think visually," Mr. Black says. Potential terror targets are "under the ground, over the ground and in the air." Among them: natural gas pipes and distribution areas, local electrical grids, local telephone distribution systems, telephone switching stations, the local reservoir.

Appoint yourself a member of the Neighborhood Civilian Defense Patrol, the kind we used to have during World War II, and need again. (Memo to Tom Ridge: This is a good idea, bring it back.)

Find out what sensitive infrastructure you have locally, find out where it is, and keep your eye on it. Case the joint. Get a bunch of folks together to watch things. If you see anything funny—say, guys with box cutters who look like they could be Mideastern terrorists and who happen to be videotaping the main office of the local nuclear power plant—take out your weapon: your camera.

Snap a photo of the possible bad man. Snap a photo of his car, and his plates, and his confederates.

Use a digital camera if you can (about $50, available in your basic electronics and camera stores). If you do it with a digital camera you won't have to wait for the film to be developed, you can call 911 or the FBI, tell them what you saw, and tell them you can download pictures of it into your computer and shoot it to them right away. "The FBI is amassing a cross-referenced data base," Mr. Black told me, and it holds real potential for finding the bad men.

Mr. Black makes a point that deserves making: While we were as a nation on an extended commercial lark the past ten years, our obsession with getting our hands on the newest and latest and best new toy helped build an extraordinary array of items that now can be put to a more serious purpose.

So: keep your eye on the world outside and carry a camera. What else?

Half the people in New York now use this phrase: "my Israeli guy." We all know someone from Israel who has lived a life a bit like the one we are entering. "Do what we do in Israel. We have what we call a safe room." This was my Israeli guy, an elderly fellow at my local hardware store, on September 13. I told him I needed advice on how to make my son and myself safer at the margins as we entered a difficult unknowable time.

He told me what to do. I've checked it with people. it seems to be good advice for anyone caught in the middle of terror, and needing a place to gather and duck.

So: a safe room. Find the room with the thickest walls and fewest or smallest windows and doors in your house or apartment. Make do with what you have. If you live in a one-room studio apartment, that's your safe room. If you have a secure room in the middle of the house, that's your safe room. Basement with thick walls and little windows? Safe room. (If you live in a big apartment building, ask the owner/super/board head, Whatever happened to the old fallout shelters big buildings used to have? They still exist. They're often the laundry room. Maybe the one in your building can be turned into a communal safe room.)

Okay. You've figured out where your safe room is. What to have in it? You start with tape. My Israeli guy told me to buy two-inch-wide blue 3M Scotch tape, and tape any openings that allow air into the safe room. Tape the window frames, the door frames. I asked him if I could use gray gaffer's tape as it seems sturdier and more . . . fume-stopping. He said: Sure. So I bought both. And two big rolls of blue and two big rolls of gray are in my safe room, along with heavy scissors, a utility knife and a box cutter.

Question: Um, if you tape everything shut and sit there with your kids and breathe, won't you, um, run out of oxygen?

You probably won't be there long enough.

If we are hit by a chemical attack, the chemicals will in time disperse into the air. If we are hit by a bio attack, you'll stay there as long as you can and then get out. If it's a dirty bomb with radioactive material, you get into the safe room soon as you can and stay there a few hours after the blast. And then you get out of Dodge.

A safe room isn't a place to live but a place to duck the incoming.

Still, you want to have plenty of stuff in it in case you need it, and as the place where everyone in the family knows you keep it. Get big plastic containers of water—enough for everyone in your family for a few days to a week. (I think: Get too much. Too much bottled water may turn out to be a good thing, and in any case will likely get drunk along the way.)

Keep flashlights in the safe room, with backup batteries and backups to the backups.

Have bandages and medicines—can't hurt, might help. Whatever prescription medication you may be on, get a month's supply and put it in the safe room. In California they call this making an earthquake pack: everything you need to get through a few days with systems going down.

For communications, you want a battery-operated radio, a ham radio if you have it. Two good ideas. Get a crankable radio in case your electricity goes down—you can get them off the shelf at consumer electronics stores. Those walkie-talkies that people started using the past few years (I think the most well-known is made by Motorola) could be a great thing to have in a safe room or outside it. They have a radius of a mile or two, a lot of people use them, and you can find out a lot on their shared channels. Peter Black again: "They can be a short-term communications network if the lights go off for a while." A lot of us noted a few weeks ago that when the World Trade Center was hit, the phones in New York stopped working reliably—but the Internet stayed up. Why? Because it was, essentially, designed by our defense establishment to stay up. If you have wireless Internet access, a Blackberry or whatever, it goes into the safe room with you.

By the way: Keep making sure all battery-operated and electrical operated items are fully charged. Just keep making sure everything's charged.

Have enough canned goods to last you and your family a week or so. Canned franks and beans are not delicious, but they can withstand any blow, and if you get nuked they'll come out fully cooked. (Sorry—New York moment.)

Memo to our wonderful television networks: Do the safe-room segment. Do a piece on how to get through a rough few days if a rough few days happen in your town. *PrimeTime Live, 20/20, 60 Minutes, Dateline, Oprah, The View:* This means you. As you are all in the entertainment/information business, make it not only helpful but fun. Do interviews with Israelis and get safe-room stories—they've used them. Oprah, go to Martha Stewart, a hardy and quick-thinking woman who hasn't constructed her career by being careless, and ask her what she has in her safe room. This might be helpful and will surely be amusing. (Frank Rich will make fun of it. So what? In the making fun of it he'll spread the word.)

I am told it would be wise to take some money out of the bank and keep it in a safe place. The bad men may and many think will attempt to destabilize and disrupt our financial and banking institutions and systems through cyber warfare, etc. Everyone tells me to get $1,000 or more, a mix of small and large bills but more small than large. Also have change. "Have silver," another Israeli told me, "it can come in handy—phones, and things."

Keep your wallet, cards, keys, license and a good bit of cash near one another, always, in a regular place so you know where to find them quickly if you need them. Take them into the safe room and out of the safe room with you.

I suspect we should be making sure the barbecue grill in the garage has a lot of charcoal and a lot of lighter fluid. If you can, have a lot of frozen food in the freezer; if you lose electricity, the food will last longer if there's a lot and not a little. And if it turns out you have to cook a lot of it on a peaceful day, you can invite the neighbors.

I suspect we should all be getting together with our neighbors and friends and family and attempting to plan or coordinate what might be called . . . The Escape. Or: The Fleeing. If something bad happens, where do you all meet? If Mom and Dad are at work and the three kids are at three different schools, who picks who up and meets who where? Make out a phone contact list, with everyone's home and office and cell numbers; an e-mail contact list too. Have copies made, laminate them, and give to family and friends.

Have an escape plan. If you had to flee, how would you do it? Think about it. Think about people in the neighborhood.

It's a good idea for the most vulnerable—the old who live alone, single people, single mothers with kids, or those who live with people who are not fully functioning—to be looked out for by neighbors, or groups, or organizations. Local churches and police could keep a drop-by list for the most vulnerable.

Another idea, again from Peter Black: Why not approach your local doctor and ask him if he would stock up on all needed medicines, and the neighborhood will pay him now, in advance to get them and organize it all. Raise the money at a cake sale, get him what he needs; he'll help you on a terrible day.

A friend who would know tells me, "You need a dozen gas masks." I said, "Oh no, it's just me and my son." He said, "No! The most embarrassing thing that can happen is you're having friends over and you're attacked. You and your son get your gas masks and put them on and say, 'We are safe, I am sorry you are not.' Terrible! You have to have gas masks for your guests!"

Well I guess you do, and I'll save up. (The unpopular have a real advantage here, and should take some deserved satisfaction.) Like everyone else in New York, I have the kind of gas mask you get at the local hardware store. I have tried to get a better one. I still have no idea if this is a good idea, as smarter people than I are disagreeing on it. But I mean to get one if I can.

The subject of guns has come up. Everyone has an opinion. Here's mine: If you know how to use a gun, and you can get it legally, get a gun. If you want to learn how to use it, go to the NRA, and they'll tell you what ranges and instructors are available. Learn really well how to use it, store it, handle it, hide it. The number of people registering for gun ownership is skyrocketing, and understandably. Worst-case scenario: A "dirty bomb"—a big, hunking so-called suitcase bomb with radioactive material—goes off in the middle of your city. Everyone ducks and covers; those close to the blast die. Chaos ensues. You're in the safe room trying to figure out when to leave, but you can't find out on the short-wave and the battery-operated radio isn't working. Some people go out, though—vandals, criminals, the marginally sane, and they gather together and become an ambulatory little miniriot. The various branches of government move and bungle, help and make mistakes. You are at the mercy of luck, chance, geography. You are threatened. This is where you and your neighbors with guns come in.

The present crisis is a great blow to the antigun forces, and they know it. That's why they have nothing to say right now. It is a boost for the right to bear arms, for everyone knows they well may be needed, not now but longer down the rocky road.

But it won't help if you don't know how to use a gun, or are afraid to use it, or brandish it ineffectually. After you scare the bad rioter and then show you're incompetent he will be very, very angry with you, and perhaps "act out his anger," as we say at school meetings.

So, do what you can. Think. We're at war; think like a warrior and a survivor. This is not only a good idea, it will make you feel better, or at least a little bit safer, which is not a bad way to feel.

Then when you're done planning, get dressed and go out to dinner, and have a nice time.

But remember as you get organized not to let your kids know, "This is what we're doing because we're scared." It's, "This is what I'm doing to make sure we're safe."

This is just a first pass at what to do now. I'll be returning to it, and I ask you all to write in with your ideas. Because we're all in it together.

9

The Phony War

That was an interesting speech President Bush gave last night in Georgia. Its subject was homeland security, and in terms of content, style and tone it seemed to be, essentially, nothing new. And yet by the end and after reading it, I thought: He's telling us a great deal here.

The terrorists "want to kill Americans, Jews and Christians"; we've seen this hatred before in history, and "the only possible response is to confront it and defeat it." The bad men "have no religion, have no conscience and have no mercy"; it is a war "to save civilization itself"; the way to win peace is "to take the battle to the enemy and to stop them."

He talked at length—at too great length, I think—about how we as a people are buoyed by faith and family, how flags are flying everywhere, how Americans have contributed a billion dollars to relief efforts and charities, and how this would be a good time to mentor or tutor a child.

This has already been said, but it allowed him to underscore what he wants us to absorb, and every day: that the terrorists brought out the very best in our people, and the very best is what it will take to defeat them.

It was a speech in which the president was determined not to announce but to underscore, and to leave his audience inferring. Inferring that yes we're in a heck of a war, and yes we'll get through, yes the government is on the case and yes, we must continue to live and love life and refuse to let the terrorists diminish the simple joys of dailiness.

It was a long-haul speech, not a review-the-current-crisis speech. It was the kind of thing we're going to be hearing from him for a long time, because the war will go a long time. Along the way he announced as his subject "how to live"—Tolstoy's great question, which suggests someone in speechwriting has been hitting *War and Peace*. Mr. Bush continued to accent the importance of viewing Islam as peaceful and the terrorists as its abusive misinterpreters.

Most interestingly, I thought, he seemed to suggest along the way that 9/11 has given us as a people an opportunity to revisit our long history, and understand better what it is we are fighting for. "Ours is a great story, and we must tell it," he said. I suspect very soon now he will be expanding on that thought, and asking our public schools to return to the old history curriculum, the one that told our story from prerevolutionary days through the Civil War through the age of invention to all the great social and moral movements that have swept the past century. Our children, that is, for the first time in twenty-five years, may be taught our history again. What a boon this would be for our country.

In the middle of the speech Mr. Bush touched on ways to mobilize the interest and energy of our newly aroused country. Most significantly, he said he will ask state and local officials "to create a modern civil-defense service," to help us win the war at home. Well done, hooray, and just in time.

Where we are right now is 1939, and what we're in right now is the Phony War. That was the placid time that followed Britain's declaration of war against Germany, after Germany invaded Poland. Everyone knew that what would soon be called World War II had begun, and yet things were relatively quiet. John Bull found his daily life undisturbed and actually quite pleasant in the way that walking out of a funeral on a pretty summer day makes you see the buds on a tree more brilliantly and receive them more gratefully. That was the autumn of 1939; it was followed by 1940, and the German invasion of Paris, and the Blitz.

But for now and until the next shoe drops—I like that phrase, which people use to mean "until the next terrorist attack," but it's not really the right phrase unless you are envisioning a centipede with a lot of different shoes—the phony war is what we're in. Difficult times loom ahead, and most of us know it, but tonight we're on our way to the movies or to dinner or to buy a new car to take advantage of the fantastic values being offered.

A phony war is better than a real one. We'll be happy as long as it lasts and safe as long as we remember it's phony.

The other night I heard a man say, "While we're in a war . . . ," and I said, "No, we're not in a war. We're at war, but we'll be in it soon enough."

It is a question of time, and timing.

Tony Blair, who has been bold and stouthearted in his support of America, is reported in the London *Independent* to be urging the Bush administration not to widen the American bombing campaign to include Iraq. At the same time *The New York Times* reports (and *The Wall Street Journal Europe* reported three weeks ago) that two highly placed defectors from Iraq's own intelligence agency have revealed that Iraq has been hard at work training Islamic terrorists at a local terror camp since 1995. The defectors said they knew of a highly guarded compound within the training camp where Iraqi scientists, led by a German, produced biological agents. One of the defectors told the *Times* the terrorists receiving training came from Algeria, Egypt, Morocco, Saudi Arabia, Yemen and other countries. "We were training these people to attack installations important to the United States," he said. "The Gulf War never ended for Saddam Hussein. He is at war with the United States. We were repeatedly told this."

This report is of course not surprising. It is just more data that backs up what we already know. It's the kind of thing Richard Butler, the former United Nations weapons inspector, has been talking about for years. Now people listen.

The argument about targeting is an argument about timing. The argument about whether to bomb and take Iraq is not an argument about whether to take Iraq, it is an argument about when, in this long war, it will be best to move on Iraq. If Secretary of State Colin Powell does not know this he will know it soon enough; if President Bush does not know (I believe he knows, in spades), he will find out; if Mr. Blair doesn't know, he will find out too.

Why is it only a question about the timing of the effort and not the size and scope of the effort? Because we cannot survive—the West in its entirety cannot survive—in a world in which Saddam and his friends are able to unleash what they desire to unleash. We cannot last in a world in which those whom Christopher Hitchens aptly calls Islamic fascists mean to and can kill us by inches, or yards.

There is another question about time, and timing. I know people who think this struggle may last years. I will be grateful and surprised if it does not last decades. Some of that will depend on whether we widen the war quickly or not. If we don't, history will widen it for us.

The enemy has already bombed our country and unleashed biological warfare on us, clear acts of war. We are now bombing the Afghan areas in which we believe the terrorists are hiding, and feeling impressed and rather taken aback at the sight of hardy Northern Alliance soldiers charging would-be terror enclaves on horseback. They remind me of the Polish cavalry, whose efforts in defense of their country in World War II were as gallant as they were doomed. (More heartening thought: They put one in mind of the fearless and quite crazy Arab tribesmen who charged Aqaba during World War I. They took it. Still, as I watched what appeared to be a Northern Alliance cavalry charge on the news last night, I thought: This is how David Lean would have shot it in *Lawrence of Arabia* if his producer, Sam Spiegel, had drastically cut the budget. Mr. Lean had a cast of thousands; the Northern Alliance looked like dozens.)

Let me tell you why I have a hunch that Mr. Bush sees it all, in his head, as ultimately a matter of timing and not mere targets.

On the morning of 9/11, when he was in Florida with his top staff unveiling an education initiative at a local public school, the second World Trade Center tower was hit. This was exactly the moment at which all the most sophisticated people understood, and said, "This is terrorism. This is no accident. This is a terrorist incident. It's Arab terrorists."

That was the smart and obvious thing to think.

But at the point where most sophisticated people were saying, "This is terrorism," he said, "We are at war."

He jumped ahead of the obvious and went straight to the not-so-obvious. I found it interesting that his heart-head-and-spirit apprehended immediately the fix we were in. (And let me tell you, presidents are not quick to say sentences like "We are at war.") I found it interesting when, on Tuesday, Mr. Bush told European leaders that the terrorists are trying to get their hands on nuclear, biological and chemical weapons to use against the West, though I did not understand why he said "are trying to," as opposed to "have acquired and are attempting to acquire." Some accused him of scare-mongering, but he was not. He was underscoring the obvious. And underscoring the obvious is a good thing to do when the obvious is not obvious to everyone.

Everything I hear about him and of him, everything he says that I watch or read, tells me he is ahead of the curve in his thinking on what we are in. This is only a hunch—I have neither seen nor asked—but let me tell you what I feel certain he knows.

It will not only be a long war, he will probably be only the first (though perhaps the most crucial) president who fights it. It will be a terrible war, too. This war happens to be the reason he is president: because something big and bad and dark was coming, and he was the man to lead us through it. He didn't, you will remember, really hunger for the presidency only two years ago, did not have the famous fire in the belly; when the local preacher talked about what God wants us to do to help our country, his mother really turned to him and said—I paraphrase—*He's talking to you, George.* It is interesting that she felt she had to say it. But the president feels none of his old ambivalence now. The new war has given shape, form and historical purpose to his presidency. My sense is that he walked into office knowing huge history was coming but not knowing when, what, where. Now he knows. I can quite imagine him thinking, *This is the reason I'm here.*

I'll tell you something else I keep thinking about him. It is the thing he did, or that happened to him, that no modern president has ever done, that no past president is reported to have done. As George W. Bush took the oath of office on the steps of the Capitol last January, his eyes filled with tears. You could see them on TV, and the people around him saw them up close.

And I remember thinking: Those tears have meaning, those tears are about something, and I wonder if he knows exactly what. Because sometimes people have presentiments they don't even understand until later.

10

The President Within

He walked into history an obscure, flat-footed, bantamy little fellow in a light gray suit, the inhabitant of an eloquence-free zone who gave boring speeches in a flat voice. He was not compelling. This was more obvious because he followed a charismatic leader who did big things and filled the screen. He was quickly defined and dismissed by the opinion elite as "a first-rate second-rate man." And maybe at the beginning he feared the appraisal was correct, for when he became president he said very frankly that he felt the moon and the stars had fallen upon him.

Why would he expect people to be impressed by him, to see him as a leader? His background: a failed businessman who wanted to rise in politics but was forced to do it through a corrupt local political machine. He worked and rose within it, doing his best to hold on to his integrity. He achieved local office, and then shocked everyone when the machine picked him to run for the U.S. Senate and he actually won. He served a term with mild distinction and then through an accident of history became president because—well, because history can be antic, unknowable, full of tricks.

His name of course was Harry Truman, and to him fell the hard and hellish job of keeping the world up at a terrible time. He made tough decisions at the toughest moments—admitting, as his predecessor never did or could, exactly who "Uncle Joe" Stalin was and what he wanted, stopping him in Greece, pushing through the Marshall Plan to save Europe and get-

61

ting the money for it from a depleted American public, fighting a land war in Korea. All this when his exhausted nation—we had been through two world wars in twenty-five years—did not want another war, and needed to be rallied. He stopped or thwarted communism wherever he could, fought like a tiger, faced down the most admired American general of the day and canned him for overstepping his bounds, made the crucial and horrific decision to drop the atom bomb on Hiroshima and Nagasaki and took the responsibility himself to the extent that when the head of the Manhattan Project came to him and said he feared he had blood on his hands, Truman took out his handkerchief and wiped J. Robert Oppenheimer's hands, and said no, I made the decision, the responsibility is mine.

Harry Truman was a great man. And I believe we are seeing the makings of a similar greatness in George W. Bush, the bantamy, plainspoken, originally uninspiring man who through a good heart and a good head, through gut and character, simple well-meaningness and love of country is, in his own noncompelling way, doing the right tough things at a terrible time.

And he faces stakes as high as Truman faced, if not, as many think, higher. Truman had to stand for freedom and keep the West together while keeping Stalin from getting and then using weapons that he could, in his evil, use to blow up half the world. Mr. Bush has to stand for freedom and keep an alliance together while moving against a dozen madmen who have it within their power to deploy weapons of mass destruction that can blow up half the world. He has to see to it that this great mission doesn't end with getting or killing Osama and his men. He must lead the civilized world now to root out, get and remove every weapon of mass destruction— every chemical and bio depot and laboratory in every rogue nation—and banish this scourge from the world. It will be hard to keep the allies on board and supportive, hard to keep the American people behind him, because it's going to be a long war.

Mr. Bush also followed a charismatic leader, and I do not mean Mr. Clinton. Mr. Clinton, whose eight years in the presidency could be compressed like an accordion into one inch of meaning, was no FDR. The charismatic figure Mr. Bush follows is the last big American president, the last who had the massive presence of a battleship, Ronald Reagan.

People kept wondering last year during the election if Mr. Bush had it in him to be a Reagan. I thought maybe he did. But now as I watch him I think: Truman.

Harry Truman did it all through gut and instinct and character. He was a good man who loved his country. He loved to read history and could quote Ovid, but he was no intellectual, not a man of strikingly original thought; his mind wasn't so much creative as quick, and solid as a rock. He grew into the job, on a steep learning curve, forced by history to absorb facts and decide quickly. He didn't know about the atom bomb until the first week of his presidency.

Mr. Bush has been on a similar steep curve, forced to absorb and decide quickly, and his decisions too seem to have been issued from a mind that's quick and solid as a rock. In the early days of the current struggle he immediately understood the situation—"We are at war"—but did not immediately strike back. He seemed, at first, in the day after 9/11, to have been as shocked by history as Harry Truman—the moon and the stars had fallen upon him. He was eight months into a new presidency, and now all the facts of the world changed. But he righted himself as Truman did, and he made his plans. There were no showy and meaningless kabooms with our missiles hitting aspirin factories in the desert. Instead Mr. Bush prepared, pushed, waited and struck—and now the Taliban are on the run and Afghanistan is teetering on something that whatever it is will surely be better than what it had been. Al Qaeda is not done, but as Mr. Bush said again yesterday in his news conference with President Vladimir Putin, we will not rest until it is.

It was in that remarkable news conference that Mr. Bush displayed once again in public what is reported of him in private—that he has an instinctive command in his private dealings, a way of appealing to his guests with a well-meaning warmth that is both ingenuous and . . . yet another little weapon in the Bush armory, an armory whose job it is to provide him with what he needs to get what he wants. In this case and for some time now what he wants has been a personal bond with President Putin that both reflects and promotes a new and deep alliance between America and Russia.

"It all starts with the human element," he said yesterday. And of course that personal element was much in evidence, and yielded a news conference between an American president and a Russian leader the likes of which has never been seen in history. "Yesterday we tasted steak and listened to music and did all of this to increase the understanding between peoples," said Mr. Putin. He especially liked the barbecue: "When I asked the president he said, 'Indeed this cannot be done except for in Texas.'" It would be naïve to see this as anything more than a charming routine by two men in a charming mood if it were not also clear that, as Mr. Putin said, serious discussions had been held. And though some issues remained open, Mr. Putin announced, "We will arrive at a conclusion acceptable to Russia, the United States and indeed the entire world."

Mr. Bush was at his best, and I realized there is a way you can tell that he is and knows he is in full command. He signals it by talking the way he talks; that is, he signals it through bad grammar, or if you will highly colloquial usage. When Mr. Bush is uncomfortable or being formal he says, "The tax structure in Russia is exemplary in many ways." When Mr. Bush is in full command he says, as he did yesterday, "And by the way they got a flat tax in Russia." They got one indeed, and it's turnin' that country 'round big-time. (English teachers across the country are going to have to get used to saying, "It is good to listen to this nice man's thoughts but not to adopt his usage.") You also know when Mr. Bush is in full command when he's not afraid to let his merriness out. His natural verbal style is Texas wise guy: asked by a student if he had any advice for her life he said, "Yeah, listen to your mother." This got a lot of laughter but then, to show respect for a child who asked an honest question, he turned serious, and what he said was moving. "Follow your dreams. . . . You never know where life's gonna take ya. I never sat and thought, 'Gosh, if I work hard I'll be president of the United States.' It wasn't in my vocabulary. But you never know. You never know. Trust the Lord."

Harry Truman couldn't have said it better himself.

I wrote to one of Mr. Bush's aides the other day, a smart and gifted man, and he sent back a note saying the most moving thing that has happened to him the past two months is "seeing that George Bush is a great man—a truly great man."

He meant it sincerely, and would not have said it to me if he did not think it. And it reminded me of something. I spent a lot of the year 2000 writing about Mr. Bush when he was running for president, and stating in these pages and elsewhere that I felt he had potential greatness in him. This seemed to some of my friends absurd. He didn't look great or act great; he looked like an aging preppy fortunate son.

But there's an odd thing about presidents. Sometimes you can meet a man on his way up in politics and you can see the president within. There were people who met Ronald Reagan in the 1950s and '60s and who saw—one wrote a notarized letter so he could prove decades hence that he had seen it—that Ronald Reagan would be president one day, and a great one. There were people who met Jack Kennedy and thought: president. But no one met young Harry Truman and started hearing "Hail to the Chief," and no one even thirteen years ago, in 1988, met George Bush Jr., as he was then called, and saw the president within. I certainly didn't.

But life is funny, and what matters is that Mr. Bush has found the president within. I think he knows he's going to be a great one, and that's significant because all the great ones always know it somewhere inside. Even Truman did, eventually.

11

What We Have Learned

"We gather together to ask the Lord's blessing," the old hymn says and children still sing. This Thanksgiving some of us have felt a greater than usual desire to gather, and ask. Our first big national coming together since the attacks on America has taken on a heightened feel. There's a lot of tenderness out there, and a lot of gratitude, too. One way or another we'll all probably be talking about the things we've learned about ourselves, and our country, since that extraordinary day, September 11.

Trauma educates. We've been reminded that life is short, and probably more beautiful for the brevity: Maybe we wouldn't appreciate flowers so much if we thought that they, and we, would last forever. To know it's temporary is to want to see life more sharply, to breathe it in. Tragedy can leave you hungry for life.

We have learned that Americans are nimble: We crossed the divide between the old world and the new in about forty-eight hours. In the much used phrase we wrapped our brains around it, and quickly. We reordered our minds, and stepped into the new reality.

We are newly aware that as a nation we are both fragile and strong. Because we are technologically highly evolved we are dependent on the maintenance of a certain infrastructure. It took only nineteen men only two hours to down the power lines, cause chaos, crash markets, strike fear. We were vulnerable.

We also learned we are stronger than we knew. A nation that had spent

66

the past few decades trying to decide what kind of cashmere slippers to buy found out it was, still, tough as old boots.

We found some things that had been lost. Our love of country, for instance. Not everyone found it because not everyone had lost it but some had. They hadn't thought in a long time about why America is worthy of their love and protectiveness. But it's been on their mind since 9/11. They are like the character Tom at the end of Tennessee Williams's *The Glass Menagerie,* who said of the family he could not forget, "I was more loyal than I meant to be." Maybe a lot of people have found they were more loyal to America than they knew.

We have learned that the baby boom generation was up to the crisis history finally handed it. From the White House to the media to the Pentagon to Ground Zero the salt-and-peppered ones met the challenge. We may have to stop calling them babies now.

We have learned, as a minister put it, that the age of the genius is over and the age of the hero begun. The observation is that of Father George Rutler, a Roman Catholic priest who ran to the Trade Center when the towers were hit. As New York's firemen, the first and still greatest warriors of World War IV, passed the priest on the way to the buildings they'd pause for a moment and ask for prayers, for a blessing, for the sacrament of confession. Soon they were lined up to talk to him in rows, "like troops before battle," he told me. He took quick confessions, and finally gave general absolution "the way you do in a war, for this was a war."

When I heard this story it stopped me dead in my tracks because it told me what I'd wondered. They knew. The firemen knew exactly what they were running into, knew the odds, and yet they stood in line, received the sacrament, hoisted the hoses on their backs and charged.

When Father Rutler hears sirens now his eyes fill with tears. There was so much goodness in that terrible place! And he saw it, saw the huge towers burning, melting, saw a thousand Americans hit the scene and lead what is now known, in New York, as the greatest and most successful rescue effort on American soil in all of American history.

We have learned, perhaps in a new way, that we are one people. In the past fifty years we have seen our country inch closer each day to greater affection, regard and understanding among our many races. For half a century we've seen Americans of all colors in the office, at Bible study, on the playground, in school negotiating the new respect in a million private transactions every day.

But something in the events of 9/11, something in the fact that all the different colors and faiths and races were helping one another, were in it together, were mutually dependent and mutually supportive, made you realize: We sealed it that day. We sealed the pact, sealed the promise we made long ago. We went from respecting our differences to having, essentially, no differences. We are Americans. That's a lot to have in common.

If you need one stray bit of proof: Helping to run the war, negotiate the diplomatic aspects, standing and speaking for the administration, said to be the most trusted longtime counselor of the president of the United States is a forty-six-year-old black woman who was born when black girls had to be escorted to public schools by federal marshals.

Nobody really mentions this about Condi Rice because it's not big news. And it's not big news because it's what we do now.

What kind of country does this? A great country. That's a good thing to learn, or relearn, too.

We learned or were reminded that in America the toughest moments become, within weeks, tough jokes about the fix we're in. And we still know better than almost anyone how to laugh at ourselves. A small for instance: It was said by a late-night comedian that since Americans can't keep all the "istans" straight—Uzbekistan, Tajikistan, Afghanistan—the best plan was to invade them all, turn them into one country and call it JenniferAnistan, as that way we'd both remember it and like it.

We have learned that in the life of this nation faith trumps everything. Faith trumps culture, faith trumps politics, faith in God is simply at the heart of the American experience and has been from the very beginning, from the first Thanksgiving, which was a giving thanks to God.

The men and women in their twenties and thirties who are on the ships, in the jets, in the troops on the ground: They wear crosses and Miraculous Medals and Stars of David. America taught them to be ambitious, but life taught them to be religious, because it teaches that rising is not enough. They are like the firemen: They believe. And their belief may lead them to heroism, and their heroism may win the day.

Individually many of us have learned what was said the other night at a dinner for the widows and children of New York's firemen and police. That when you're with the grieving you don't have to say the right thing because there is no right thing. You just have to be there. Just be "there," not distracted and daydreaming but loyally there and consciously there.

And we have learned that people experience things in different ways, draw different conclusions. The priest, Father Rutler, who was at Ground Zero, was, a few days later, on a train on the East Coast. He fell into conversation with a young man on his way back to college. He told the young man what he'd seen, what the firemen had done, how none of them turned back or turned away. And the boy listened and said, "They must have been sick." The priest was startled; he thought to himself that the boy was a victim of modern philosophy, of the deconstructionist spirit, of modernity.

"They were heroes." "They were sick." That's a division, but it's not a question, because most of us know what they were. It's something else we've learned since 9/11. And I don't think we'll be forgetting it any time soon.

12

A Wing and a Prayer

FRIDAY, NOVEMBER 30, 2001

I flew this week. It was A-OK.

I flew from La Guardia Airport in New York to Chicago's O'Hare and then back, and it was good.

In New York, scene of three air disasters in six weeks, everyone asks everyone else, "Have you flown yet?" They don't have to say, "since September 11." Up till today the answer for me had been "No." I had canceled all business that required long-distance traveling and was happily at home, sitting with my son in the warm glow of the TV as I fielded calls from hardy souls who had, just days after 9/11, been up and flying to speeches in Miami and Massachusetts.

They all had tales, but the tales were always introduced with "Have you flown yet?," which came to sound to my ears like the challenge the hard-bitten paratrooper makes of the rookie in the outfit: "You jump yet?"

"No, sir!"

"Well, come talk to me when you have, son."

Finally duty called and a book tour beckoned, and there I was at La Guardia breezing past the porters with my overnight carry-on.

La Guardia was calm, about half populated, and had an echoy quiet to it. It was Tuesday morning, and I had arrived two hours early as everyone told me was now necessary. But I only stood in line to check in for fifteen minutes, and when a customer service rep at the counter told me I was in the wrong line, she let it go and gave me my ticket anyway. She was so courteous. I was grateful, and as she was the first human interaction I'd had since walking into the airport I asked for her name so I could put it in this article. Roberta Spinosa gave her name, and asked if this was my first flight. I said yes.

"Are you nervous?"

I said, "Yes. Is that kind of over, being nervous at the airport?"

She said, "Oh no, people are just starting to come back, believe me."

Then I stood in line to get through security and found that some things have changed. You have to take off your coat now and put everything through the magnetometer, including your watch and earrings and rings. Remember the little white plastic container they used to give you to put change and bracelets and wallet and phone in? Now they give it to you but it has to go through the machine, and you watch it nervously until you get it in your hands again.

The line went slowly, but everyone seemed peaceful and accepting about it, and everyone joked and shrugged. I think they were thinking, as I was: This is good, this makes me feel safer. And if you can't have real safety, the appearance of safety, the illusion of it, is better than nothing.

Anyway, it worked for me.

I did not experience the intrusive and wacky searches that people, especially women, keep reporting—the little nail clipper taken from the makeup case, the tweezers seized as if they were daggers. I did see some people getting wanded, and I was wanded too, at O'Hare, on my way home. There seemed no reason for it, no logic to it; I think it was random.

My coat and bags and wallet and jewelry were traveling through the magnetometer when suddenly a young woman security screener was arguing with another woman security guard over the exact nature of a shadowed portion of my overnight bag. In the X ray it looked like something exotic to the first woman. The second insisted it was just a hanger. I backed her up. They argued some more, and then the second woman took the bag from the machine, opened it, found the hanger and shouted to the first woman, "See? Hanger!" The first woman looked away angrily.

Then I guess because I was there they gave me a thorough wanding. One has the impression the security people well know that they are wanding, searching and holding up people who—how to put it?—do not appear to be part of a conspiracy to attack America.

But they have to show they are not profiling anyone, so they inspect Grandma as closely as a twenty-five-year-old man. But somehow it doesn't seem obnoxious; it seems okay. When I was wanded, the wand made its crazy beep sounds in odd places like the back of my head, where I keep the explosives, and we laughed as the security woman frisked my neck and patted her hands against my hair to find the gun.

I did not experience the level of intrusion a friend of mine who is a reporter has. She is on planes a lot because she travels both for work and to see her family; she has an elderly mother on one end of the continent and a daughter just starting out in business on the other. Because my friend works in TV her face is well known, and the minute security people see her inching closer to the magnetometer they think: *Huh, I bet she's doing an investigative piece on faulty security at airports. She's probably got a gun on her that she's trying to get through. Well, I'll give her a search she won't forget!*

This poor woman almost gets thrown against the wall and given a full cavity search every time she travels; her bags are searched inch by inch, she is wanded top to bottom, her nail clippers are taken, her jewelry inspected.

When she told me about it, we started to laugh. She has been profiled. She is a victim of Flying While Famous.

When I got past the security checkpoint in La Guardia and walked toward the gate, I passed two U.S. Army reservists in fatigues and black berets slouching with M-16s and chatting with each other. They looked European, like NATO troops; they were both young guys from Long Island who had volunteered for duty after 9/11. I asked them if they'd seen anything interesting since they started patrolling. One, a tall young man with a black mustache, said no, "except for when the pilots and crew come through. They don't like to be searched. They really let you know! Otherwise everyone is just easygoing."

On the plane, a 737, I took my seat in coach and smiled at the person next to me, a young Chinese woman. She smiled and said hello. I went into my briefcase and got out my Blessed Faustina Chaplet card and opened it up. It has a picture of Jesus on the front. When my seatmate saw it she said, "This is your first time?" I nodded. She said, "My first time too, I'm a little nervous!" I said, "Me too."

Soon a steward stood next to us and with graceful ballet movements acted out with points and gestures the safety instructions the stewardess up front was reading aloud. I had never seen anyone so gracefully act out the safety features, and I smiled and clapped when he was done. He leaned down and chatted with us, and I asked him what had changed for him since 9/11. He told me the job had lost a little of its fun. "We used to be able, the crew, in the middle of a flight, we could gather sometimes in the galley and have coffee and talk. Now we just can't. I have to have my eyes on the passengers at all times—I can't turn my back." He gave me a tough little look and leaned close to my ear. "And let me tell you, if anyone starts any trouble on my flight he is going down, I mean I will break his legs!"

I laughed and thanked him.

We took off. I almost always pray on planes and have a standard prayer: "Oh dear Lord please pick up this plane in your big hands and carry it safely through the air and place it down so gently in Fill-in-the-Blank. Thank you, Lord." I thought those words and said them, and said more. And within ten minutes of a smooth and eventless takeoff it was just like old times. I was sound asleep.

We landed gently, I did my work, went to interviews and a book signing and met delightful and warmhearted people, and came back Wednesday evening. Our takeoff was smooth and our flight was smooth and our landing was smooth right up until we were about twenty feet above the tarmac. Then the pilot pulled back and we went up and up and over a bit and circled the airport again. The pilot soon came on to tell us there was a little too much traffic on the runway, and he was going to give it some time to clear.

We landed safely. And I went happily home.

The extra security precautions seem to make people feel not worse but better. I got the sense a lot of people didn't mind it so much that things have slowed down. And I wondered if some, like me, weren't quietly relieved and made happy by the partial slowing down of America. Slower and safer sounds good to me.

It's fine to see the young national guardsmen who wanted to do something to help be there, and be polite and friendly with everyone, and be able to potentially eyeball bad men and deter them from their path.

But I wonder. Since American civilians are the target or at least a major target in this war, why don't we put one soldier or one Marine on each flight? We have enough soldiers and Marines, and most everyone would feel safer with one on board.

Second, my friend who is wanded within an inch of her life, the reporter, told me that on a recent flight the pilot sought her out to tell her what he was really afraid of. He didn't fear bad men with paper cutters anymore. He was afraid that the next trouble would be the guy in seat 23-C, a guy who presses a remote control button which sets off a bomb in a bag in the hold. "That's what I fear," he told her, hoping she would do a piece on it.

It's what I fear too. This week Transportation Secretary Norm Mineta said the U.S. isn't able yet to search and have dogs sniff each and every bag that goes into the hold of a plane.

But why not have the armed forces do it? We have the means and the manpower and it would make everyone safer, which is part of their job.

We want to get people flying again, moving around America making deals and appearances and selling things and finding new things to sell. The airlines are still in financial trouble, and a lot of people need to be reassured that to fly is not to take a huge personal risk. It seems odd to me that the administration has not moved more forcefully in this matter. Heck, Harry Truman got so mad one day that he threatened to have soldiers run the railways. And he almost did it. And he didn't have a war on terrorism to give him fire.

As for me, I just felt better for having flown and witnessed the same old essential boringness of it. It was good to fall asleep somewhere over New Jersey as we headed west, an unread magazine open on my lap, just like the old days.

13

From September 11 to Eternity

For America for Christmas this year there's only one gift, a history book. And we should all get busy writing it.

Today is the sixtieth anniversary of "the day that will live in infamy," the sneak attack on the American fleet at Pearl Harbor. We know a lot about what happened on December 7, 1941, but not enough. Some of the best of what we know came from a work of fiction, James Jones's great classic novel, *From Here to Eternity.* Jones had been there that day, a young enlisted man at Hawaii's Scofield Barracks, a nascent novelist looking for experience. He got it. He wrote the great novel of World War II. It is amazing to realize that unlike the great novels of World War I, *From Here to Eternity* hinges on the day the war began, at least for America, and never touches upon the war's execution or ending—and it was published near the end of the era in which novels really, truly mattered, when they were seen not as a tributary off the great river of American literature but the river itself.

It was a great book with wide cultural impact. People knew the names of its characters; I can still remember my father watching TV once about twenty years ago as someone played taps on a bugle, and my father said, "Play it, Prewitt." A reference to Private Robert E. Lee Prewitt, the broken-hearted Southern boxer who wouldn't fight but who could make a bugle sing. The great novel was made into a great movie directed by Fred Zinnemann. Like the novel of course but unlike the recently released movie *Pearl Harbor,* it actually had a story, a wonderful story of a lonely wife in a

75

bad marriage and a tough man in a cold barracks, not to mention Private Angelo Maggio, Prewitt's best friend, a tough little Brooklyn boy who had issues with authority.

Sixty years later we are at war again, and I happen to think the estate of James Jones should flood the market with a new paperback version of *From Here to Eternity*. It would become a great best-seller again, would speak to our times and would give America a sense once again of what it is to be a soldier in the army of our country. Modern novelists don't know about those things.

But none of this is, strictly speaking, today's subject.

Today's subject is the subject that will not go away, September 11, 2001, and what we know of what happened then, and there. I hope there will be great novels about it—it is nothing if not rich material—but until then there are data that we have that must be saved, and soon.

Do you know what it was like to be a secretary in the White House on the morning of 9/11 and to hear, as you passed him in the hall, a Secret Service man's radio squawk that there is an incoming airliner aimed at the White House and everyone must run, now? Do you know what it was like for Lynne Cheney, the wife of the vice president, to be hurried down into a secret room in the deepest innards under the White House? Do you know what it was like for the desk assistants at CNN who spent that morning at their posts doing live TV while, for at least part of the time, they had reason to believe the next suicide bomber was coming for them?

Do you know what it was like for anyone beside yourself and your family and magazine and newspaper writers and those you saw talking about it all on TV?

You don't. And we have to do something about that.

I was in the White House the other day as part of a weekly series in which writers and journalists meet with whoever in the White House staff is free to talk about whatever is on their minds.

Before I spoke, I chatted with some staffers and asked them if they had yet written down what they had experienced during the extraordinary events of 9/11 and after. They all said no. And they shook their heads as if to say, "Surprising but true," and "I haven't had time," and "Only fools keep diaries in government."

One man told me his story of that day. I asked if he'd evacuated the White House and he said yes, and I asked how it happened, who told him to leave, and he said, "No one." It was fairly early in the morning of course and he'd been holding a staff meeting in the Old Executive Office Building, just across from the west entrance of the White House. Suddenly he noticed people running by. Then a lot of people. Then he overheard from a walkie-talkie words that seemed to mean the White House is the expected target of a terror plane. Then he realized what everyone else seemed to know but no one had formally announced: We have to get out of here, quick. One thing he remembers hearing: Someone telling women to take off their high heels and run.

They ran. They got out of the complex and ran down the street looking back and then running forward again. Someone once noted of truckers that after they park their rig at a highway rest stop, they take the keys, get out of the cab, walk about five yards and then turn to make sure the truck is there before they walk on. That's how it was with people fleeing the White House, I gather. They'd run ten yards and then stop and look back to make sure it was there, run ten yards, stop and look back.

What a moment in American history. I suppose there had been nothing like it since the War of 1812—that night in August 1814 when whoever was in the White House scrammed as British troops, carrying torches, marched down Pennsylvania Avenue for the White House, which they soon set ablaze. (When I worked in the White House for Ronald Reagan they were repainting the façade. In order to do it right they had to strip centuries-old paint. They stripped it right down to the burn marks left by the British soldiers. You could go by and touch them.) That was the night President Madison's wife, Dolley, saved the portrait of George Washington that hangs, still, in the East Room of the White House. Dolley Madison is said to have cut it from its ornate frame and hid the canvas under her skirt as she escaped in a coach.

That was quite a moment too.

But not enough people took notes on it. We still don't know enough about that night, and the days and weeks afterward as America recovered, and won back its executive mansion.

What we need from White House staffers now is notes, memories, stories, oral histories of 9/11. History needs these things. As William Safire once said, the one thing history doesn't have enough of is first-person testimony.

And not only from the White House, and not only from Washington. Everyone in American media that day has a story, from the people reporting live the collapse of the first tower—Aaron Brown of CNN watched, aghast, and called the great rush of smoke and ash "a mushroom cloud," and I realized at that moment that in the first few seconds of the collapse people didn't know if they were witnessing a suitcase nuclear explosion within the building.

Everyone in the Pentagon has a story. So does everyone in the armed forces, from sailors on aircraft carriers to the pilots who scrambled to force planes down if they had to that day.

The children of our country—they will be writing novels (well, probably screenplays, but let's hope novels) about what they saw and heard on 9/11. But their novels and screenplays will be better, more realistic, more richly observed, if they write it all down now. The testimony of a bright ten-year-old can be a raw and beautiful thing.

So: Everyone should write down, or record, for history, what happened on 9/11. And I think everyone should be given a few hours or a day at work to do it. It could be called "The 9/11 History Project," could be declared a public duty, could be given a special day at schools across the country, and could be led by, say, the Office of the 9/11 History Project within the White House office of Homeland Defense. Just to make it official, and just to have a central place where everyone could send their memories before they're sent on to the Smithsonian, which might consider building a special room for them.

The record of that day should include the kinds of things people wrote and drew afterward, too. This was the first disaster of the e-mail era, and we've all received cartoons and poems and essays and columns sent through cyberspace, with subject lines that say things like "You HAVE to See This."

Here's one I received this week, a poem by an apparently unknown author. The acquaintance who sent it wrote, "This is a must read. This person should step forward and claim this poem.* The words are very powerful!"

It's called "Two Thousand One, Nine Eleven":

> *Two thousand one, nine eleven*
> *Four thousand plus enter heaven.*
> *A bearded man with stovepipe hat*
> *Steps forward saying, "Let's sit and chat."*
>
> *They settle down in seats of clouds*
> *And a man named Martin shouts out proud,*
> *"I have a dream!" And once he did,*
> *The Newcomers said, "Your dream still lives."*
>
> *Groups of soldiers in blue and gray*
> *Others in khaki, and green then say*
> *"We're from Bull Run, Yorktown, the Maine."*
> *And the Newcomers said, "You died not in vain."*
>
> *From a man on sticks one could hear*
> *"The only thing we have to fear—"*
> *And a Newcomer said, "We know the rest,*
> *trust us sir, we've passed that test."*
>
> *"Courage doesn't hide in caves*
> *You can't bury freedom in a grave,"*
> *The Newcomers had heard this voice before*
> *A Yankee twang from Hyannis shore.*

*Peggy Noonan, Wall Street Journal Books and Free Press gratefully acknowledge Paul Spreadbury's permission to reprint his poem, which previously had been published without attribution. Paul Spreadbury can be reached at beesboy@earthlink.net.

A silence fell within the midst
And somehow a Newcomer knew that this
Meant time had come for her to say
What was in the hearts of the four thousand that day.

"Back on Earth, we wrote reports,
Watched our children play in sports
Worked our gardens, sang our songs
Went to church, walked along.
We smiled, we laughed, knew love and hate,
But unlike you we were not great."

The tall man in the stovepipe hat
Stood and said, "Don't talk like that.
Look at your country, look and see—
You died for freedom, just like me."

Then, before them appeared a scene
Of rubbled streets and twisted beams
Death, destruction, smoke and dust
And people working because they must.
Hauling ash, lifting stones,
Knee deep in hell, but not alone.

"Blackman, Whiteman, Brownman, Yellowman
Side by side helping their fellow man!"
So said Martin, as he watched the scene. Then:
"Even from nightmares, can be born a dream."

And down below three firemen raised
The colors high in the ashen haze
The soldiers above had seen it before—
On Iwo Jima in '44.†

---

† The photograph was shot February 23, 1945.

The man on sticks studied everything closely
Then shared his perceptions on what he saw mostly
"I see pain, I see tears,
I see sorrow—but I don't see fear.

"You left behind husbands and wives
Daughters and sons and so many lives
are suffering now because of this wrong.
But look very closely. You're not really gone.

"All of those people, even those who've never met you
All of their lives, they'll never forget you
Don't you see what has happened?
Don't you see what you've done?
You've brought them together, together as one."
With that the man in the stovepipe hat said
"Take my hand," and from there he led
four thousand Newcomers on into heaven
On this day, two thousand one, nine eleven.

Now you might see that poem as moving and simple, as outsider art, and you might call it cringe-inducing kitsch, but it's part of the record of our time, because it's part of how Americans experienced and reacted to 9/11. And so it ought to be saved.

Here in New York we've elected a new public advocate, Betsy Gotbaum. She is an impressive person, a woman who knows and loves New York and who in the past few years helped save the New-York Historical Society as a vital institution.

Betsy Gotbaum and her friends at the historical society too should turn their minds to getting and saving as much as they can from 9/11.

The huge canvas sheets that people write on, in Magic Marker, at the Ground Zero memorials. They hang on the gates of St. Paul's Church, for instance, one of the churches near Ground Zero that didn't burn. I was there one night watching the volunteers change the sheets and put out new markers. The messages people left on them—from the strangers of New York to the dead of New York—were and are priceless. They were like notes left on the side of the road at Gettysburg. Some of those canvas sheets could be bronzed like baby shoes and put in an eventual memorial.

(Two memories. One: The woman who ran the St. Paul volunteer service the night I was there, in October, insisted on putting a new canvas sheet out at midnight even though there was not much foot traffic and no one who walked by seemed eager to be writing notes. But the woman told me, "The bars close at two and four, and people who've been drinking need to write." And you know, she was completely correct, and by 3 A.M. the empty sheet was half full. Two: A young Hispanic woman, a newcomer to America or a visitor, came by with her friends. She wrote a long note on the canvas in black Magic Marker. When she finished she turned and said to no one, in English, "I was here.")

There's a lot more to be saved. The hundreds of thousands of cards from children all over the country to the survivors of the Towers and the Pentagon. In New York there were a lot of crayon drawings sent from second-graders in California of the Twin Towers with sad faces being saved by firemen carrying flags. We should collect them too, and bronze 'em up, and put them in an eventual memorial.

There's a lot that still needs saving. The remaining bottom of one of the Trade Center towers, for instance—which is still there, with the ironwork like a cathedral. That piece of metal is emblematic of so much, and must be cut down in one piece, and saved for the memorial. And the gear of a cop, a fireman, an EMS worker; the gear of a construction worker—all of it should be saved.

The oral memories of everyone in the Towers and nearby are valuable too. Including the terrible memories of those in buildings around the Towers who saw the people who fell from the top floors. They were called jumpers. They were not jumpers. Jumpers are suicides; they decide to die. These people were on a windowsill with roaring flames on one side and on the other a hundred floors of air. They didn't decide, the flames decided.

We have to remember. We have to save these things. We can't lose them. History needs them. Children will learn from them. Scholars will ponder them.

Here in New York we call what happened on 9/11 the greatest and most successful rescue effort on American soil in all of U.S. history.

But there's more rescuing to be done, and it's from a thief called time, which robs memories of their vividness, and from the Dumpster, which is daily carting history away from Ground Zero and the Pentagon.

I wish I could hear my father talk about what it was like sixty years ago, on December 7, 1941, when he was fifteen and living in a little apartment near the old Brooklyn Navy Yard, and hearing the tough men who worked there react to Tojo's deeds. He and his memories of those days are gone. I wish I'd asked him; wish he'd written it all down; wish someone had asked him to save what he thought and heard and witnessed and feared.

So President Bush and Mr. Ridge, and Betsy Gotbaum and everyone else, as a Christmas present to history I hope you get this project going. Some day long from now when America is "old and gray and full of sleep" and "nodding by the fire," it can "take down this book" of memories and slowly read about the hardy and inspiring country that got through that terrible day together, and the war that followed.

14

Miracle on Fulton Street

FRIDAY, DECEMBER 14, 2001

My friends, this is the kind of column I used to do now and then before the world changed. I tell you what I've been doing and thinking and if you're interested you get a cup of coffee and sit down and read along, and if you're not you can go back to OpinionJournal's main page, or Drudge, or Salon, or Free Republic.

It is Christmas in New York. The weather as you know has been soft, nice and not freezing but often overcast. A friend who comes into New York each week from Chicago told me yesterday that on Michigan Avenue it's hustle and bustle and the world hasn't changed at all, it's Christmas, but on Madison Avenue it's dead. It happens that I often walk along Madison Avenue and hadn't noticed that, but there's some truth in what he said. Our great high-end commercial avenue doesn't have quite the cheery bustle of years past. But there's more love on it, more flags and more friendliness in the shops, and at a big expensive handmade furniture place in the Eighties they still have the pictures of every fireman who died on 9/11, each face highlighted in the middle of a paper star, all the stars filling the store's main window. (In New York there has been a slight below-the-radar anti-fireman reaction to this kind of thing. Some people are tired of hearing the firemen praised, and they have a brother-in-law who's a fireman who's a worthless oaf who can't even pick up his shorts. The other day an Internet executive told me this. I said: "Believe me, as soon as 343 Internet executives rush into a burning building and die so that strangers can live, I'm gonna drop the firemen like a rock and celebrate executives.")

I have had a Christmas party week, a very social week. I am not an especially social person but it's been a time for big gatherings, and I am grateful for it. In Brooklyn in my new neighborhood a house party in a grand brownstone mansion, thrown for the neighbors by a gentleman who in the 1980s and 1990s became rich. When I walked in I had the oddest sense of having been in this great home, or having been in a place very much like it, long ago. The huge rounded doorways, the height of the ceilings, the size of the rooms and placement of the windows.

I was born in Brooklyn half a century ago and not far from here, but in those days Brooklyn wasn't rich. It was still full of the families Betty Smith wrote about in *A Tree Grows in Brooklyn,* only two generations older than Francie, the schoolgirl in the book, and not impoverished but working class. We lived in an Irish and Italian ghetto that was turning African American and Puerto Rican. Living with our family were old aunts who'd been maids and cooks in Manhattan, and an uncle who was a carpenter. My grandmother was the coat attendant at a dance hall in Brooklyn called the Lenruth Room when I was a little girl. And I remember being there with her when I was a child, and seeing people dance and touching the coats.

My grandparents lived in an apartment on Myrtle Avenue, in a walkup on the fourth or fifth floor, and their bedroom faced the Myrtle Avenue el, which was about ten feet outside their window. The whole apartment shook, literally shook, when the elevated trains came by. When I was with my grandparents I would put my arms on the windowsill like the old ladies of the neighborhood and watch the trains go by.

I'll tell you who else did this, a generation or two before. The actor Tony Curtis, who a few years ago wrote a wonderful memoir of his years as New York street urchin and Hollywood hellion. He told this story. As a boy he would sit each morning at the window of his parents' apartment and watch the elevated trains. Every morning he'd see a man on the 8 A.M. train sitting in the same seat, wearing a brown hat and reading the *Herald Tribune.* The train would stop, young Tony would glance at the man and the man would glance at Tony. Then he'd go back to reading the paper and the train would roar off. One morning the train stops and the man isn't in his seat. Next day he's not there, next week. Then ten days later he's back in his same seat with the paper and the brown hat. And he glances over at Tony and Tony glances at him. And for once they maintain their gaze. And the man lowers the paper and mouths, "I've been sick!" And the train roars off.

I love that story. It's a metaphor for how we know each other and don't know each other, how we have relationships we don't even remark upon and barely notice until they leave. Did I have a relationship with the house of the rich man whose home I was in this week? I didn't see how I could, but I mentioned to the man's friend, standing in his great hallway, that I had the oddest feeling of knowing this place even though there had been no mansions in our lives when I was a kid. The man said, "Oh, this wasn't a mansion when you were a kid. He restored it to the way it was when it was first built. When you were a kid it was all broken up into ten apartments. Regular people lived here."

So I could have been there before. And now I am here as an adult, as a person who writes of presidents, and the house is a mansion. Brooklyn is, has been, will ever be a place of miracles.

At a party in Manhattan, I spoke to a close aide to Rudy Giuliani, our king. He told me Rudy doesn't want to leave until the fire's out. Mr. Giuliani, of course, leaves as mayor in January, but his aide told me he is obsessed with putting out, as his final act, the infernal fires of Ground Zero, which still burn. Rudy wants the fires out by his last day as mayor. The city, the aide tells me, has been using satellite heat-finding imagery to pinpoint exactly where in the dead zone the fires are. "We find out where, we force foam in from one direction and the fire goes in another. We force foam in from the other direction and the fire goes up or down."

I asked him what, after three months, is still burning.

"Computers," he said.

"Computers?" I said.

He said the wires of computers, the innards and machinery of computers—they keep burning. "There isn't a piece of glass in the ruins, not a single piece," he said. The glass was melted and pulverized, turned to ash. There isn't a desk or chair in the ruins either, he said—from two towers full of desks and chairs. Again, they were burned and pulverized by heat and force.

He mentioned another odd thing I'd noticed, we'd all noticed: paper survived. Paper from the offices of the Trade Center—merger agreements, divorce decrees, memos that Sandra in Accounting had a baby boy, custody petitions—the paper of the Towers shot into the air. When the towers tumbled it created a reverse vacuum and papers were sucked up into the gathering cloud and dispersed all over downtown, the rivers, Brooklyn and Queens. But the binders the papers were in—the legal binders, the metal rings inside them—they didn't survive.

What he told me made me think of a telephone repairman who wrote his memories of 9/11 and sent them to me after last week's column. He had been working on a telephone pole in Queens. He heard the explosions, the lines went down, and soon paper was raining down on him and everyone else. One fluttered down and he caught it. It was a business card. A few days later he called the number on the card and asked for the name. A young woman answered. Yes, she said, she was alive, she had made it out of the building. No, she didn't know her business cards had made it to Queens. (Hollywood: Use this. In your version they fall in love.)

I went to a book party in downtown Manhattan, in the spacious condo of a man and woman who had been walking their children to the first day of school when the Towers were hit. They have three gorgeous kids, one of whom, aged about four, asked to stay up to see the guests this evening and then, overwhelmed by the smiles, crinkles, wrinkles, earrings and perfume of adults bending down to kiss, and frightened perhaps by the gooney look old people sometimes get when they look at childhood beauty, hid in her mother's skirt and then her father's arms. The guest of honor, a wonderful man of depth and charm, arrived late, from a television appearance. I hugged him, congratulated him, asked how he was. "My whole life is work," he said, softly. Then he sucked in his abs, turned, shook hands with friends and worked the room.

We all feel that way so often: "My whole life is work." We all work so hard. But it is, as they say, a choice. We wouldn't have to work so hard if we would take everything we have and rent a $600-a-month apartment just outside a suburb of Tulsa, and join a local church and get a job in a hardware store and be peaceful and kind and take the elderly neighbor to the hospital every other week for chemo.

But it is not the American dream to want to live outside a suburb of Tulsa in a $600-a-month apartment. It is the American dream to, among other things, be at the book party celebrating your friend's best-seller surrounded by brilliant, accomplished and interesting Americans who take part in the world, who are immersed in it and try to turn it this way and that.

We work so hard to find happiness. But more and more I think of what a friend told me on the phone ten years ago after I had written an essay on the subject. He called and said: "This is a famous quote from someone, I forget who, and this is what you mean. 'Happiness is a cat. Chase it and it will elude you, it will hide. But sit and peacefully do your work, live your life and show your love and it will silently come to you and curl itself upon your feet.'"

After the book party, I went to a dinner party in upper Manhattan, at the home of a writer and thinker and his smart, bubbly wife. It was the three-month anniversary of September 11, and naturally the talk was: 9/11. Normally these conversations end in something like resolve and laughter, with someone saying something upbeat. But not this night, and I was glad of it. I spoke to a man, a dynamic businessman and a good person who was, to my surprise, utterly changed. I hadn't seen him in more than a year. I found out that until recently he had been at Ground Zero every day since 9/11. He had lost his office, scores of friends and coworkers, had rushed to the site and worked there for months as a helper and organizer.

Now he is a changed man. He used to carry success on his shoulders like a well-padded suit, and now in his eyes there is grief, grief, a deep well of grief. "I had to go to a doctor because I couldn't stop smelling the smell," he tells me. It is the olfactory disorder of Ground Zero: Work there long enough and you can't lose the acrid burning smell, your nose absorbs it as if it were a memory, and won't let go. You wake up thirty miles away at home in your bed and it's 4 A.M. and you smell it and you think you're going mad. He told me how 9/11 had changed his life. "I am more religious," he said. He looked like he wasn't sure what that meant and was surprised to find it happening to him, didn't fully understand it but knew it was true: He's more religious. And, he said, what he wants to do now is not make money but help people, serve the public, do good.

And he meant it. It wasn't post-traumatic virtue disorder, it was: A life in change.

I find myself drawn to and heartened by people who can't get over 9/11. Because I can't either, and I never will. But then I talk to them and realize: They're here, and I'm here, and we're at the party, so we'll get over it.

On the way home and for no particular reason I remembered something I was told a few weeks ago by a friend who had in another time and for other reasons become a changed person.

I have known him for years but had not known the story he told me. He had been a roaring alcoholic, a man who'd lived to drink and gamble. But something was changing in him, and one night he was at home drinking by himself when he saw something on TV—something someone said, something that moved him deeply. And suddenly he knew his life must change. He picked up the phone and called the twenty-four-hour hot line at a local rehab hospital. And he said, slurring, "I want to spick to a dahkter, I think I'm an alcaholic."

"Is that you Billy?" said the woman who answered the phone.

He was shocked. Someone must have reported him! They must keep the numbers of known local alcoholics!

"How did you know my name?" he demanded.

"Because you call every night at two A.M. How's your daughter?"

For two weeks he'd been getting drunk every night and calling the rehab line and having long conversations with whoever answered. And it was news to him. The next day he entered rehab, and for many years he has been a changed man.

People change. It's not true that they don't. It is true that it is more unusual than it is usual.

At the dinner party a friend told me of his son, a Marine at Camp Lejeune. My friend and his wife may or may not see their boy for Christmas, it depends on his orders. The mother, a beautiful lady, frankly admitted her fear for her son. The father was proud and wistful. I mentioned an acquaintance of ours who has a handsome young son in ROTC, and who will join the armed forces when he graduates in June. I bumped into her and she told me that this is where parenthood makes hypocrites of us all—you know our country needs men like this, you know we must fight, but not my boy, not my son.

The father and mother I was talking to smiled and nodded. It's the same for them. "Let me tell you what my son said to me when I told him how worried I was about him," the father said. "Dad, I am fully capable, fully trained and armed to defend myself, and I am not the target. You are not armed and trained and you are the target. Worry about you."

I worry about all of us, and so no doubt do you. But Wednesday I had a wonderful, heartening experience online that I will share with you because it may help you too. I like to go to Christian Web sites such as www.redeemer.com, where you can find the Reverend Tim Keller's inspiring and informative sermons. I go to Catholic Web sites too, and Wednesday I marked a great feast day of the church at one.

It was the feast of Our Lady of Guadalupe, a celebration of the event 500 years ago in which the Mother of Christ appeared before an earnest and loving Mexican peasant named Juan Diego. The appearance and the miracles that followed sparked what was probably the biggest mass religious conversion in the history of the Americas. And indeed Our Lady of Guadalupe is considered by Catholics to be our country's patroness. As America becomes more Latin and Hispanic the feast has become bigger, grander. It was marked in Washington with a mass at the Shrine of the Immaculate Conception, and there were masses and festivities in Albuquerque, New Mexico, Houston and Phoenix, and Tucson, Arizona. But according to an article in *Crisis* magazine on a Catholic Web site the biggest celebration in the United States took place in Los Angeles. "Following a procession through the city's streets, Cardinal Roger Mahony celebrated a mass for nearly 20,000 who gathered on the football field in the Cal State Los Angeles Stadium." Twenty thousand.

And, most delightfully to me of all, yesterday in Rome, at the end of a general audience, Pope John Paul II for the first time ever activated a Web page. They brought him a laptop and he hit a key with his Parkinson-pained finger and suddenly www.virgendeguadalupe.org.mx was born.

At another site I found that people were writing prayers of gratitude and petition to mark the feast, and I read them. They were so moving and beautiful.

There is so much going on in America, in churches and on Internet sites, that no one in normal media, elite media or any media really seems to touch. But I continually discover and rediscover that there is a whole world of people who exist apart from the *New York Times,* the *Washington Post* and our beloved *Wall Street Journal,* who exist as part of a real and strong and authentic American community, and indeed a world community.

At the site I visited the prayers and petitions to Our Lady were in English, Spanish and French.

They asked for consolation for those who died or lost loved ones in the Trade Center attacks, they asked for protection for our country and peace for the world. "I pray for the people and kids in Afghanistan," said one.

Most were in one way or another personal: "Dear Blessed Lady, intercede for me and pray for me that with your help I can get the money to save my home. Ask your divine son to show his infinite mercy."

"Dear Lady, please . . . pray for dj's, entertainers, artists, performers and media and writers."

"Mama Mary . . . please pray for . . . all the teachers, everyone serving in the armed forces, President Bush, all the leaders especially of the Philippines, all the terrorists, bin Laden, all the priests and religious and our Holy Father."

"Dear Lady of Guadalupe, please let all my friends forgive me for all that I have done."

"Pour les enfants abandonnés."

"Señora, en tu dia te recuerdo y te amo. Gracias madre por todos tus bienes."

"Je t'aime et merci d'être avec moi et ma petite famille je t'aime très fort dis bonjour à Padre Pio pour moi."

"Happy Feast Day, my Lady Mother. You seem so close today, telling me to let the desire of my heart be that of your Son's, and to let his desire be mine . . . bring me back to my monastic community, my Lady, though I have failed and fallen so many times."

"Jesus, Son of Mary, our Mother—forgive me and help me to know and love her more. I desire to be just like her . . . Mama Mary, help me to let go of covetousness, vanity, lust for the flesh and food . . . and all the vices and weaknesses that separate me from your son . . . [help] all my students, especially John."

"Blessed Mother on this, your feast day, please free [my loved one] from the bondage of drug addiction."

"I beg for my estranged husband and for the purity and sanctity of my children . . . Please, my Mama, obtain a miracle for my family."

"Dearest Lady Thank you for all the trials I have received these past few years for in them I have found a new love of God."

There were men praying to be better husbands, wives to be better wives, prayers to be freed of alcoholism and healed after infidelity, for runaway children and broken families. All were marked by humility and gratitude, many by pain and anxiety. They prayed so hard for our country, and there was a sense that they knew that they were praying at a time of heightened alert, and during Ramadan and in a time of extraordinary need.

I found it all so moving. So now I go there and pray along with them, and feel enlivened by their community. It's as good as, better than, a wonderful dinner party.

I will leave you with a happy thought. The other day into my imagination popped a scene that I dearly hope will happen. I imagined that I was walking along Fulton Street in Brooklyn. It was a pretty afternoon, just pre-dusk, and the street was full of shoppers. And suddenly a woman came running from The Wiz, and she shouted to no one, to everyone, "They found Osama! They caught bin Laden!" And the street stopped stock still and then someone cheered and then we all cheered, and we went into The Wiz and watched the reporters telling the story on all the big TV monitors, row after row of them. And strangers talked to strangers and people who hadn't wept since 9/11 found themselves with tears in their eyes, and it was an unforgettable moment in American history.

Actually I shared this scene with my table at the dinner party earlier in the week.

"Dead or alive?" someone asked. I shook my head. "The way you imagined it, is Osama dead or alive?"

I said I didn't know and didn't care. A man said I should care, it's bad if he's alive, that means crazy hostage things and suicide bomber nuts. Someone else said, "I feel sure that when they get him if they get him it will be an unknown CIA agent who gets him, and we'll never know his name." He will be invited to the White House and shake the president's hand and be assigned somewhere far away, and it will be one of the great secrets of all time. He will be The Man Who Got Osama. And we won't even know his name.

I thought, Oh no, we must know his name and dedicate things to him like mountains and libraries. I said we have to know and she said no, if he is known he will be in danger, and so will his family: "the Jihad never forgets."

Well, we'll see how it goes.

We'll see how it ends.

For me today more prayer sites, and a visit to the pained and peaceful people of faith. And then on to Fulton Street, where there's a big Macy's and a Wiz and television and appliance stores. On to the great street bustle of Brooklyn in 2001, where miracles still happen, and have.

15

Give Them a Medal

We wind up the year. It has been full of drama. We now prepare for fun. Christmas is coming, very soon, and whatever religious holiday you celebrate, you've probably got some cheer and downtime coming. And this is good.

Shall we have some fun? One thing we could do, together, is sit down for a minute, read this, and take part in a bit of constructive mischief.

The Presidential Medal of Freedom was created in 1945 by Harry Truman to recognize high and heroic civilian contributions in time of war. President Kennedy reinstituted it shortly before he died in 1963; he continued it as the highest civilian award in the country but wanted it given to those who give great service to their country in time of peace. Many great artists, scientists, civic leaders, entertainers, novelists, union leaders and political figures of all stripes have received the award, which happens to be very pretty: a red-white-and-blue enameled star on a round gold filigreed medal, with a navy blue ribbon trimmed in white. About a dozen Americans receive them every year or so, usually in a colorful ceremony in which the president personally hands it to you in the White House, lauds your great work and thanks you on behalf of a grateful nation.

I saw Mother Teresa win it; they waived the requirement that you be an American citizen for her, in part because so many of her convents did so much work in America's cities. She was given the award in a special Rose Garden ceremony, and afterward, pressed by a reporter on what she thought

94

of Ronald Reagan, she uttered a few words that carried a real definitional wallop. "In him greatness and simplicity are one," she said. Then she and a bevy of nuns hurried away, but not before pressing into my hand a pamphlet with a drawing of Christ and inside a poem she had written about him. She looked at me and said two words: *Luff Gott.* Love God. Then she walked softly and quickly into a black White House car and was gone.

I love the Presidential Medal of Freedom. To me it's like a Medal of Honor for civilians, only without the physical derring-do. The ceremony itself is always full of high feeling, marked by the delight that comes with seeing excellence recognized, celebrated and applauded. (It should be broadcast in its entirety on television, so children can be inspired.) And it's an open and egalitarian award: you just have to be a citizen who has done great things that have been a great benefit.

In 1984 or '85, as a speechwriter to President Reagan, I wrote a series of memos putting forth the name of those I thought deserved it, and made what I felt was a strong case for Stephen Sondheim and, my special hope, the novelist Walker Percy, whose *The Moviegoer* was in my view the great novel of the second half of the twentieth century. (In it, greatness and simplicity are one.) My nominees were not chosen; I think that was the year Frank Sinatra won. He too had been in his career a great contributor to the pleasure of the people, so what the heck. But Percy was alive then, and I think it might have meant something.

It happens that our busy president is coming up on his first anniversary as chief executive. It happens that he has not yet awarded any Medals of Freedom. He and his staff are preoccupied with a hot war and a cold recession and are busy. There's no rush; the medals don't have to be given every year. But right about now the White House should have in it someone who is . . . thinking about it. I have not been able to find that person.

I think we should help. I think we should make our own list, don't you?

It seems to me obvious that George Bush's first Medals of Freedom should be given to the men and women who one way or another pulled us through September 11, 2001.

I have my list. Take a look at it, and add a name or two if you want. (We don't have to be limited to the events of 9/11, I just think we should.) The hardy and incredibly devoted James Taranto and Brendan Miniter, editors of OpinionJournal, will post here as many of your ideas as they can. Then we will forward the whole bundle to the White House in an e-mail whose subject line is: "The People Have Spoken."

I feel certain that the White House will listen to us, as we are the millions of men and women who read OpinionJournal, and we are not to be ignored.

All right, my list, not in order of importance or even love, just as they come to me.

1. *The New York City Fire Department*. On their medals: "The hero comes when he is needed. When our belief gets pale and weak there comes a man out of that need who is bright and shining, and everyone around him reflects some of that glow, and stores some up against the day when he is gone."

2. *The men and women, the airline staff and passengers, on the planes that went into the Towers and the Pentagon*. We'll never know the exact dimensions of the heroism on those planes, but we know it was there. See quote above.

3. *The New York City Police Department and Emergency Medical Services personnel*. Not as celebrated as the FDNY, but full of people who put it all on the line that day.

4. *The men and women of the Pentagon, who lived and led through what happened there*. This includes Donald Rumsfeld, who ran not from the scene but to the scene and helped the wounded. I don't know if that's a good thing in a defense secretary the day a war starts, but it's hard to think of a better symbol of the goodness and egalitarianism that people displayed that terrible day.

5. *Rudy*. It was said of the great Japanese film director Akira Kurosawa that his work was marked by this dynamic: "The villains have arrived while the hero is evolving." Rudy had a lot of time to evolve over his two terms, and he did. By the time the bad guys came, he was ready; he had become the

man he was intended to be. He used all his gifts. He led with perfect integration of head and heart.

6. *The flag raisers.* The three firemen in New York who lifted the colors, and whose Iwo Jima–like moment was immortalized on the front page of the *New York Post,* among other papers, with the headline "Proof Through the Night That Our Flag Was Still There." Ditto the men at Ground Zero who unfurled a huge flag from a broken building. Ditto the man at the Pentagon who, the night of the attack, put up a huge flag and trained a spotlight on it so everyone going by would see the proof through the night.

7. *Paul McCartney.* While Rock Hollywood went somewhat goth and dark in its all-network fund-raiser and tribute to heroes, it was the fireman's son from Liverpool who, a few weeks later, really got it right. He came into New York, got the room, put on the show, electrified hundreds of thousands of tired and sad New Yorkers, and reminded them they could rock again. The former Beatle is already Sir Paul McCartney. America can do the Brits one better. After giving him the Medal of Freedom we can, by act of Congress, give him honorary citizenship of the United States of America. Paul McCartney, American. That just sounds right.

8. *Michael Moran.* I know it was vulgar; I know it wasn't dignified; I suspect it wasn't sober. But don't you think Mr. Moran, a fireman, got it right when he informed Osama bin Laden that he, Mr. Moran, was from Rockaway, and OBL could kiss his royal Irish ass? It was so old-fashioned ethnic, so old-fashioned Brooklyn and Queens. It was the authentic voice of the old New York, which was newly back in style. It captured what so many of us feel, whether of the Hibernian persuasion or not. And it's always nice to give a nod to royalty.

9. *The cheerers.* The men and women and kids who lined up on the West Side Highway in Manhattan for a month to cheer on the workers going into Ground Zero and the workers coming out after a twelve-hour shift. I will never forget the middle-aged Hispanic woman I saw with her two little grandchildren, one in a stroller. They were standing in the dark by themselves just off the highway. The child in the stroller held a little American

flag. The mother held a hand-lettered sign torn from a cardboard box. It said, "America You Are Not Alone, Mexico Is with You!" When people under stress see things like that, it means everything.

10. **Oprah.** I don't know how many shows she did helping people get through the horror of 9/11—and I mean everyone, from those who lost loved ones to young people who can't work in skyscrapers anymore, and people who started to descend into all sorts of emotional dark places. Oprah would not give up on 9/11; she stuck with it as the only subject matter of our day, she got people on her show who could help people. It was a stupendous public service, done with no eye to the ratings and against the common wisdom that we have to move on. Her show didn't move on until it moved people on. Also she came to New York and did, with Bette Midler, a fabulous stadium show. So:

11. **Bette Midler** too.

12. **The men and women of the media.** They drive us so crazy with their lockstep view of the world; they consciously and unconsciously skew the news; they see the world through the very same lens and ask the very same questions and rarely and only for entertainment or under cultural duress allow other points of view on their air. These are people who badly need *real* diversity-training sessions. And for all that, they did the work of heroes on 9/11. They were cool and tough and unstoppable; they hit the sites and got the news and risked their lives. And the brightest of them understood for at least the first twenty-four hours of this war that they might be hit live, on the air, kaboom! The great symbols of American commerce and military might had already been hit; only the media remained. They did their jobs and held their ground. Well done, crazy-making and courageous journos.

That's my list of the people who made all the difference that day, who got covered in grit and ran to the trouble. They're my dirty dozen. Add some of your own. We'll send it to the White House, to help them. And yes, we are talking about a heck of a lot of medals. But then a heck of a lot of people earned them.

16

A Nod from God

I have not read a newspaper in seven days, nor heard a news report, gone online, or called the States in four. Apparently you're all well, or I would have heard about it on the beach. I find it very easy, for the first time in three months, not to know what is going on. It is a real pleasure. When the young man at the beach comes to sell newspapers, I do not call out to him as I did last year. I have no idea what columnists are saying. Shortly before I left home I heard that Charles Krauthammer had compared the American Battle of Afghanistan, in terms of historical impact and implications, to the Battle of Agincourt. I mentioned this at dinner on Christmas night to a large table of beloved friends. A teenager piped up, "We few, we happy few, we band of Afghans." The educational system of our country is not a complete dud.

I am in Mexico. It is warm, in the high eighties, and humid, but softly so. We are on a little bay in a little town on the western coast. In the Spanish-language daily there is no talk of Osama and war, only of Argentina and its financial/political crisis, which for those who live here is of great importance.

On the porch this morning there were hummingbirds floating above the pink-red bougainvilleas. A big ceiling fan turned slowly. A little boy, the three-year-old son of friends, walked in with tiny, half-inch-wide lemons and oranges. "Smell," he said as he put them to my nose. They had a full,

99

sweet citrus smell. I told him they were fruits specially grown for infants. He thought about this and walked away.

Overnight a huge white cruise ship dropped anchor in the bay. It looks very important and mighty. A local friend told me that it doesn't dock because the town would charge it too much, so instead the ship sends little launches full of tourists to town. But they don't walk through the town and buy things, they are met by a bus at the docks which takes them to a local and newly discovered archaeological dig. There they walk around and look at it and ask questions and then get back in the bus and back to the ship. This all strikes me as not fully courteous. It is only fair if you're going to use the town's roads also to go to its shops, which are very nice, and give them money in return for products.

There is a little local agitation about all this. But it made me think of a subplot for a movie. A small and obscure town in Mexico is going broke. It is never frequented by tourists or cruise ships, for there is nothing there. The locals decide they must change this, or they will all have to leave and seek a living elsewhere. And they don't want to as they love their sleepy little town. So they decide to make their own archaeological site. The mayor claims they have found great archaeological discoveries ten feet underground beneath the old bus station. It appears to be a 600-year-old Spanish mission. It has old bricks and old crucifixes and old friar's shoes. Word gets around and tourists start coming. The locals create the dig site in a really professional way, with little dug-up and pre-dug-up areas, and little brushes for gently brushing dirt off bricks and pieces of masonry; and everyone wears big-pocket khaki Gap shorts and eyeglasses and baseball caps bearing the names of movie studios and media outfits. When the buses arrive they are there, doing their work quietly and diligently, except when one of them exclaims, "But this could be pre-Columbian!" Another calls over the government site-control official and says, "It is barely legible, but look—I think the lettering says C-O-R . . ." And someone else says, wisely, "This is too exciting, do you understand what this might be?" There is silence. And then the oldest man there, soft white hair and a face baked for a century in the sun, says softly, "Cortez."

Every day heavy launches full of tourists are met at the dock by local people with donkeys and old carriages. They charge a small amount to take the rich Americans and Germans and Asians to the site. They are well

tipped. At the site the tourists ooh and aah, and watch as priceless old trea-
sures are unearthed. A man playing the part of the local wise guy takes one
of the tourists aside. "There is loads of this stuff. No one will miss anything. We haven't even catalogued it. You want to buy an old crucifix? I
have one. Here, fifty dollars." The tourist pays.

Everyone goes home, the tourists happily to the ship, the locals back to
the little house where they make the old crucifixes, beating them with ham-
mers and putting them on the stove for burn marks. They hammer out
some new Cortez signs on old tin.

The town is saved, the tourists are happy, and one woman from Wies-
baden, holding her little burnt-up cross, experiences a religious conversion
and attributes it ever after to the Crucifix of Cortez. I like this story.

Actually there has been one bit of local news, and I know of it because the
people here who witnessed it haven't stopped talking about it. It is what
happened with the moon. Two nights before Christmas, people were outside walking along when suddenly they looked up and saw the moon and
saw an amazing thing. There was a perfect brilliant white ring around it. As
one who was there told me, if you imagine the moon as a one-inch-round
ball of whiteness, about four inches from its circumference and making a
perfect circle was a perfect white ring. "It was like a ring you would put on
your finger," a young man who saw it told me. His mother added: "It had
that sort of shine to it." And a doctor who has lived here for a decade told
me, with a look of real wonder, "I've never seen anything like it."

They all discussed it as a meteorological oddity, but I of course immediately apprehended what it was: a celestial gift. A nod from God. For three
days earlier, in Rome, Pope John Paul II had approved the canonization of
Juan Diego.

Juan Diego of Mexico, the loving and humble Indian peasant who five
centuries ago saw the Blessed Mother, talked to the beautiful lady and,
through a series of amazing occurrences, convinced the local bishop and
even ultimately the Vatican that the Lady was real and the Lady wanted a
great church built. Her appearance to Juan Diego sparked what has been
called the greatest religious conversion in all of Western history; it is the
point at which Mexico became wedded to Catholicism.

In 1990 Juan Diego was beatified. And soon he will be recognized a saint.

And on that night, around the moon, a wedding ring to mark a marriage that for all its ups and downs endures, and was that evening acknowledged in a spectacular manner.

This is a wonderful time to be alive. I just thought I'd add that.

17

2001: A Bush Odyssey

FRIDAY, JANUARY 4, 2002

One year ago he stood before us, right hand raised, a new president chosen by a shade less than half the American adults who are responsible enough to bother to vote. He had been certain of victory and shocked by the closeness and the Florida aftermath. The weekend before the polls opened, Al Gore strained for every vote; George Bush went home early, making the almost fatal decision of responding with what seemed wan disinterest to a well-wired last-minute revelation of a drunk-driving incident in his past.

And it all seems so long ago.

He is not the minority president anymore, he is the president. His approval ratings are in the 90s. He saw that happen to his father, whose popularity was at 90 percent a year before he was voted out. Because George W. Bush remembers this well he does not operate under the illusion that 90 percent of the people think he's just great, and mean to rehire him in 2004. He thinks of polls as thermometers: Today he is at 98.6, hale and healthy. Tomorrow he may run a fever. Things change.

He knows his father's popularity slid in part because his father saw his numbers as a jewel you could wear. He didn't have to do anything with his popularity, he just had to wear it. This works if your luck holds and doesn't if it doesn't. The economy began to falter. People looked at him and thought: "I'm getting laid off and he's walking around with a jewel called 'The American People Love Me.' I think I'll take it away from him." They did.

George W. Bush watched and learned.

A year ago he stood before us and spoke of "the angel in the whirlwind." In the last year he found whirlwind and angel, and the finding changed everything.

September 11 did many important things. Somewhere on the list is this: It gave shape, purpose and meaning to the new president's presidency. On September 10 the Bush administration was about faith-based social assistance, tax cuts, an improved military—the modern conservative agenda. And like all agendas it had many parts, and the parts became a blur. That happens in politics. September 11 blew the blur away. The presidency is now about two things: ridding the world of madmen who seek to terrorize, and making America safer from weapons of mass destruction. Everything else comes after that.

He has become, as everyone has pointed out, a leader. Our leader, the American president. There are some who knew he always had this potential, had the gift of figuring things out quickly, deciding, delegating, saying what he was doing and why, getting folks to see things his way. A year or so before he announced he would run for president I read a quote about him from the Texas Democrat Bob Bullock. He and George W. had become friends as they worked together during Mr. Bush's first year as governor. Bullock was smart and tough. And when he was asked about Mr. Bush, shortly before he died, he said, "Let me tell you about that fellow. He's going to be a president, and he's going to be a great one." I watched him closely after that and read everything about him. In time, I came to think: Bullock is going to be proved right.

One of the things I realized about Mr. Bush in the late 1990s was that his politics were different from his father's. His father was a low-budget liberal who accepted liberalism's assumptions but thought Democrats spent and taxed too much. George W. is a high-budget conservative, who believes in conservatism but doesn't worry too much about spending money to, say, reform the military. And, it seems, a high-budget conservative is what he will continue to be as president.

Mr. Bush continues to prove that he is not eloquent, and that he does not have to be. People need a plain speaker who'll tell them what he thinks and why. Mr. Bush does this. He does it with the words of the average American, simple flat words. I like the way he talks because I understand it.

Bill Clinton was always issuing great smoggy clouds whose meaning I could not fully decipher. Mr. Bush gives you arrows of speech that have a target. It's good.

Mr. Bush is not obsessed with his legacy. This is good because it suggests he is emotionally and intellectually mature, which is how we want our presidents to be. When you walk into the presidency as a fully formed adult your first thought is "What should I do first and how and when?" When you walk into it with more vanity than sense, more hunger than purpose, your first thought is of what history will say of you. This is like moving into a new neighborhood and deciding the first thing you'll do is find out if the neighbors like you, as opposed to the more constructive, "I think I'll cut the grass, paint the house and join the civic organization." Mr. Clinton spent all his time thinking about his legacy, and by the end he had one: He was the president who spent his time thinking about his legacy while Osama made his plans. He wasted history's time. Mr. Bush isn't like this. Be grateful.

Mr. Bush works well with the competing personalities around him. He keeps Colin Powell and Don Rumsfeld and Dick Cheney and Condi Rice and Paul Wolfowitz close, listens, seems to have an acute sense of what each can give him. He appreciates Mr. Powell's power as a leader and man of respect, and means to keep him close. He will have to, in 2002, which he has called "a war year." That war has many fronts and there are many ways to move forward on each; the war can become bigger or smaller, hotter or cooler, wider or narrower. When he makes his decisions he will announce them, explain them and argue for them with a striking plainness. The quality will be needed, and it is good that the president has it.

18

"Everybody's Been Shot"

There's a small but telling scene in Ridley Scott's *Black Hawk Down* that contains some dialogue that reverberates, at least for me. In the spirit of Samuel Johnson, who said man needs more often to be reminded than instructed, I offer it to all, including myself, who might benefit from its message.

The movie, as you know, is about the Battle of the Bakara Market in Mogadishu, Somalia, in October 1993. In the scene, the actor Tom Sizemore, playing your basic tough-guy U.S. Army Ranger colonel, is in charge of a small convoy of Humvees trying to make its way back to base under heavy gun and rocket fire. The colonel stops the convoy, takes in some wounded, tears a dead driver out of a driver's seat, and barks at a bleeding sergeant who's standing in shock nearby:

COLONEL: Get into that truck and drive.

SERGEANT: But I'm shot, Colonel.

COLONEL: Everybody's shot, get in and drive.

"Everybody's shot." Those are great metaphoric words.

Let me tell you how they seem to apply metaphorically. An hour before I saw the movie, I was with friends at lunch, and they filled me in on the latest doings in our beloved country while I was away. Cornel West is very,

very angry at Larry Summers for suggesting that Professor West shouldn't essentially perp-walk his way through the halls of academe. A Secret Service agent—a presidential Secret Service agent!—had a hissy fit when an airline pilot refused to let him board a plane carrying his gun with dubious paperwork. The agent is not only threatening a lawsuit, he says he doesn't want money when he wins. He wants the airline to be forced to give sensitivity training. I thought: I think someone needs sensitivity training all right, but I don't think it's the airline.

Just after the movie, I picked up Ellis Cose's latest book, *The Envy of the World,* about the "daunting challenges" that face black men in twenty-first-century America. I read and thought, Earth to Ellis: Everyone faces daunting challenges in twenty-first-century America. Because everybody's been shot.

What does that mean? It means something we used to know. It means everyone has it hard, everyone takes hits, everyone's been fragged, everyone gets tagged, life isn't easy for anyone.

I turn on morning television and see Rosie O'Donnell referring again to the fact that her mother died when she was young. This of course is very sad, and Rosie has spoken of its sadness very often, and with a great whoosh of self-regard. Her sympathy for her loss made me think, the other day: She doesn't really know that other people lost their mothers when they were young. She doesn't really know that some people never even had mothers.

She doesn't know everybody's been shot.

I put on HBO and see their new young poets' show. Young poets—well, they say they're poets; I guess they're more like performance artists—come on and sort of strut around a stage and yell, and the more authentic their anger seems, the more the audience applauds and hoots. These poets seem attached to their separateness and in love with their grievance. "I am one angry Lebanese lesbian," "I am one angry NewYorican mother-lovin' whatever." They pour out their pain. But they don't actually seem to be in pain. They all look like they went to Brown and hang out downtown and have invested fully and happily in the Misery Industrial Complex. They look like they want an agent. They're not old enough or, in spite of Brown, bright enough to know: Everybody's been shot.

A young friend of a friend is still so depressed by 9/11 that school and social life and going to a show are now out of the question. "I'm staying home. I'm hurting."

I know, I said a few days ago when we talked. But everyone's hurting, I explain. Then I thought of Tom Sizemore. "Everyone's been shot," I said. "Ya gotta get in and drive anyway."

When I was a child in the old America, people said things like, "It ain't easy." Then they'd shrug. Or, "Whatta ya want, life ain't easy!" I think people actually sighed more in those days, issued forth big long sighs that said: Life is hard. There was a sort of general knowledge that each day would not necessarily be a sleigh ride, and that everyone hits bumps along the way, and some of them are really hard, and everyone sooner or later hits them.

But now, more so than in the past, something has grown in our country, grown perhaps because of good things like psychotherapy and bad things like group-identity politics. And that something is an increasing tender regard for one's own sensitivities and quirks and problems and woes—twinned with a growing insensitivity to everyone else's quirks and problems and woes.

This is not progress. If we became more aware of others instead of demanding that others be more aware of our needs, we would probably get a better fix on life, a better perspective, a better sense of everyone's context. We'd wind up more patient with others, more sympathetic. We could actually wind up sensitive to someone other than ourselves.

I sound earnest today. I am earnest today. But I will make this more fun. The week included the story of a congressman, who through no fault of his own, was humiliated, treated with great insensitivity. I am speaking of John Dingell, the Democrat from Michigan. Mr. Dingell, as you know, is an important veteran congressman who has grown used to—how to put it?—asserting his needs and seeing to it that they are met. John Dingell was trying to get on a plane the other day when his artificial hip set off a magnetometer. He pointed out that it was an artificial hip, and I suspect he pointed out that he was a member of Congress who does not fit the prevailing terror profile. But you know what the security guards did? They took him into a side room, made him take off his pants and wanded him. John Dingell had to stand there in his underpants proving he wasn't carrying a gun.

When the story became public, the secretary of transportation called him and apologized. Mr. Dingell waved him off and told him it was okay, he understands, everyone's doing his job.

Now that's someone who knows that everybody's been shot.

19

Loose Lips, Pink Slips

Someone once said the White House is the only sieve that leaks from the top, but the Bush White House is, so far, famously leakproof. Or rather almost leak-free.

And that is amazing.

How could it be? How did it happen? And is there any chance it will continue?

The Bush White House doesn't leak because George W. actively and affirmatively does not want it to.

From 1981 to 1993, George W. Bush spent twelve years of his life, from the ages of thirty-five to forty-seven—the years of full adulthood when you absorb Life's Major Lessons—watching leaks almost kill the administration in which his father was vice president, and then arguably destroy the administration in which his father was president.

Dubya learned to hate leaks. And to hate leakers. And boy do his people know.

Here are some of the leaks Dubya witnessed in the Reagan-Bush era. A year into Ronald Reagan's first term, his most influential domestic adviser, David Stockman, went to the liberal *Atlantic Monthly* magazine and spilled into its pages the darkest night of his dark soul. The tax cuts were evil, the deficit irresponsible; spending can't be controlled; we're in "an economic Dunkirk"; supply-side theory is nothing more than "trickle-down economics." Mr. Stockman was speaking of course at the exact moment in history when the economy, as Mr. Reagan prophesied, was beginning to burst from its old constraints and yield the Great Abundance, which, for all its ups and downs, is with us still. But Mr. Stockman's leak was truly destructive, not only to Mr. Reagan personally but to his administration's standing as an earnest and believable entity. For it gave Mr. Reagan's great nemesis, the American establishment, enough ammunition for the next twenty years of propaganda. "It was all smoke and mirrors, his own budget director admitted it." Mr. Reagan soon said he'd had it "up to my keister" with leaks, but, being Ronald Reagan, he ultimately treated Mr. Stockman with mercy. Mr. Stockman repaid him by suggesting in his memoirs that if Mr. Reagan had been a real leader he would have canned him. Mr. Stockman then left for Wall Street, where he prospered in the greatest peacetime economic expansion in all of U.S. history—which resulted from the policies he'd done so much to denigrate. Life is funny.

George W. Bush saw that leak and more. He saw the ketchup-is-a-vegetable leak, the White-House-staff-in-constant-turmoil leaks, the Iran-contra leaks in which operatives on Capitol Hill and in the independent counsel's office whispered to the press that Vice President Bush was soon to be named, subpoenaed, indicted.

It was all so damaging. The Reagan-Bush years were a leak feast, and every morning sophisticated White Houseians woke up to grab the *Washington Post* to find out what reporter David Hoffman had today. They'd read, interpret, analyze, deconstruct. I can remember conversations in the halls of the Old Executive Office Building in which Joe would say to Bob, "I know that was Frank's unattributed quote in the Hoffman piece, no one else around here would use a word like *coruscating*."

I knew a man who was an infrequent but truly gifted leaker. He was so good at it that he managed to leak in other people's language. One of the man's enemies was a guy down the hall who had the habit of punctuating other people's remarks with "Absolutely!" My friend the leaker would use "Absolutely!" in his unattributed quotes so his enemy would be the first suspect.

George W. Bush in those days witnessed a political culture in which Lee Atwater was leaking against Ed Rollins to *Time* in one office and Ed was simultaneously leaking against Lee to *Newsweek* in another. I remember hearing one story of a 1984 Reagan campaign staffer who leaked so much and so often about strategy—he never came up with any strategy, he just heard about it at meetings and then spent the rest of the morning on the phone telling reporters what we were going to do next—that one day one of his bureaucratic foes locked him in his office and told him he was going to watch the outside lines, and if one of them lit up he'd come in and drag him straight to his boss. Everything was strangely quiet for a few hours, so the fellow poked his head into the leaker's office and found him under his desk—literally under his desk—with someone else's phone in his hand, leaking.

This really happened.

Part of the reason for the leaking in the Reagan-Bush era, especially the Reagan era, was that both White Houses were riven by a left-right split, by philosophical and ideological divisions. People leaked bad stuff about Team Conservative to help Team Liberal. In the Bush administration it all culminated in the most destructive leak of all.

In 1991–92, when Budget Director Dick Darman, a liberal Republican, wished to give his version and view of Bush 41's tax-cut pledge and its rescission, he went to his friend Bob Woodward, of *The Washington Post*. The *Post* of course is the Washington establishment newspaper, read by all Washington powers and all embassy staffs, which wire home its contents. And so when Mr. Darman leaked to the *Post*, part of his intention was to make his claims, memories and point of view the Official Version.

But Mr. Darman got tripped up. Mr. Woodward had told Mr. Darman he was interviewing him for a book to be published down the road and Mr. Darman, as an old friend, took this at face value. But once Mr. Woodward had everything he wanted from Mr. Darman and others, he informed the budget director that, unfortunately, he has an agreement with *The Washington Post* that any time he discovers major news while working on a book he has to share it with the paper's news desk.

And so, shortly before Election Day 1992, with President Bush struggling against the odds to hold on to his presidency, the *Post* published a series saying that Mr. Bush never meant the tax pledge, never intended to keep it, and the president's own pollster had been eager to raise taxes from day one.

It was devastating. And Dubya was watching it all. And he hated what he saw.

One of the things he saw, by the way, was not only that leaks were destructive, but they were uniquely destructive to conservatism. Liberals had big media, elite media, establishment media, from the newspapers to the networks, to leak to. It was the liberal pipeline: Turn it on in the *Post* or *Times* and it will flow into ABC and CBS. Conservatives didn't have a media structure to effectively leak to. They had small weekly papers like *Human Events,* the fortnightly *National Review,* the brand-new *Washington Times, The Wall Street Journal's* editorial page. But there was no non-liberal news alternative in those days, no conservative media infrastructure, no Rush, no Drudge, no Internet, no Fox News Channel.

So Dubya learned that not only did leaks destroy but they tended to destroy conservatives. And Dubya was a conservative.

From the minute he went into politics, in Texas, at the top, the governorship, George W. Bush let his people know: *Leak and you are out.* He told them they could be frank with him and frank with one another in meetings, that he needed their candor and expected disagreement. But as soon as he read about it on the front page of the *Houston Chronicle,* you are out of here. He let them know he would find out who did the leaking, for leaking is something he understood. He had spent twelve years watching the masters.

Mr. Bush also surrounded himself in Texas with tight, talented and competent people as opposed to visionaries and venturesome thinkers. Visionaries and venturesome thinkers talk; communicating is what they do. They fall in love with their ideas, and come to dislike those who oppose them. They sometimes lash out at them; they sometimes leak. When he got to the White House, Mr. Bush kept his Texas staff and added on people he respected from his father's term—people who to a man hated the culture of leaks and had been damaged by them in their previous lives.

· · ·

So: Mr. Bush's White House doesn't leak. But how does Mr. Bush enforce his No Leak Law? In a way he doesn't have to. It enforces itself. It's in place; he brought it with him; it's there.

But there's more. On deep background I spoke to someone I know/have never met/once had lunch with in the Bush White House/Executive Office Building/Cabinet. He/she/it did not want to be identified. I asked, "How do you guys/gals/things get the word that you can't leak? How does the White House enforce it?"

The man/woman/top aide/peon answered—this is a real quote, which on the rules of background I'm not supposed to use but so what: "Let me close my door. The reason this place doesn't leak is because people have to look up and down the hall before they talk. Killing leakers might have a deterrent effect!"

But he/she/it said it was interesting, no one ever tells you not to leak, it's just something you pick up. There are signs and signals. They are expressed institutionally.

Certainly Mr. Bush showed his resolve on leaks when, after 9/11, classified information he'd shared with some congressmen wound up in the press. Mr. Bush came down hard, spared no feelings, slammed the Hill and ordered a directive limiting the dissemination of U.S. intelligence. Jake Tapper of Salon compared him to "a master hitting his dog with a rolled-up newspaper."

The Bush White House is a White House of empires—Karen Hughes's empire, Karl Rove's, Josh Bolton's, Andy Card's. The people who work for them take their cues from them. If Ms. Hughes doesn't leak, her empire doesn't leak. And Karen doesn't leak.

I called Mary Matalin and asked her why this White House doesn't leak when every other White House she ever worked in did. She said, "There's this notion [in the press] that this White House is just so well disciplined and well organized. They think it's run like a camp!" But the real key to the success of the No Leak Law is simple: "Because we have a common agenda we're not trying to advance any position but the president's. So we don't use the vehicle of leaks to advance our own agenda. The Washington press thinks of leaking as 'conflict leaking'—you leak to them to advance an agenda that is apart from the president's, or to force an argument in a certain direction. We don't have that. There aren't any separate ideological or policy vents, we're here to advance his policy. Previous administrations, you didn't like the way it was going you'd leak it out in the press."

Then she said something no White House aide in modern history has ever felt compelled to say. "We do leak!" she insisted. "We leak stuff all the time about what we're doing and why, but it's not conflict leaking."

And they leak what Mr. Bush wants leaked. "He speaks in English not just to America but to us. He makes the agenda clear. It's not unclear, there's no guessing, what he's thinking or wanting or going—he's straightforward."

There's another way Mr. Bush enforces the No Leak Law, and it's that he appears to obey it himself. He doesn't leak. He doesn't share with an aide details of a conversation he had with a Democratic senator and then wave his hand as if to say, "Make sure the *Post* finds out." He doesn't leak against Democrats. He doesn't leak against Republicans. He doesn't against his staff.

Previous presidents have, thinking they had to become part of the game. Mr. Bush just thinks he had to shut the game down.

What is the public benefit of the No Leak Law?

During the Cuban Missile Crisis, President Kennedy often chose not to meet with his top military and civilian advisers as they gathered down the hall trying to come up with options on what to do about the Soviet missiles aimed at America from ninety miles off the Florida coast. JFK's instinct: When the president is in the meeting some people become inhibited, some are afraid to be candid. And what he needed was their uninhibited candor. So he didn't go. He was briefed later, by his brother and others, and made his best choices based on the best thinking.

In the Bush White House it's the press that isn't there, at the meeting. It is "briefed later," by "others," such as Don Rumsfeld in his daily news conferences.

The president gets what he needs to hear, the public gets what it needs to hear, and there are fewer harum-scarum headlines, which in wartime even more than at other times is a good thing.

But—a big but—has a bright and industrious little serpent attempted to invade this leakless Eden?

Yes.

Guess who's working on a book on Dubya's first year, or Dubya's first year and the war, or the Afghan war, or the continual fighting among State, Defense and the National Security Council over Dubya's first year, the war and Afghanistan?

Big Bad Bob. Woodward, that is. He is reported to be hammering all over the place looking for leaks, trying to make them spring. Who would be his sources? I can guess and so can you, but the more sophisticated and experienced guesser would be one George W. Bush.

I wonder how he intends to handle it. I wonder what he's doing about it. I wonder if the No Leak Law will prevail or, if it doesn't, I wonder if Mr. Bush will choose to cooperate, and have his people cooperate, on the old theory that if you cooperate with certain people you're paying a kind of protection money: Talk and the whole story won't be told to your disadvantage, refuse to talk and you'll be portrayed as the fool. "In this town," as Bob Novak once famously said, "you're either a source or a target."

Wonder what Mr. Bush and his people will choose to be. Wonder if they'll figure out a way to be neither.

20

Plainspoken Eloquence

THURSDAY, JANUARY 31, 2002

State of the Union addresses are usually reviewed in terms of "eloquence," or "drama," or how the overnight polls register the public's reaction. But for sheer seriousness, for the depth and scope of the information imparted, the president's State of the Union the other night was, simply, staggering.

I'm not sure everyone fully noticed, but about five minutes into it George W. Bush laid the predicate for what will no doubt prove a costly war marked by high casualties some of which, perhaps many, will likely be civilian.

That is what he was saying when Mr. Bush asserted that North Korea has weapons of mass destruction aimed at the West, that Iraq continues to hide its WMDs, that old allies such as the Philippines are increasingly over-run by those who want the West dead, that the Mideast and Africa are the home of similar and connected terror movements. Nineteen men caused havoc on 9/11, he said, but the camps they were trained in have pumped out ten thousand more, "each one a ticking time bomb."

The president was blunt in unveiling what will perhaps be known as the Bush Doctrine. And that is that the United States will no longer hope for the best in the world and respond only after being attacked; we will, instead, admit and act on the facts of the WMD era and actively search out our would-be killers wherever they are and whoever supports them and shut them down dead. The Clinton model of inadequate response based on ambivalent feeling is over; likewise the Bush I model of cat-herding

117

coalitions and anxious diplomacy is over, though coalitions and diplomacy are nice, especially when everyone agrees to do the same thing at the same time in the same way.

This is about as big as presidential statements get. Where and when will America move next? Mr. Bush did not say. How long will it take? Ten years. Or, as he put it, this "decade" will be "decisive" in "the history of human liberty." This was not rhetoric. In fact, the speech was blessedly free of the faux poetry that is often mistaken for eloquence. Mr. Bush's eloquence is in his plainspokenness, in the fact that each word is a simple coin with a definite worth. The speech was fact-filled, dense and not airy. Its main point was to tell the American people we are in the fight of our lives and that we had better win, and will.

It was not a laundry-list speech, as State of the Union addresses usually are. It was not a laundry list because we are at war, and so there are essentially only two items on the president's list, the war and reviving the economy that, among other things, supports the war.

Mr. Bush also is not by nature given to laundry-list speeches. One senses he understands that politicians who do them are trying to obscure the fact that they don't have a philosophy. They hope the adding up of program upon program will give the appearance of philosophy. But Mr. Bush has a philosophy. It is conservative. Freedom is the God-given and natural state of man, the government exists to protect man's freedom, and the greatest and most reliable freedom protector in all of human history is: us.

That's what "Let's roll" means to him. Let's be us.

For a man who is famously not smart Mr. Bush certainly is smart. The president seems to me these days to be operating as a person of essentially two halves. The first half is Sheer Gut—a sharp and intelligent instinct, an inner shrewdness, an ability to see the bottom line, decide priorities, and see the difference between what is desired and what is needed. The second half, as the liberal pundit Bill Schneider said on CNN after the speech, is "character." People can tell, Mr. Schneider said, that when Mr. Bush says he's going to do something he actually means to do it.

A great gut plus a reliable character is maybe the exact perfect mix for any president, but certainly for a wartime president.

On nonwar issues the president continued to paint himself merrily and sympathetically as a man who stands for giving the little guy the tax cuts he needs . . . for using honest faith to answer public problems . . . for a strong defense, a strong military, a pay increase for the soldiers, sailors and Marines who put themselves in harm's way so we can sleep safely at night. He put himself forward as the man who stands for winning the war and encouraging the rise in well-grounded patriotic feeling.

Mr. Bush's opposition at the moment appears to have been reduced to agreeing with the president on just about everything and then saying, "But let's make sure we don't run a deficit!" Mr. Bush is talking life and death, love and honor and they're running around talking like accountants. The Democrats of Congress seem at the moment to be acting like liberal Republicans during the Great Society, always worried about the cost of things and never the meaning. Without a message they wince; they are acting like what H. L. Mencken said of the Puritans, that they lived in constant fear that someone, somewhere is having a good time.

And I am not sure the coming deficit will have much traction as a political issue for the Democrats. The public by and large seems to know that (a) there's a war on, (b) we all want whatever defense systems or weapons that can keep us alive to be bought and deployed, and we'll worry about the cost later when we're still alive, as opposed to dead, and (c) oh heck, Ronald Reagan said we'd grow our way out of the last deficit and we did, let it go.

I quoted Bill Schneider praising Mr. Bush. After his speech, the liberal historian Doris Kearns Goodwin said the president's words were "galvanizing." Chris Matthews compared him to Jack Kennedy. *The New York Times* said Mr. Bush has "soared to new heights."

In the old days elite opinion held that Mr. Bush was a scripted trust-fund dullard whose rise was greased by luck and birth. Those were the days. Those of us who stood with Mr. Bush then were a small and hardy band of criticized contrarians. It was fun. We had secret handshakes and everything. Now everyone's in on the act.

It is not, in general, good for presidents to be so universally praised. Politicians are made dizzy by love. They lose their edge, their purpose, and coast. But Mr. Bush has earned this support, and in any case wartime is a good time to unify behind a president—particularly this war, particularly this president.

And it's also true that those who once dismissed Mr. Bush and now praise him are demonstrating an honesty and high-mindedness that is wonderful to behold after the sapping, sour 1990s. It really is refreshing—literally refreshing—to have a president people admire and can follow cleanly again.

21

Why We Talk About Reagan

FRIDAY, FEBRUARY 8, 2002

A small band of former aides and friends of Ronald Reagan were all over TV this week talking about the former president on his ninety-first birthday. Our memories and reflections were treated with thoughtfulness and respect by the media. It wasn't always this way but I'm glad it is now, and I think there are reasons for it.

Journalists feel an honest compassion for Mr. Reagan's condition—everyone is saddened by the thought that this great man who was once so much a part of our lives no longer knows he was great, no longer remembers us. It's big enough to be called tragic: this towering figure so reduced by illness. Part of it too is a growing appreciation of Nancy Reagan, who is doing now what she did for fifty years, protecting him, protecting his memory and his privacy. Only now she does it 24/7 at the age of seventy-eight, and without the help and comfort of the best friend of her life: him. She told me some months ago how to this day she'll think of something and want to say, "Honey, remember the time . . ." Or something will happen and she'll want to ask him what he thinks. And of course she can't.

It is also true—I am sorry to be cynical, but I have worked in media, have enjoyed and even shared its cynicism—that the hungry maw of every network and cable news show is hoping, on the day the former president leaves us, to get the Get. To get Mrs. Reagan on the air, or the former president's children, or his associates in history. The more sympathetic they are now, the better the chance they'll get the Big Get. And this is understand-able. It's what newspeople want to do: Get the story.

Whatever the reasons, it's good to see Mr. Reagan's memory held high by those who admire and understand him, and have the arguments for his greatness heard with respect in the media.

But let me tell you why we make those arguments as often as we can. When I talk about Mr. Reagan, media people often preface my remarks, or close them, with words like this: "You adore him." Or, "You of course have great affection for him and so it's your view that . . ."

These are not unfriendly words, but they're a warning to the viewer: Take what you hear with a grain of salt. Needless to say the grain-of-salt warning doesn't come when the subject is, say, JFK or FDR or Martin Luther King, all of whom had friends, supporters and biographers who have spent decades advancing their causes with affection and respect.

And that's why those of us who talk about Mr. Reagan talk about Mr. Reagan, why we stick to the subject. After he leaves us the media may well conclude that they have no particular reason to listen politely when we speak of him. So we do it now.

And we do it because history is watching. Because young people are com-ing up. Because new generations rise and look at the past and think: Who was great, who was worthy of emulation, who can I learn from? Children whose parents have not for whatever reason led them or nurtured them suffi-ciently sometimes feel a particular need to look at the historical past and think: Who can I learn from there as I try to put together a good life?

Who indeed. There is something the past few days I've found difficult to communicate on TV, in part because it sounds pretentious in the chatty atmosphere of the news-nook, but it's at the heart of what I'm trying to say. Laurens van der Post, in a memoir of his relationship with Carl Jung, said that we all forget the obvious: "We live not only our own lives but, whether we know it or not, also the life of our time." We add to that larger life or detract; we give or withhold, we lead or shrink back, we put ourselves on the line for the truth or we ignore the summons, we meet the great chal-lenge of our age or we retreat to our gardens. It is not bad to tend your gar-den, and is in fact necessary; you can find wholeness, solace and truth there too. But to tend it and also step forward into history, to step into the life of your age, to step onto history's stage and seek to take part constructively, to try to make your era better—that is a very great thing. And that is what Mr. Reagan did, and successfully. He helped his world.

Ronald Reagan's old foes, the political and ideological left, retain a certain control of the words and ways by which stories are told. They run the academy, the media; they control many of the means by which the young— that nice, strong twenty-year-old boy walking down the street, that thoughtful girl making some money by yanking the levers of the coffee machine at Starbucks—will receive and understand history.

But the academy and the media may not in time tell Mr. Reagan's story straight; and if they do not tell the truth it will be for the simple reason that they cannot see it. They have been trained in a point of view. It's hard to break out of your training.

Those of us who lived in and feel we understood the age of Ronald Reagan have a great responsibility: to explain and tell and communicate who he was and what he did and how he did it and why. Where he came from and what it meant that he came from there. What it meant, for instance, that he came from the political left, was trained in it, and then left it—for serious reasons, reasons as serious as life gets. And: what it cost him to stand where he stood. That is always one of the great questions of history, of the story of a political or cultural figure—"What did it cost him to stand where he stood?" You learn a lot when you learn the cost.

If we don't tell the young they'll never know.

That is why we don't let the subject pass. It's too rich with meaning. To speak of Mr. Reagan honestly, to speak of his fabled life and his flaws, is to make a contribution to the young, who ten and twenty and forty years from now will be running history, and who will need lives on which to pattern their own, lives from which to draw strength.

The young could do worse. The young often have.

22

The Great Iraq Debate

FRIDAY, FEBRUARY 15, 2002

The other night in New York, the Council on Foreign Relations hosted a fascinating debate between the always interesting Richard Perle, an assistant secretary of defense in the Reagan administration who now serves as an adviser to the administration on the Defense Science Policy Board, and Leon Fuerth, whose career in foreign affairs has taken him from Capitol Hill advising Democrats to the office of the vice president, where he was Al Gore's national security adviser.

The subject of the debate was Iraq, and what the Bush administration's plans and attitude toward it ought to be.

In the spirit of Kausfiles' "Series Skipper," which as a public service boils down the information in long newspaper series, I will attempt to capture the more than hour-long debate. (I was not there but listened to reports from friends who were, and later read the transcript.)

Mr. Fuerth began with a striking directness. American policy toward Iraq begins here: "We need to get rid of Saddam Hussein." But we need to get rid of him on our schedule—"at a time that we have prepared under conditions that we have set in motion." Mr. Fuerth opposed "pivoting out of Afghanistan and moving on to the attack in Iraq."

The current crisis, he continued, began with an attack by a terrorist network, not a state. What happened in New York and Washington was an international event, plotted in Germany, financed by money from around the globe, executed by operatives trained in the United States. This is a global network. It didn't come out of Baghdad or Tehran. We must focus our time and resources on preventing terror networks from using weapons of mass destruction against us. They had attacked us before—our embassies in Africa, the U.S.S *Cole*. Because it is a global network, the fight against it must be global.

At the same time we cannot ignore Saddam. We should see to it that he is forced to spend time and effort "defending himself" from internal challenges that the United States can help set in motion. Perhaps the anti-Saddam Iraqi National Congress could become a force; perhaps internal opposition will rise. A return to "draconian weapons-inspection rules" under U.N. auspices is also needed.

Also, America must "prepare a homeland defense against the moment when we take on" a nation-state such as Iraq. This job will not be finished in six weeks or six months. But yes, he said, ultimately we'll have to reckon with Saddam. "A moment does have to be picked. Right now, exactly now, coming out of Afghanistan, is not the right moment." Now is the time to focus on the global terror network.

Now Mr. Perle spoke, with the bluntness and occasional sarcasm that characterize his rhetorical style.

"We cannot wait," he said. Saddam is "attempting to acquire nuclear weapons." He may have them in a year or two. He does already, as we know, have chemical and biological weapons and has already, alone among nations, used chemical weapons against civilians, Mr. Perle said.

Saddam's hatred for the United States is murderous. "He is a threat to us," argued Mr. Perle. He is a tyrant whose loathing is "undisguised." He is "in contact with networks of terror." He is in a position to use weapons of mass destruction against us "delivered anonymously." We cannot wait and hope he'll do nothing, Mr. Perle said. As we wait, we risk giving Saddam time to distribute his biological weapons to Al Qaeda.

As for the Iraqi National Congress, the Clinton administration in eight years and the Bush administration in one year have done nothing to make them ready to help on the ground in Iraq. They are not ready and indeed will not be ready to rise against Saddam until America moves on Saddam,

Mr. Perle said. "At that point we will set in motion what it takes to make them ready." Only then, once we move, will they be "our allies on the ground."

Mr. Perle concludes: "We waited too long to deal with Osama, and he struck. We must not repeat this mistake with Saddam."

Mr. Fuerth answers. Yes, he agrees that Saddam is "malevolent and danger-ous." But why then march on Iraq and not Iran, which is also dangerous? Mr. Perle speaks of the risk of waiting, says Mr. Fuerth. But what about the risk of "premature action"?

The INC is not at this time a fighting force, it is fractious and untrained.

Intriguingly, Mr. Fuerth seemed to imply that the Joint Chiefs of Staff would have to be "overruled" by President Bush if he ordered a fast military action out of Afghanistan and into Iraq.

Mr. Perle replies. If Mr. Fuerth thinks Iran is as big a threat as Iraq, why doesn't he recommend action against Iran? "I don't think he's prepared to take any action against any state," Mr. Perle says. Which, he implies, is the real reason Mr. Fuerth puts emphasis on moving against a nonstate entity, the international terror network.

Mr. Perle says it is good that Leon Fuerth agrees we must win the war against terror. But we must "take that war to the states that harbor and sup-port terrorists." Once those states know they will have no peace until they throw the terrorists out, the terrorists will be thrown out, be exposed, and we will get them. If we "shy away" from taking on "the states that support them" the terrorists will continue to find and enjoy state sanctuary from countries such as Iraq. Which is to say, they will continue as a real threat.

As for homeland defense, Mr. Perle's definition of it was limited, and his attitude fatalistic. "An open society" such as ours has "poor prospects in making this country impermeable," Mr. Perle says. Now the most ringing and direct Perleism: "We have to take the war to them because of our inability to prevent them from bringing it to us." Mr. Perle said he is not advocating making a move a month from now, or two months from now. But we must make the decision to move, and choose strategy and tactics now. Mr. Fuerth, he said, doesn't want to take the risks. But the greater risk is doing nothing and leaving Saddam more time to plan, gain strength, take the initiative.

Moderator Les Gelb asked the question of the hour. If Saddam believes the United States is coming after him—and with the administration's "axis of evil" rhetoric and the strong poll numbers supporting the president, Saddam might certainly likely conclude the United States is coming—then why shouldn't Saddam come after us now?

Mr. Perle's reply was both low-key and chilling. "He may." Saddam may indeed "act preemptively." But we cannot let that fear stop us. Indeed, it should stiffen our resolve: Saddam has got to go.

In the question-and-answer session that followed, *Slate*'s Jacob Weisberg asked what we knew, essentially, about Saddam's sanity. "It seems to me an important question in this debate is the extent to which Saddam is rational," he said. Will Saddam refrain from attacking us in a way that would cause us to remove him from power?

Mr. Perle replied. "I tried to suggest earlier, and let me make it more precise, Saddam has available to him the option of empowering anonymous terrorists to do great damage in this country. There's a great deal of evidence that suggests he would be immensely pleased if damage were in fact done. So working deterrents against an anonymous threat is extraordinarily difficult. Suppose a significant quantity, a few pounds, of anthrax were released over this city from a tall building. Suppose we suspected that Saddam was behind it, and suppose the terrorists who did it committed suicide in the course of it. Could we then act, and how?

"We might have the option of a brutal attack against civilians in Baghdad," Mr. Perle said, but that "hardly seems to me an appropriate or an effective way of protecting the United States. Which is why I think it's essential that we get ahead of the problem, since he has the capacity to do something like that, and conventional deterrents cannot be made effective."

So, that's the Series Skipper version.

Some thoughts. One does get a sense of what a Gore administration foreign policy might have been from Mr. Fuerth, who himself might have become an NSC adviser for President Gore. One senses that policy would be marked by talking, hoping, waiting and worrying. There's a lot to worry about so that's not all bad, but it's not all good either. From Mr. Perle, on the other hand, we get a sense of impatience: move, and now! But he did not communicate an impression that he is thinking of the civilian cost that might be incurred by the operatives of an invaded and enraged Saddam.

It is interesting, the tradition whereby the very best, most imaginative and textured discussions and delvings into world politics have come not, as a rule, from the elected officials of the world's democracies but from, if you will, the hired hands of diplomacy—those who do not run for office but help those who do. Part of the reason is obvious—elected officials have real reason to avoid dramatic thoughts colorfully put. And part is less obvious. The hired hands are almost always cleverer, and often deeper, than their principals. St. Thomas More was, in all ways but power, the superior of Henry VIII, and George Kennan—who among other things developed the policy of containment—is a cleverer man than most of the presidents he served. This isn't surprising, but it's always interesting.

As for the debate itself, Mr. Fuerth did not elaborate on exactly what he meant by "homeland security," and Mr. Perle chose to define it for him, and narrowly. Homeland security, he suggested, is the daily effort of our government to keep terrorists off our planes, away from our nuclear plants, out of our country. With our famously porous borders and our famous personal openness, this is indeed difficult. A determined bad guy has many points of entry.

But I thought that when Mr. Fuerth referred to homeland security he was speaking not only of law enforcement. I thought he was also referring to what I think of homeland defense, which includes the putting in place of systems whereby American citizens are made safer when an attack has come. This would include but not be limited to increased efforts to produce various vaccines and medicines, the return of some kind of fallout shelters with independent ventilation systems, etc., and increased production and availability of nuclear-biological-chemical suits and masks. Whatever will make our citizens a little safer, or a little safer a little longer, is a good thing. If it means taking some time to help people survive a dirty bomb or the unleashing of smallpox, and the time can be taken, why not take it?

That is my first point. My second is more frivolous but I've been meaning to mention this for a while, and actually it's not frivolous. Since we have
entered the age of weapons of mass destruction, since we are immersed in
the fact of them and will no doubt be shaped in part by their existence, we
need a way of speaking of them with a phrase that is easier to say and easier
to grasp than "weapons of mass destruction" or WMDs. Ideas for a new
name for WMDs are welcome, and will be forwarded to the administration.

Third, and as important as the first point: The Perle-Fuerth debate, for
all its disagreement, underscored what most observers have sensed the past
few months but few have clearly said. The debate reflected a most extraordinary change in our foreign policy. Only a year ago the idea that left, right
and center in America would be saying "Saddam must go" would be too far-
fetched. The idea that a year ago we would be engaged in a war in Afghanistan
with left, right and center behind it would be similarly unthinkable. The
idea that all would back hunting down and killing the head of a terror network—again unthinkable. The idea that the only real question on moving
on Iraq is how and when—unthinkable.

How did this all happen? It happened after we all woke up happily on
September 10, 2001, and went to bed happily that night. And then, a few
hours into the next morning, the world changed forever. Talk about the law
of unintended consequences. The man who planned and created the terrible deed that day signed his own death warrant, signed the death warrant of
his movement, may well have signed Saddam's, and left an America stronger
and more united than it had been in a very long time.

This is fortunate indeed. May our good fortune continue.

23

A Message for Rumsfeld

FRIDAY, FEBRUARY 22, 2002

On Wednesday Defense Secretary Donald Rumsfeld met with the troops at Nevada's Nellis Air Force Base to grip and grin, take questions and fill them in on the war so far. The troops were gathered photogenically in what CNN called the living and dining area of the base and what looked like a big cavernous hangar, which happened to have a jet parked in the background.

It was billed as a town-hall meeting with American airmen, and it reminded me of what Richard Brookhiser once said of presidential campaigns, that it's the outside story—the public statements and speeches, the things voters can see and are meant to see—that tends to be more interesting and important than the inside story of who said what at the meeting.

Mr. Rumsfeld's appearance gave rise to some thoughts, mostly about him. He has of course, since 9/11, emerged as a singular presence in the war. At first it was startling: all that interestingness wrapped up in such blandness. Mr. Rumsfeld looks like the competent mayor of a midsize metropolis, or the savvy CEO of a midlevel company. Gray hair, gray suit, silver-rimmed glasses. He looked the other day like a beige and silver guy in a tired red tie.

And yet these days he seems, as leaders go, a natural. Much has been written about his skills, and though the amount of interest being paid to him is inevitable—he's a WASP wartime consigliere, an interesting thing in itself—a lot of it misses the point.

As a communicator he's clear as clean water. He seems ingenuous. He talks with his hands. He's thought it through and knows a lot and tells you what he knows. At first you sense his candor and clarity and enjoy it without realizing it. Then you realize you must be enjoying it because you're still listening. Then you sense that his candor and clarity are in the service of intelligence and clean intentions. You find yourself following what he says, following the logic and the argument. Which makes you ultimately lean toward following him.

He's Bushian, but he seems more interesting than George W. Bush, and not only because he is more experienced, an accomplished veteran of past governments. (He was first elected to the House forty years ago; the first time he was Defense Secretary was in 1975, when he was the youngest ever.) He has a certain merriness, which is a good thing in a war leader when it is not a sign of idiocy, and it is a knowing merriness. Mr. Bush in contrast has comic, joshing moments, and Dick Cheney has genuine wit.

Mr. Rumsfeld, like Mr. Bush, uses plain words to say big things. He can use plain words because he isn't using words to hide. He can afford to be frank, and in any case it appears to be his natural impulse. He can afford to be frank because we are at war, and part of winning is going to be remembering that we're fighting, and why, which is not easy when there's so much on sale at the mall. Part of Mr. Rumsfeld's job is to tell the American fighting man and woman, and the American people who pay for the defense establishment, what is going on in the war, and how, and where, and why, and what the future holds. It's his job, in effect, to be blunt, to increase consciousness, and to enhance our determination while damping down pointless anxiety. It's a delicate dance, and yet he doesn't seem to be dancing.

When asked by an airman how long the war will last, Mr. Rumsfeld said that question is quite close to him because every morning when his wife wakes up she asks about Osama. "Don, where is he?" He tells the airmen, "There's no way to know how long. It's not days, weeks, months; it's years for sure."

Asked if the U.S. military will wind up occupying Afghanistan, he calls that "unlikely," but says the United States wants to help Afghanistan build and train its own army. He foresees "a military-to-military relationship."

It's clear when he speaks, and because it's clear you can follow it, and because you can follow it you consider following him.

This as we all know is not always the way with leaders. Usually people like secretaries of defense and secretaries of state and United Nations representatives say things like this: "We have to remember, Tim, that the infrastructure of the multinational coalition in conjunction with the multilateral leadership entities inevitably creates potential for a disjunction of views that requires cooperation, coordination and cohesion from member states."

Some of them talk like that because they're hopelessly stupid and are trying to hide it. Some of them are just boring. But a lot of leaders talk like this because they don't want to communicate clearly. They want instead to create a great cloud of words in which the listeners' attention and imagination will get lost.

They're not trying to break through with thought, they're trying to obfuscate. They are boring not by accident but by design. Because they don't want people to understand fully what they're doing. Because they know what they're doing won't work, or is wrongheaded, or confused, or cowardly, or cynical, or just another way to dither, or will more likely yield bad outcomes than good.

We should all try to keep this in mind when we watch *Meet the Press* and someone is being especially boring. Henry Kissinger once joked that the great thing about being famous is that when you're boring people think it's their fault. But it's almost never "their fault."

Anyway, instead of giving a dull, windy and dissembling answer when asked about the war coalition, Mr. Rumsfeld cut through to the heart of it. He said it exists to do a job, and the job, not the coalition, is what counts. "You have to let the mission determine the coalition, you don't let the coalition determine the mission."

So that's the key to Mr. Rumsfeld: candor and clarity plus specificity, and all of it within a context of a war that itself, so far, makes sense and is just.

Mr. Rumsfeld offered one answer that, while demonstrating a grasp of the question's many different layers, failed to capture something that probably needs capturing. Asked by an airman what the armed forces are going to do to retain experienced personnel, Mr. Rumsfeld spoke of pay raises, spare parts, morale—"every one of you has to know that you're needed." He said we need a military command that has enough imagination to see who's good at what and make sure they're assigned to it.

All good as far as it went—pay and parts and a psychological sense that one is noticed and appreciated are key, always. But so is something else that one senses has gone by the boards the past decade or so, and it has to do with the whole mysterious tangle of motivations that leads a man (or woman) to join up to defend his country. The thing that makes him take as his job protecting the strangers who are sometimes ungrateful countrymen; the thing that tells him to put himself in harm's way and live the loneliness of the job; that tells him to risk his life so that my son and yours can sleep peacefully through the night. The whole mysterious tangle that leads them to join is also, in part, what leads them to stay. And to my mind it comes down to sissy words like love. "Only love will make you walk through fire," it was said of the firemen of New York on 9/11; only love will make you enter that cave in Afghanistan, too. We just don't call it love. We call it a solid job and a good pension system.

The other day I got a letter from a guy in the army in Bosnia, telling me about his duty there and including an essay about the Christmas party the troops at his base threw for the badly damaged children in an orphanage west of Tuzla. Friends and relatives of the American troops had sent wonderful gifts for each of the hundred or so children; the children in turn had dressed up in paper party hats and put on angel wings and sung songs and recited poetry. When it was over, the American soldier thought of something his history teacher back home in Michigan had taught him. You cannot escape history, the teacher had said, for history is not what happens in books, history is what will happen to you.

The American thought of how history had smashed the lives of the children in the orphanage. And then he thought of how history, in the form of "the treasure and sweat of America's finest" had also given those same children a new chance "to grow in peace." It was American troops acting through history who had done that.

It was clear from what the soldier wrote that his spirit and intelligence were engaged not only in the fight in Bosnia but in protecting Bosnian children, and therefore Bosnia's future. What that knowledge did to his pride and sense of mission was obvious. He didn't use the word *love*—he is a soldier—but that's what he was writing about.

Last summer I went on a U.S. Army Web site, a recruiting site actually. I'd gone there because I wanted to write something about Medal of Honor citations, and I wanted to read them. I found to my surprise that when you go to a U.S. Army Web site what you mostly see is how much money they pay and how they'll put you through school. That's good and needed information, but there wasn't any of the deeper meaning of serving—no history of the U.S. Army, no Medal of Honor citations, no essays from Bosnia. It was all slogans and salaries. It was all about pay. Which recruitment specialists apparently think is the prime motivator for joining up. Surely it's part of it, but it couldn't be all, and if it is we're in trouble. An army runs on its stomach, Napoleon famously said. But it fights with its heart and its spirit and soul.

Mr. Rumsfeld (U.S. Navy, 1954–57) seems the kind of leader who would appreciate this, and give it some thought. Maybe there are things that can be done to remind the world—and the members of the armed forces—who they really are, and have been, and can be. It may be in part a whole mysterious tangle, the motivation of the men and women who fight for us, but Mr. Rumsfeld better than most could probably see that it's addressed with clarity and candor.

24

Break Out the Bubbly

FRIDAY, MARCH 1, 2002

A good little scandal this week and just when we needed it, when things were getting a little slow. *The West Wing* producer Aaron Sorkin perked things up by telling Tad Friend of *The New Yorker* that it's good we're "laying off the bubblehead jokes" about President Bush but let's face it, we're all just "being polite" and making believe Mr. Bush is a substantial figure. He added that it's too bad NBC's Tom Brokaw agreed to let the White House rearrange the president's schedule to make him look "more engaged" when NBC aired its "A Day in the Life of the President," which was broadcast after a recent *West Wing* episode.

When Matt Drudge got hold of *The New Yorker* interview, he headlined it on his site, spicing it with comments from an unnamed NBC executive who said, "Sorkin does not speak for us." Soon NBC president Jeff Zucker came forward to defend Aaron's criticisms of Mr. Bush, saying he has every right to his views although he was wrong to criticize Mr. Brokaw, as everyone knows all presidents change their schedules for day-in-the-life shows. (And good thing, too. Cameras need action. You can't show a president discussing national-security secrets or sitting in the offices daydreaming or answering the mail. You have to show them dashing into important meetings or burrowing quickly through the halls, which is how Aaron shows President Bartlet on *The West Wing*.)

I call him Aaron because I know him and I know him because I am an adviser or contributor to *The West Wing*. I'm not sure which because I can't find the letter of agreement. I am, as far as I know, the only conservative who works on the show, though maybe there are more. I send Aaron e-mails from New York with ideas and suggestions. About every fourth show someone says something conservative. That's usually me. Two weeks ago, for instance, Press Secretary C.J. was talking to Presidential Conscience Tobey about affirmative action. When Tobey pressed C.J. for her views, she said she was the wrong Democrat to ask. She explained that her father had once been denied a job when someone else got it in an affirmative action decision. Tobey nodded and asked, "How's he doing?" C.J. said, lightly, "Fine."

In my version, C.J.'s father had suffered. He was an idealist who believed everyone has an equal shot at success in America, a public school-teacher who wanted to help kids and was gifted in his work with them; now he saw a less qualified and implicitly less loving person elevated at his expense, and only because he was the wrong color. It left him shattered. The flag on which he'd stood had been pulled from under him, and he never fully regained his balance.

When Aaron wrote it, C.J.'s father was not a victim of government but a fellow doing fine. In part because that's how Aaron thinks about affirmative action, and it's his show. And in part perhaps because C.J.'s terse "he's fine" is dramatically interesting—a man is treated badly and he's fine. Life is strange.

Aaron is a really interesting man. He is brilliant to begin with, and he has more wit than he displays on his show. He works like a dog and is deeply committed to excellence in his work. He is, in my view, an incipient artist who has not fully decided whether he is a political operative who does art or an artist who does politics.

The show he produces each week is a hymn to the American political process. I love it. I think one of the most constructive things it does for our culture is help young people feel romantic about adulthood. It tells them that no matter who they are or where they're from, they can work hard and rise and come to walk the halls of the White House, helping a great president lead his country well. It is a hymn, too, to professionalism, to the joy of being a professional operating at the height of one's powers "along the lines of excellence" as JFK used to say.

It is a show about friendship and loyalty. No one cares about people like the chief of staff, Leo, a pained and sensitive man who's earned his furrowed brow. It is compassionate about people in trouble (see Leo's relapse into active alcoholism during the New Hampshire primaries) and respectful of people who struggle (see Josh's secretary attempt, with respect for her own real if not heightened intelligence, to puzzle through the great issues of the day). It is not a highly sexualized show, it is not violent, and it is wonderfully dramatic.

The shows in which Bartlet, reeling from the death of his beloved secretary in a car crash, struggling with his multiple sclerosis, trying to decide whether and how to run for reelection, and remembering his childhood with a bullying father who showed one face to the public and another to his son—well, this is a very long sentence but when it all came to a head with Bartlet having a semi-unhinged argument with God in the National Cathedral and then a semidelirious colloquy with the dead secretary in a lightning-lit Oval Office as a storm raged without—I thought it was as big and terrific and absorbing as TV gets. Some people put down the argument with God, but I thought it was beautiful because you don't argue with one who does not exist. The estimable President Bartlet knows there is a great God. This is not bad.

Some episodes are not so good. The dreary lecture-show that followed 9/11 was an intellectual's attempt to evade the truth of 9/11 by avoiding the emotions 9/11 elicited. It yielded lifeless drama, because the emotions of 9/11 contained within them the great truth of 9/11: Bad men did bad things, leaving us wounded and furious. A prim little history of terrorism that was wholly somber and yet lacked seriousness was just what no one needed. I thought it was an example of how stupid intellectuals can be, missing the obvious point that the neighborhood dunce apprehends in a second.

But back to what Aaron said about Bush. It is surprising that it caused so much comment, even in a relatively slow news week. Because Aaron Sorkin was only saying what Aaron Sorkin thinks. And Aaron Sorkin thinks the thoughts of a left-liberal.

Because he is a left-liberal. And the show he writes and produces each week, the show whose story lines and dialogue he dreams up, reflects his views, utterly.

No one has every accused *West Wing* of being a conservative show or a right-wing show—no one, ever. That's because it's not. It's a left-liberal show that propounds left-liberal ideas through the acting of such left-liberals as the gifted Martin Sheen. I know this. Aaron Sorkin knows it. And you know it too if you're paying attention.

A reporter once asked me if I thought, as John Podhoretz had written, that *The West Wing* is, essentially, left-wing pornography. I said no, that's completely wrong. *The West Wing* is a left-wing nocturnal emission—undriven by facts, based on dreams, its impulses as passionate as they are involuntary and as unreflective as they are genuine. After I sent the answer in an e-mail to a reporter, I showed it to Aaron so he could have a response ready. I told him he was completely free to fire me and I could hardly complain, but he should fire me right away before the comment was published or down the road when no one remembers it. He laughed and said no, and the comment in any case was never printed.

Which left me mildly relieved. I continued sending my e-mails, and soon there was a rumor that the character of Ainsley Hayes, the young, blond, chic, fair-minded, miniskirt-wearing Republican lawyer, was based on me. I loved that rumor. I certainly enjoyed spreading it. I told my friends of course she's based on me, it's obvious, I have legs exactly like her legs, inside my legs. (Ainsley, alas, was dreamed up and in the Sorkinian creative pipeline long before I got there. However if you tell people she's based on me that's really all right.)

But back to what Aaron said about President Bush. I think his comments were bubbleheaded. But they were not "wrong" or "terrible," or "scandalous," and not only because everyone in America has the right to insult the president, or any politician anywhere for that matter.

His comments were, to me, a step toward clarity and candor, which are good things. Aaron Sorkin thinks Republicans in general are bubbleheads. He thinks conservatives tend toward evil and cynicism, although I think some stubborn little part of his brain knows it isn't quite that easy.

But it isn't bad that Aaron was frank, and it isn't bad that he put his political heart on his sleeve. He writes what is arguably the most important political show in America. He shouldn't have to hide where he stands. His *New Yorker* comments reminded me of the flap following the disclosure that my old boss Dan Rather had hosted a Democratic fund-raiser in Texas.

He's a liberal, why shouldn't he go to a Democratic fund-raiser? And why shouldn't we know it, and factor it in as he reports the news?

Tony Snow of Fox News Channel got in a small amount of trouble last year for making a speech to a conservative group. So what? Why shouldn't he speak to a conservative group? One of the great things about the explosion of media in our time—all the TV and radio and talk shows and Internet sites— is that everyone gets a voice. There isn't only one media funnel now, as there used to be, and the people at the networks don't have to pretend anymore that they don't hold political views when they do, and passionately.

The West Wing is liberal. I like it. I am not a liberal. I am a conservative. I watch it each week and enjoy it because I am capable of ignoring its political slant and filtering out its political propaganda. Once I push past them, and I do not as a rule find it difficult, I can find out how the Bartlet campaign is going and whether Sam is getting a personal life and whether Tobey will get back with his former wife and C.J. fall in love with the reporter. You just have to push past the slant to get to the drama. Then you can sit back and enjoy not only the characters but the actors, like Martin Sheen, who happens to be a wonderful Dorothy Day kind of Catholic and whose politics are intransigently leftist and therefore quite stupid.

A note on Aaron's art. If he screened out the propaganda on his own it would not only make it easier on a lot of us, it would put him that much closer to being a dramatist of the stature of a William Inge or Tennessee Williams or Paddy Chayefsky. With a first-rate artist you can often guess his politics. Walker Percy, who wrote about the secret brokenness and lostness of our selves, which is to say our souls, was probably in many ways a conservative. Tennessee Williams with his great tugging heart toward the outsider, the outrider, the one who doesn't fit, was probably a liberal. Eugene O'Neill, if he had lived twenty years longer, through the 1970s, would probably have completed the transit from socialist to right-wing nut.

Or so I imagine.

But I have to guess. Their work doesn't bludgeon me with the political views of the dramatist (or, in Percy's case, the novelist.) Their work stands, speaks and stays, untethered to passing political views and positions. Which is one reason they're great. His show would be better if Aaron Sorkin tried to be great.

25

My Brothers and Sisters

Hello my friends, or rather my brothers and sisters, which I'll explain later. This is going to be one of those long pieces, so park it and come back later, or make some coffee and settle in.

Our thought for today: This is the age of miracles and wonders, and of signs and symbols too.

I am experiencing a change of temperament, if that is the word. I have mostly gone through life as a short-term pessimist and a long-term optimist, but now I find, and perhaps it's only temporary, that I am increasingly a short-term optimist and a long-term pessimist. That's not quite right. I am certain there is a heaven, which is not a pessimistic belief. But my long-term thoughts about the world are not as sunny as once they were.

And yet I am happy each day and enjoy my life.

While I am worried about the future in a way I cannot shake.

The first e-mail I opened this morning was from a friend who said this: Peggy, the government fears a nuke has been smuggled into the United States, the Mideast is boiling, the weather is roiling, the church is reeling from sexual corruption in the clergy, and last night came a report that a statue of Padre Pio in Sicily is weeping blood. "I'm feeling very apocalyptic, and I'm serious," he wrote. He's sane, sound, not usually excitable. He reminded me of Andrew Sullivan, who wrote Wednesday on his blog that for the first time since 9/11 he is having nightmares. The next day he posted Senate testimony that a dirty bomb would render Manhattan uninhabitable for decades.

So many of us, at least so many of my New York friends, are experiencing a Second Great Wave of anxiety. Maybe it is connected to or heightened by the approaching milestone, six months after 9/11, maybe it is that and other things. The friend who had e'd me followed up with news that the Chinese are creating dozens of cloned embryos in their labs. The British medical journal *New Scientist* has reported a Chinese team "based at Shanghai No. 2 Medical University" says it has "derived stem cells from hybrid embryos composed of human cells and rabbit eggs." The journal said scientists throughout the world fear similar research in the United States and the United Kingdom has been "bogged down" by "ethical concerns."

Ah, those pesky ethical concerns. They slow you up just when you could be creating in a petri dish the recipe for Rabbit Man. And then of course you could grow him, bring him into being, for all but dunces know that what man can do he will do. And then perhaps once you've grown him you can have Rabbit Man for dinner.

My friend sent the story because once, in conversation, I had told him I feared cloning was the key, that the big headline I feared is "First Cloned Human Being Born: 'We Call Him Adam!' Says Scientist." I had told my friend I thought there would be few happy headlines after that one. Because, as the Bible says and Sam Ervin quoted, God is not mocked.

And so today, after the morning mail, I thought again as I often do these days of Langston Hughes. "God gave Noah the rainbow sign, No more water, the fire next time." If it comes, I feel we will have to thank, among so many others, the good men and women of Shanghai No. 2 Medical University.

I found the Padre Pio story on a Catholic Web site and didn't know what to make of it. As Kevin Orlin Johnson, the great writer on Catholic mysticism, has said, there are few stories the church dislikes more than levitating house-wives and bleeding statues. And yet. The BBC report, based on an Italian news-agency story, said that thousands of people flocked earlier this week to the city of Messina, in Sicily, after reports that a statue of the Catholic mystic had begun to weep blood. The seven-foot-tall bronze statue stands across the square from Our Lady of Pompei Church in Messina. Tuesday night a passerby looked up and saw that it seemed to be weeping. A local priest was called. The BBC said he tried to wipe away "a red substance leaking from the eyes" of the statue. Padre Pio, who died in 1968, bore the stigmata, the wounds of Christ, an extremely unusual mystical phenomenon in spite of what Hollywood movies suggest. There have been only a handful of such men and women in all of human history. Padre Pio was a great man, a gifted confessor, an ascetic, a mystic, a saint; he has quite a following in the church, and is to be canonized in Rome in June by Pope John Paul II, who knew the padre when he was a young cardinal from Poland.

The weeping statue was reported on Tuesday. On Wednesday John Paul, who is suffering among other things from persistent pain in his knees, which has no doubt been made worse by his continued habit of kneeling and praying, greeted a Vatican audience from his papal study. He spoke on Psalm 64: "Hear my voice, O God in my prayer: reserve my life from fear of the enemy. Hide me from the secret counsel of the evil-doers."

The pope told the audience, in his commentary: "In the Bible, creation is the seat of humanity and sin is an attack on the order and perfection of the world. Conversion and forgiveness, therefore, restore integrity and harmony to the cosmos." It is amazing that this eighty-two-year-old man who suffers from Parkinson's, who has lived an arduous, effortful, searing life, who was born during war, who endured Nazism and communism, who is fighting now materialism and fatalism, who has been shot, who suffers, is still with us, and occasionally with a startling vitality.

It is interesting to me too that so many Catholics, at least ones I know, seem to feel that while he is alive they are safe. It will be hard when he leaves. Although I must say Catholics can be merry even about that. A few months ago I was talking with a priest about the prophecies of St. Malachy, a mystic who, 1,000 years ago, wrote a line of prophecy about each future pope. The next one, the priest told me, is described by Malachy as "the joy of the olive." I didn't know that, and asked him what he thought it might suggest. He said, "It suggests we should keep our eye on Cardinal Martini." When I told another friend he laughed and added, "But the olive tree is also the symbol of Israel. It may mean the next pope will be a son of Israel." Such as the retired Cardinal Lustiger of Paris, a convert from Judaism.

. . .

But back to my subject, which may be the six-month mark since 9/11. The papers in New York have been carrying reports that the emotional after-shocks of trauma tend to be most intense six to twelve months after the event. Which would possibly explain both my friends' apocalyptic jitters and what I've been seeing on the subway.

I notice that people on the subway in just the past few days have been— well, I am seeing less beauty in our subways, after months of finding them the best place to be.

I love my darling subway and feel great tenderness toward the people crowded into it. We're all together in the noise and clamor and crowded-ness, with lights flickering on and off and the public-address system hissing inadequately and the train jerking to a stop in the middle of the tunnel. I sit there—I almost always get a seat—and say the rosary and am happy. How could I not be? I have progressed in my prayer life from praying for myself and my loved ones to praying for others. This took a solid twelve years. Twelve years to learn to pray consistently for others! (This is, I know, an amazingly personal thing to say, but I don't imagine it can harm anyone, and this is not a time for reticence in such matters.) I now pray for strangers, happily. I am so proud of this, and relieved. The subway gives me constant new people to pray for.

It's like the Canterbury Tales down there, like the great procession, so many different kinds of people doing different things, thinking fabulous things, on their way to different places, living different lives. It's like a Broadway show. I wish people would stand and share their reveries, or sing whatever song is in their heads. On the No. 4 train there is the man with no legs. He pushes himself along on a little roller-blade sort of rig, pushing himself through the cars with a paper cup, saying nothing. He looks like Porgy in *Porgy and Bess*. The tall white men almost uniformly ignore him, the shorter darker people, especially the women, give him quarters and dol-lars. The ones who have least give quickest, and most.

Last week a woman was walking car to car as the train rushed along. She was in her forties, black, heavy, with a little white wool hat on her head. She was preaching Christ and him crucified. You looked at her and you really couldn't tell if she was filled with the Holy Spirit or off her meds. You didn't know if she was in the full sway of evangelical fervor or in full psychotic break. But there was a lovely tolerance with which everyone looked up, observed, listened and then went back to their papers or back to sleep.

There are crazy people who won't harm you, and friendly old people, and kids. There is an Asian woman whom I've seen a few times, dead asleep, with her two children, each under ten, sleeping soundly next to her.

I sit and pray and feel my prayers bring greater peace wherever I am. And lately this is good, for in just the past few days, as we approach the six-month point, things are getting snarkier in our underground. There is more disturbance down there in the dark, more tension than in December and January and February. Or so it seems to me. Yesterday a man was haranguing a young stranger in a loud voice, verbally harassing her on the need for friendliness between people who don't know each other. He was aggressive, hectoring. The poor young woman just nodded, smiled and tried to placate. I prayed on him, and he got off the train.

Earlier this week there was a more dramatic moment. A woman—hyper, in her twenties, tall, strong, Jamaican accent, tight black pants, high boots—got into an argument with a young Asian woman. I couldn't make out what it was about, but the Jamaican woman was very angry. Then she turned her anger on a young man, who intervened for the Asian woman. In a loud and dominating voice she called him "rude" and "inappropriate" and "incapable of facing" his own lack of manners. She was very articulate and quite forceful, and she seemed on the edge of out of control.

Finally, pale with anger, the man snapped, "You'd be a lot better off if you'd lay off the heroin. I'm a doctor, and I know what I'm talking about."

She became enraged, stood and yelled, "What do you know? You're a doctor? I'll show you my needle-pocked arm as I knock your block off!" And she went toward him. And ever so smoothly, ever so massively, a young black man wearing earphones blocked her way, as if by accident.

"Yes, my sister, he is rude, ignore him. I know you're not on H. He has no idea the charge he's making."

She looked at him. She pleaded her case to him. She started to simmer down. He said soothing words.

She was utterly unconscious of her own aggression, and experienced herself as a person under siege, forced to stand up for her own humanity. She couldn't see that she was pushing people around.

But he understood, and befriended her. And now they stood talking, finally chuckling, as we bumped along from station to station through the darkness. She got off at 33rd Street. We all let out sighs of relief. The man who'd helped her moved to get off at the next stop. I patted his arm. "My friend," I said.

He removed his earphones and looked at me.

"You are a diplomat," I said. He shook his head in the noise. "You are a born diplomat," I said louder.

His face broke into a smile. Now the man sitting next to me joined in. "Did good, man," he said. He looked like a cop.

The diplomat smiled, nodded, shrugged. "All just tryin' get home, man. Just doin' our best."

I switched trains at 14 Street, stood a few stops. A seat opened up and a man who was drinking from a bottle in a brown paper bag gestured to me to take it. I smiled my thanks, and a few stops later the seat next to me opened and I moved over and he sat down. When I got to my stop I asked him if he wanted my paper and he said no, and then yes, and thanked me with a sweet smile. I said, "Good-bye, my brother," and he said good night.

The man on HBO's *Oz* who is the leader of the prison Muslims gets to call those who share his faith "my brother." I always like the way he says it, with such dignity and respect. My faith is one whose adherents include all races and ethnic groups, and I never know who my brothers and sisters are. So I've decided they're everyone. I have taken to calling strangers with whom I interact "my brother" and "my sister." It surprises people but no one seems to dislike it, and almost everyone smiles. There is a great liberation to age. You are allowed to say anything when you are a middle-aged woman, for no one is eager to be offended by you. You're harmless, and probably well-meaning. I can't wait till I'm old. I will call strangers "my beloved little darling."

But the point, and there really was one a few score paragraphs ago: New Yorkers are getting jittery again, and the subways are getting tenser, or so it seems to me.

∙   ∙   ∙

I have been on the subway so much because I've been going into town to witness and be part of various events. One was a screening of the CBS documentary on 9/11, which airs next week. CBS was nervous about it, though it's hard to see why. It is a respectful and affectionate look at Lucky 7, the FDNY Ladder Company downtown that was among the first, if not the first, company to respond that terrible day. All of its members survived because, paradoxically, they got to the scene early. They went to the first tower that was hit, which was the second tower to fall. They milled around in the lobby. There's nothing gruesome in the documentary, no falling bodies, no people on fire. The story is told through the eyes of a "probie," a probationary fireman newly assigned to the company, and through the lens of two Frenchmen, brothers who were doing a documentary on the NYFD.

The film captures the ghost-town quality of downtown that day, with everything covered in Pompeii-like ash. It captures the lostness of the firemen massed in the lobby of the first tower, as lost as a platoon on D-Day overwhelmed with heavy fire and not knowing where anyone is or what to do. It captures one of the great strangenesses of the catastrophe, and of modern life in general. And that is that the men on the scene, in the lobby of the tower, knew less about what was going on that day than did a casual viewer of television half a world away in Taiwan. The Taiwanese anchorman had the wires, live pictures, live reports. The firemen on the scene had nothing but dead radios in their hands. They had no idea what was happening, and didn't know what to do.

It is amazing when this happens, when people a world away know what's happening 200 yards from you and you don't. But it happens in our modern, fully wired and utterly fragile world. Wires, wires everywhere, and yet when the catastrophe comes the firemen have dead radios and can't get word on what's happening.

I went to a lunch at the home of Tina Brown, whose Talk Miramax Books is publishing a memoir by a young Afghan woman who defied the Taliban and started a school for women in her home. She is young, in her early twenties, and shy. She does not speak English and seems overwhelmed, understandably so. I asked her something I have not heard fully answered. It is: What is in young men in your homeland that makes them want to join a movement as destructive of culture and violent toward women, toward their sisters and mothers, as the Taliban? But the question-and-answer became lost in translation, and I did not learn what I hoped to learn.

The women invited to meet the writer were a slice of Manhattan life—other writers and editors, publishers, media people, political people. It was a ladies' lunch, all women. In a dozen years in New York I had met many of them before, but now I see them less, and in a way I saw them anew. Erica Jong, the novelist, was there, warm and full of conversation. She told me she is hoping to be principal for a day soon at a local high school. An old friend from CBS was there, wry and funny.

I saw a woman I used to know sitting at one of the small white round tables, went to say hello and halfway there thought without thinking: Don't. I wondered afterward what had stopped me. On one level she seemed like a handsome lady at lunch. On another she was . . . like a snorting animal pawing the ground. She was glowering. In fact observing her made me think of a Lewis Carroll poem about spending Christmas Day with his extended family. "[I] thought [I] saw a Buffalo / upon the chimneypiece: / [I] looked again, and found it was / [My] sister's husband's niece."

She was a buffalo ready to charge. Later conversation with others at her table revealed that she's still smoking with rage at the failed presidency of Bill Clinton, who is her close friend of many years. "Why does Bush get good press?" she demanded of her tablemates.

I don't understand the bitterness of New York Clinton folk. They had their eight years; some of them did their best; it ended with its derelictions; we had 9/11; now it's over. You'd think they'd keep their counsel, choose a new man to back for president and back him, help him, tout him, fund him.

Instead they waste their time simmering, resenting, as if Clinton had been their only shot. If he was, they're in worse trouble than I thought.

And there was a woman who was once my friend, who backed and worked for the Clintons and who thought being loyal to them meant we must no longer be friends after I wrote so much against them. She approached me, kissed me hello and kept walking. When I first met her ten years ago she was humorous, modest, hopeful. Now she is sharp featured and tough. No, hard. She is hard.

The odd thing about these people is that they have everything. They are rich, accomplished, healthy; they have marriages, children, love; they don't have to be up nights worrying about paying the rent or the electric bill. And they are not really happy. They have been lucky so long they don't even know they're lucky anymore. That's the bad thing that can happen to you when you've been lucky too long: You start to think it's not luck, it's what you deserve. And instead of being grateful you get a bitter-tinged sense of entitlement. You start to think you deserve it, you made the right choices. You're smarter than the dumb people, or more accomplished than the lazy people.

When the truth is you're lucky and blessed and should be on your knees saying thank you for your good fortune, and giving out twenties on the subway.

Instead they have a sense of being cheated. *Why isn't my life perfect? Why don't we have $2 billion instead of $1 billion? Why isn't Al Gore president? Why can't everyone love Bill, he deserves it!*

But back to the topic of this piece, which appears at one point to have been that we're coming up on six months after 9/11.

I think the untold, unmentioned story about New York right now, as I wrote in a British newspaper earlier this week, is the disjunction between what we truly think and how we act.

Each day we reenact normality. We reenact life before 9/11. That woman hurrying along Fifth Avenue in the coat with the mink collar, rushing with shopping bags from Barneys and Saks into the place where they do your nails. She thinks a nuke may go off in midtown this afternoon. But she also knows she needs a manicure.

She gets her nails done and muses on what will happen when the big thunderclap comes, and the sky fills with light and the wind begins to whip.

I don't think the world fully appreciates how targeted we feel in New York, but then I don't think we fully appreciate it either. But it occurs to us now and then, as we rush through the streets in our busy, distracted way, that we've got a target on our backs. You can walk along Madison Avenue, or First, and look and see: Nothing has changed since September 10. We're all still hurrying along, walking briskly through the world with our distractions and our plans. And yet every one of us knows it's quite possible—oh, it's quite likely—that we'll be hit again, and worse next time than last.

It is odd and interesting that everyone thinks it will be midtown next time, not downtown or uptown. Times Square, or Broadway, or Fiftieth and Fifth.

If we think this, why don't we leave?

You'd think we'd always be asking each other this question. We're not. We don't talk about it much at all. We keep our thoughts to ourselves. We don't want to be the morbid person at the lunch, or the downer at dinner. We maintain our cheerfulness. And it isn't even a mindless good cheer, it's something else.

There is no really good answer to why we don't leave, but there are a million understandable ones. "My life is here." "My job is here." "The kids are in school here." A friend told me she doesn't want to live in a world without New York; she'll go down with the ship.

And, "We don't know anyone in Topeka/Laramie/Tuscaloosa." We only know people here.

The people who lived at the bottom of Vesuvius didn't leave Pompeii while the volcano simmered and smoked. How could they? They didn't know anyone in Messina, or Rome. They had their lives in Pompeii, their ties in Pompeii.

But there's another thing New Yorkers are thinking. It's that deep in their hearts they don't really think there is a safe place. They don't think there's any safety anymore. They only think there's time, right now, this second. So they have their nails done, and do their work, and go to the lunch, and file the story, and argue the case. There's a gallantry, a cool courage, to New Yorkers now, and I wonder if they see it, if they appreciate it in themselves. I do. It's part of why I want to call them my brother, and my sister.

26

Quiet, Please, on the Western Front

FRIDAY, MARCH 15, 2002

I have a small thought. I would like to speak of it in a low-key manner. My thought is that we are all talking too much, or rather too dramatically—too colorfully, and carelessly—about things that are really quite dreadful. And we should stop it.

I will start with this: I have been thinking about hospitals for the psychologically and emotionally unwell, and how they run.

Now, there are many wicked people in the world, and some of them are stone evil, but some are also not at all sane. They are frighteningly obsessed or delusional; they have illusions of omnipotence, or no control over their impulses and desires; they hear voices, are unhinged by fantasies of rage and revenge, imagine that they are the reincarnation of Napoleon, or Saladin.

You can ponder whether Saddam Hussein is more evil than crazy or crazy than evil, but anyone who's seen him on the news would likely conclude that Richard Reid, the would-be shoe bomber who failed to blow himself and 400 other people out of the sky, is quite clearly unstable.

And there are of course many Richard Reids. The problem in this age of weapons of mass destruction is that we don't have one Saddam to worry about but cells of Saddams, rings of Reids, scores, hundreds of independent operators, some of whom are trying to create their own weapons of mass destruction, their own obliterates aimed at obliterating life in this place or that.

And many of them are not fully sane. Which is a problem. Which is why I'm thinking about mental institutions.

If you have ever worked in one or visited a friend in one, you've probably observed some things about how the unwell are treated. For instance: It is always wise when speaking to the unstable to speak softly if you can, and soothingly if possible. It isn't good to be loud or theatrical in your subject matter or usage. It is wise not to speak with heightened drama, because for the unstable things are quite dramatic enough. They have storms going on inside them. They don't need your howling verbal gusts. So, a general rule: Never excite the unstable.

At the same time some of the unstable are dangerous or potentially so, and this cannot be ignored. So it's always good to be planning ahead. It is wise to be preparing restraints, to have areas in which the dangerous can be segregated from the general population, to have security guards who speak softly but, as they say, carry a big stick. It is wise to have serious plans for treatment, wise to make sure that they cannot get their hands on, say, the ingredients to build a bomb.

Nurses and doctors in such hospitals know all this, especially the part about not bringing unneeded drama to their patients. They do not tell someone who may behave violently, "We hate you and plan to do terrible things to you. The next time you are bad we're going to kick you, punch you, push you in a hole and put a large cover on it. Then we're going to cover you with Italian dressing, let you marinate overnight, and cook you." That kind of language would less likely discourage dramatic action than summon it.

And that's what I think we all ought to be keeping in our minds these days, how not to summon dramatic action from the marginally stable.

We are at war. This is a grave time. And yet in some ways we are being quite careless in what we are saying and how it might be received. We are being too colorful, too vivid, and unnecessarily so. We are acting as if we are not fully aware of the gravity of the moment.

One gets the sense, reading the newspapers and columnists and Web sites, and listening to news conferences, that we are talking too much these days, saying too much and saying it too graphically.

We are being noisy and clamorous.

We are frightening the inmates. This is not good.

"Let's Nuke Em All!" Britain's *Daily Mail* headlined this week. The story was about the U.S. government review of its nuclear capabilities. Someone— Mary McGrory wondered in her column if it was "doomsday planners" or "a subversive show-off"—leaked the news that the United States may be reevaluating its nuclear posture, strategy and potential targets with an eye to breaking the taboo on tactical nuclear weapons. *The New York Times,* one of the great newspapers of the world and received by some in the world as a voice of the West, ran an editorial in which it likened America to a "rogue state." A columnist in *The Boston Globe* said President Bush is "as frightening as Al Qaeda."

All of this of course followed the previous week's story of secret plans to invade Iraq. On Wednesday, President Bush took to the airwaves in an informal news conference and refused to rule out the use of nuclear weapons in the war, explaining that his position was "a way to say to people who would harm America: Don't do it. . . . There's a consequence."

Indeed there is, and it would no doubt be terrible. But one wonders if this subject is not better confined to a grave and formal speech to the nation from a somber president, and not served up along with teasing of the press—"That you, Stretch? Oh, it's Superstretch"—and jokes about the length and complexity of follow-ups. Perhaps this is the White House's way of showing the president is utterly unrattled by the facts of the new world. But there are other ways to show that he is unrattled, if that has to be shown.

Why are we being so careless and colorful, so offhand, at a time when what faces us is so somber? Maybe we in the media are not thinking of the impression we make en masse, all together, on the world. We think of the impression we make individually, not as part of a media wave that rolls over the globe each day.

And people, even the most sophisticated, tend to project some of their inner world on the outer world around them. The unstable see themselves surrounded by threats, or secret signs. But the stable have illusions too.

People who are sane tend to project sanity onto others. Those who, like the writers at great Web sites and great newspapers, are fully stable, imagine that their thoughts and words are received by the stable. And of course that is true. Except when it isn't.

What they think and write and say is also disseminated throughout the world of America's enemies, and is not always received in a way that is sober and measured. Some of those who see, on the computer in their home outside Tehran, the headline "Let's Nuke Em All!" will take it quite literally. They will receive it as yet another reason to get back to work packing the dirty nuke into the backpack. The man who leaked the nuclear review story perhaps thought he was making the world safer—that everyone would understand it as he did. But not everyone will.

"Children will listen," the old song says. But so will the fragile and mad, and it's not good to excite them. We should not be leaking that we are reviewing our nuclear capacity; we should be quietly reviewing it. We should not be reporting in hyperventilated tones the review of nuclear policy; we should remember that this only feeds the sickness of those who mean us harm. We should be very quietly debating in the offices of government what an appropriate response would be to the bombing of America; we should reach conclusions, create a plan, and very quietly tell the leaders of the real rogue nations exactly what will happen to them, and to the terrorists who slumber within their borders, if they should dare to bomb an American city. Our words should be blunt little bombs whispered in the ears of Arab leaders in a manner that leaves them with the kind of ringing headache you sometimes get when you're told terrible news that is true.

But we should probably not be having chatty conversations about whether or not it would be a good idea to take out Mecca.

This is not censorship, it is using judgment in a time of war. It is awareness that projecting stability and sanity onto others, while polite and even touching, is not always warranted.

We should lower our voices, and be chary with words. As if we were well-meaning professionals in an asylum who want to keep everyone safe, and help the sick, and keep them safe as possible too.

27

The Pope's First Statement

This week an old giant returned to speak of what roils us. His words were welcome, heartening and necessary. But they were not, I think, sufficient.

In Rome John Paul II, our warrior-saint of a pope, addressed, finally, the sex scandals that continue to rock the American Catholic Church.

Now the pope is a great man. From almost the moment of his election to the papacy in 1978 he raised his staff—the silver crosier he carries in public, which bears at the top the crucified Christ—turned toward the east and, in effect, commanded the atheist Soviet Union to recede. And almost from that moment the Russian dictatorship began to recede like the great debris-filled wave it was. John Paul II is not only a warrior, of course; he is a mystic who believes the hand of the Mother of God literally guided the bullet away from his heart the day, twenty-one years ago, that he was shot. He is said to pray seven hours a day—alone, at mass, while doing work. He is a holy man.

In his Holy Thursday letter to the Catholic priests of the world, the pontiff spoke on the sex-abuse scandals that have engulfed the American church. His words were strong and direct. They were also brief, comprising only about 10 percent of his letter. Here in toto is what he said of the scandals:

At this time too [he refers to the new millennium] as priests we are personally and profoundly afflicted by the sins of some of our brothers who have betrayed the grace of Ordination in succumbing even to the most grievous forms of the *mysterium iniquitatis* at work in the world. Grave scandal is caused, with the result that a dark shadow of suspicion is cast over all the other fine priests who perform their ministry with honesty and integrity and often with heroic self-sacrifice. As the church shows her concern for the victims and strives to respond in truth and justice to each of these painful situations, all of us—conscious of human weakness, but trusting in the healing power of divine grace—are called to embrace the *mysterium Crucis* and to commit ourselves more fully to the search for holiness. We must beg God in his Providence to prompt a wholehearted reawakening of those ideals of total self-giving to Christ which are the very foundation of the priestly ministry.

So, the pontiff said that the priests who have abused and seduced teenage boys and adolescents had given in to the most grievous forms of "the mystery of evil." He did not call the guilty priests only disturbed or in need of therapy; he said they had done evil and betrayed God's gift to them, the gift of the priesthood.

One could not read the pope's words and doubt his dismay. One could not read them without imagining too the anguish behind them. Surely they gave heart to the good priests and seminarians who need to know the pope is on their side; certainly the bad priests, and their protectors in the hierarchy, understood what the pope thinks of them and their actions.

And yet, one must hope the pope's letter was only a beginning, only a prologue to action more grave and definitive.

To those who have campaigned on the airwaves and in the newspapers of our country, reporting the cases of abuse, payoffs and cover-ups, and attempting to force the American church toward a new honesty, a new toughness; and to those who have called on Boston's Cardinal Bernard Law to resign, to offer up his career as a sacrifice to demonstrate in a dramatic and unmistakable way that the leaders of the American church have been wrong in their cover-ups, regret them, feel shamed by the abuse of teenage boys and will begin to clean the church; to all of these people I suspect the pope's letter seemed both necessary and, sadly, insufficient.

It was heartening that the pontiff broke his silence, heartening that he did not say that priests who prey are only sick, which is how the American cardinals have treated them in the past.

The pope did not say some things that many if not most—I think almost all—Catholics here yearn to hear. He did not speak of defrocking the abusers, of defrocking serial seducers of the young and their protectors. And he did not speak of the victims of abuse and their families, except to assert the church always intends to treat them justly and with sympathy.

But it has not always treated them justly, truthfully and with sympathy, not on our shores.

Some have already said the pope's statement seems to reflect a mind-set in which the church in this drama is more victim than victimizer. I do not think that can fairly be inferred from his letter, but I'm afraid neither can this: a sense that the pope has fully absorbed that the scandal in the American church is not just a heartbreaker but a potential history-changer.

The most ardent American Catholics I know, and an imperfect and sinful lot they are, and I would know as I am one of them, but the most ardent Catholics I know, the ones who are the church—who take the sacraments, go to church, get ashes, go to confession, visit the Blessed Sacrament in the middle of a busy day, who give money to the local church to fix the roof and get new computers for the local Catholic school, who love the church, adhere to it as best they can and hold it high—are the most angry, shocked and disgusted by the scandals. They do not in this tragedy defend the leadership of the American church, as they have in the past. They are not complaining that a few cases of misbehavior are being blown up by a hostile press to attack the church, as they have in the past. Instead they send one another e-mail attachments containing new reports of abuse, and they welcome calls from prominent Catholics such as Bill Buckley and Bill Bennett to clean out the stables.

For the first time in my lifetime ardent Catholics, or perhaps I should say orthodox Catholics, no longer trust their cardinals and bishops to do what's right. They have pinned their hopes on the Vatican, and on the old warrior-saint, JPII. They want him to hold up his silver crosier with the crucified Christ on the top and demand that priests who seduce teenage boys—or who sexually abuse, molest or seduce anyone—be thrown from the church, and that their protectors, excusers and enablers be thrown from it too.

As the scandal has escalated, the language used to describe it has become more shaded, more full of euphemism. Any scandal involving sex in the modern world will become in time an ideological/political scandal, and the little dishonesties of ideological discourse have worked their way into this drama. And as usual they haven't made things any clearer. But here are some things that appear to be true of the overwhelming majority of the known cases: they involve not rape but seduction; they involve not a sole sin, mistake or indiscretion but a series of seductions by priests who are serial seducers; the seductions do not involve priests in pursuit of sexual relations with women or girls but of priests in pursuit of sexual relations with boys and young men; and most of the victims have been young male teenagers, not little boys.

How did this happen? How did we reach this pass? Perhaps great books will be written in answer to these questions. I think of the simple wisdom of an Irish Catholic grandfather in his seventies who has eleven children and thirty-five grandchildren and who always seems to be silently praying. He is a low-key leader who has led his family by example, and who is unkind about no one.

I asked him a few months ago if the church was having this trouble fifty years ago. He said no. I asked why. He said, "Because fifty years ago the church had a bigger pool from which to pick its priests."

It's true. Half a century ago in the American church the pool from which young seminarians were chosen was wide and deep, fed by belief, love, tradition and large families. But in the decades since, the world has changed, and the pool from which the church picked her priests became narrower, shallower. So much that had fed the pool dried up. America went on a toot—and I would know as I was at the party, as perhaps you were, though I must say the very best people I know seem not to have been. But America went wild in the 1970s, '80s and '90s, and the priesthood got fairly strange too.

Fifty years ago hale and eager young men entered the priesthood out of devotion and gave their celibacy and chastity to God as a gift, to join in His sufferings and deepen their commitment to serving others—to serving, that is, a family of strangers in a place called a parish. There were scandals here and there and problems; some priests left to marry, or for other reasons. But mostly it worked.

But in the past thirty years or so, many young men who were less clear-minded, who were ultimately less devoted, put themselves forth for the priesthood. And the church took them. Some, perhaps many, were sexually ambivalent, or confused, or burdened. Certainly some of them saw themselves as homosexual in their orientation, and some perhaps hoped the church's very limits and strictures might help them, might protect them from their own desires. And some no doubt became priests in part in hopes they would find comfort surrounded by those who shared their burden.

In any case some of them rose, gained power, prestige and local respect, and became sexual bullies—predators who preyed on twelve- and fourteen-year-old boys in their ambit. And they got away with it. And one priest saw another get away with it, and he tried to get away with it too.

The church turned a blind eye, not institutionally but in case after case, instance after instance, until it might as well have been institutional policy. And for a long time the church got away with it.

Why? Part of the answer is that so many of the serial seducer priests preyed on the powerless. They moved on adolescent boys in families in turmoil, teenage boys in families that had no connections, no status, no one to look out for them. They preyed on families without fathers. In fact, in some of the grimmer cases they were asked in by overwhelmed mothers who were trying to hold to the church in a rocky and dangerous world. The mothers wanted their sons to know a man they could look up to.

One wonders if those who run the American church fear that if they remove all the sex-abuser priests the church, which has a shortage of priests as it is, simply won't be able to operate anymore. Local churches would close; schools would be understaffed. And this is perhaps the central reason—not the only reason but the biggest one—the cardinals have reassigned abusive priests, and sent serial seducers for psychotherapy, sending them back to parish work when they'd been "cured."

But the pragmatism of the cardinals and bishops has resulted in scandal for the church—a scandal that will take at least a generation to heal. Now it has resulted in tragedy for the hundreds and perhaps thousands of innocent victims. And now it has resulted in shame and embarrassment for the faithful, striving and suffering priests who have done right, and not wrong, through the years. For they have been tarred by this, and badly. People who call themselves pragmatic are often the least practical of people. The cardinals thought they were pragmatic.

The other day, like a fool, I thought to myself these words: The church needs a savior. This was followed by the thought: But the church has one. He is its meaning, its purpose, its light. He threw the abusers and predators out of the temple in a great rage; He said "Suffer the little children to come unto me" and gave the innocent His love. He hangs, crucified, on the top of the crosier carried by the pope.

If the Catholic Church throws out the evil priests, its Savior will no doubt see to it that good priests come forward to take their place. That Savior is after all the God of miracles. Some cardinals have no doubt chosen to keep the sex-abuse stories quiet in order to protect the assets of the church. And in truth the church has assets that deserve protection—great cathedrals, great works of art, schools in which poor children and immigrant children are given a good education and where all are welcome no matter their faith. And local churches with high heating bills where new Americans and old Americans gather, work together, know one another.

The church does so much good! So much of what it is should be protected.

But not, of course, at the price of betraying what the church stands for. The Catholics I know, and I know all kinds, left, right and center, would rather see the cathedrals sold for condominiums than see the decay continue.

Which is where the old pope—the mover of mountains, defeater of tyrannies, killer of communism, holder to the faith, whose most special gift has been his power to show the powerless of the world, the peasants, the workers with grim hands, that he was their protector, that he loved them in the name of the church—comes in.

The powerless need his protection now. They need that old crosier held up again, to tell the dirty wave to recede.

Which is why so many of us are hoping that what we heard this week will not be remembered by history as "the pope's statement" but as "the pope's first statement—the one that led to a great shaking of the rafters in 2002."

28

Star-Spangled Evenings

FRIDAY, MARCH 29, 2002

I once saw Kevin Costner eat Raisa Gorbachev's dessert. This did not happen in a dream but in what is often called real life.

It was at *Time* magazine's seventy-fifth anniversary party, a fabulous gathering four years ago in New York City to which all who had ever appeared on *Time*'s venerable cover were invited. Many of them came—Bill Gates, Elie Wiesel, Steven Spielberg, scientists and political leaders and poets. It looked to me like a last gathering of the most famous and productive and important Americans of the twentieth century as the country trembled on the edge of the unknown twenty-first.

I was there as a contributing editor of *Time,* and I knew I must be in for a great night when I arrived and one of the magazine's editors passed me as I searched in the dark for my table. "You owe it to me," he shot out, merrily. He pointed me up front, where I found my table and introduced myself to my tablemates.

It was quite a crew. The table was for ten or twelve, I can't recall, but let me tell you who I remember: Sophia Loren, beautifully made up and gowned; she was seated next to Mikhail Gorbachev, with the pink-beige Afghanistan-looking mark on his forehead; next to him was Mrs. Gorbachev, who was smiling; next to her, Kevin Costner, beautiful in a coal-black silk jacket, his face tan and his hair combed . . . blondly, shinily. Next to him, a card with my name.

And next to me was Mr. Gorbachev's security guy, an American, a terrific kid in his twenties who was born in nowhere but was given by God a body he could make strong and capable; and now he's having dinner with movie stars and former Soviet leaders. He was happy. His happiness came right out of his face and met my happiness and we started to laugh, and communed. Next to him was an important media woman who ran either CNN or NPR, I can't recall. I think one of Ms. Loren's sons was also there. There must have been a few others, but I can't remember them because they didn't do anything as interesting as Kevin Costner.

It was a night of long speeches by and about men and women of achievement. They'd stand and bow in the lights and accept applause. It got a little long. We were all getting a little . . . bored isn't the right word, but we were starting to daydream and plan the next day.

While we daydreamed, while someone or other spoke, Kevin Costner leaned forward slightly, languidly swept his right arm to his right, and picked up Mrs. Gorbachev's dessert, a peach melba kind of thing. He picked up a spoon, and he began to eat. He did this without her permission. He did it with what seemed a sense of *what Kevin wants Kevin, by definition, should have.*

I looked to see her response. She had seen his movement from the corner of her eye, saw him make off with her dessert and smiled. It was a broad, co-quettish smile full of delight. *Thank you for taking my dessert,* it said. *I am glad it caught your fancy. Shall I open my purse? I have some change in there.*

I could tell: She felt honored by his assumption, as if his eating her dessert showed how informal they were with each other. She was friends with a movie star.

With that small act much that I had witnessed that evening seemed to come together. Mr. Gorbachev, for instance, wanted attention and engagement, but he got nowhere with Ms. Loren, who treated him with Olympian disdain, as if she'd appraised him and judged him to be a guy out of a job who hadn't exactly been a movie star for forty years. So Mr. Gorbachev turned to Kevin Costner, who doled out his attention and engagement sparingly. Mrs. Gorbachev seemed to flirt with him. The bodyguard, who by the nature of his job is on fairly intimate terms with the former leader of the Soviet Union, a man of history who bowed to its commands and ended communism's seventy-four-year reign—the body-guard too was dazzled to be with Kevin Costner.

And Mr. Costner seemed not at all surprised by any of this. He seemed used to it. Not because he's interesting or full of integrity or wonderful stories or great generosity of spirit—let me tell you, I talked to him at some length over three hours about politics, culture and movies, and Kevin Costner is one beautiful boring dullard of a man—but because he is, simply, a movie star.

And as such, he is a prince of the city, a prince of the City of Man.

And that's when it hit me: Movie stars run the world. *Movie stars trump everybody.* We all know they're world-famous and important, that they are in effect corporations whose personal success is responsible for the creation of hundreds and thousands of jobs. We all know their faces are world-famous. But I didn't realize until that night that movie stars trump everybody. The big ones—Tom Cruise, Tom Hanks—trump senators and, arguably, the entire House. They trump governors, whom they think of as men with unfortunate hair. Movie stars trump the real princes of sort-of-real thrones, such as England's. If Prince Charles and Russell Crowe walked down the street together in any city in any country on any continent in the world, the crowd would flock to Mr. Crowe and ignore the nice, well-tailored man at his side.

Any number of senators and officials can say they want a World War II monument in the mall, but if Tom Hanks wants it done, it gets done, period. It's getting done even as we speak.

The only person movie stars do not trump is the American president, while he is president, and in only one way does he trump them: He can nuke someone. Movie stars don't have that power, yet.

This was my big epiphany from the *Time* party: Mr. Gorbachev is nothing compared to a star whose movies flop. I actually hadn't known that.

There was only one man I wanted to meet that night, and he turned out to be, in my eyes, the great man of the evening. I saw him across the room at a round, white table talking to Mel Brooks. During the milling-about time between courses I went over to thank him for his excellence. Soon I was standing near him and seeing him in the bright lights—a smooth, black tuxedo on a not-so-broad back. He turned toward me; I introduced myself and asked if I might shake his hand. He smiled and said sure—I was later to find out this was amazing behavior on his part—and we talked for a few minutes about the party and about politics. I left feeling I'd just met a wonderful American man.

Later I found out that he too had done something interesting at the dinner. He had been assigned by the editor of *Time* to sit at the table of the president of the United States, Bill Clinton. When he saw where his place card had been put, in this place of honor, he ordered it moved, because he didn't want to sit at a table with a man like that.

And here's to you, Joe DiMaggio. He married a movie star half a century ago but the one thing he seems not to have liked about Marilyn Monroe was that she was a star. And that night he refused to sit with the biggest political star in the room. Joe DiMaggio trumped movie stardom. But Joltin' Joe has left and gone away.

I wish the philosopher Joseph Campbell had talked about movie stars, because I think they are received by a lot of people as having magical powers. One reason stars have such power is people tend to think that the parts they play have something to do with the people they are—with their own characters, with their personalities. You can't help but think Mel Gibson is brave. You can't help but think Tom Hanks is good. Even though you also know this is perhaps not always true, or perhaps only true now and then, or maybe not true at all.

But it's hard to keep this in your head. One of the oddest things about modern America is that we've never been so cynical about stars at the same time that we've never been so adoring of them, so aware of them, so worshipful. And we are these things in part because we often confuse the parts they play with the people they are. They do, too—the stars themselves do. Kevin Costner very much gives off the vibe of a man who sees himself on his own inner Imax as the Postman who saved the nation.

But the people most likely to confuse the part the movie star plays with the star himself are the not fully mature, the not fully developed, the not deeply intelligent, the not fully stable.

And we have more and more of these people in the modern world.

Which means stars are getting bigger and bigger. More and more famous. More and more powerful.

Which gets me to the Academy Awards. Much has been said about Sunday night's extravaganza, much of it critical, and the criticism is understandable. The ratings were historically low; the hostess, Whoopi Goldberg, while possessed of the extraordinary confidence and command necessary to host a show watched, live, by a billion people, suffers from the singular failing in a comic that she is not funny. She is smug, she plays the survivor, and when she makes off-color references she's embarrassing not because she's over the top or cutting-edge but because she's corny, old-fashioned, as if she were struck in the 1960s when it was daring to use "Down Under" as a double entendre. Corny lasciviousness is creepy.

It is also true that this year's Oscar producers appear to have no sense at all of the lives of real Americans in the real America, but instead seem to experience life through some weird, antiart prism in which everything comes down to what racial, religious or ethnic group is oppressed on a daily basis in our sad country. The show's ratings might reflect not only America's reaction to Ms. Goldberg's witlessness but also to the introduction of men such as Al Sharpton as Thinker on the Meaning of the Movies.

America knows that when Hollywood producers are giving you Al Sharpton, Hollywood is pursuing its own version of reality, and it's not yours. So why not watch *Six Feet Under*, which has the benefit of being interesting and funny and strange and beautifully acted and aesthetically pleasing.

And yet. For all of that, a good thing happened on that show, and I think we lost the good in the criticism.

It was that American kids, American teenagers, American immigrants and Americans in general got to see beautiful if over-the-top free speech as the winners referred to race. Now you might say that in a country in which African Americans are 12 percent of the population and yet our most admired leaders, such as Colin Powell, are black, and our most admired cultural figures, such as Oprah, are black, and our emcee this evening is Whoopi, and on and on—you might say that our country doesn't have as big a race problem as Hollywood thinks. You might say America has made much more progress than Hollywood understands. You might say we as a nation are unbelievably integrated compared to fifty or even twenty-five years ago.

But you could also say, and you'd be right, that it isn't perfect. And you could also say America is a country in constant pursuit of perfection, which is a good thing.

When Halle Berry bubbled and sobbed in her speech, it was understandable. She had just won an Academy Award, a billion people were watching, her career and life had been troubled and now had triumphed, and she was the first black woman ever to win in the best actress category.

And that itself is pretty wonderful. And so her words, which you might say expressed a certain wonder. "Oh my God. Oh, my God. I'm sorry, this moment is so much bigger than me." She thanked black actresses of the past for breaking ground, and of the present for sharing a sense of solidarity. She said the moment was "for every nameless, faceless woman of color that now has a chance because this door tonight has been opened."

Well, Ms. Berry didn't quite open the door. America finally did, as America finally does. But Ms. Berry passed through it, and that is cause for joy.

When Sidney Poitier won his special award for lifetime achievement, he was, as everyone said, dignified and eloquent. When he won the Oscar as best actor almost forty years ago, it was something startling and new. Now it's not. That's good. He thanked those who had helped him rise, and noted that "I benefited from their effort. America benefited from their effort."

It did indeed. I only wish he'd spoken more of his early life on Cat Island in the Bahamas, or his days as an American immigrant, washing dishes for a living and at least once sleeping in a bus station. He went from nothing to everything. He did that and America did that. They did it together.

Denzel Washington, the best actor of the evening, added context and proportion. "Oh, God is good. God is great," he began. "I thank the Academy for saying to me that on this given night I was the best that I could be."

Just so. He's a great actor, and he has real presence.

•   •   •

Conservative commentators have been especially tough on the show, again understandably, for as a group they tend to hate cant and phoniness and the untrue. They are always searching for what they believe to be true.

But a nation runs not only on certain truths but on other things, too— on warmth and fellow feeling and generosity, for instance. It means something for kids when they see, again, that everything is possible in America. This is particularly important now, as our kids have it drummed through their heads each day in school that America has been a place of bigotry and slavery and shame. Some of our children are getting a fairly eccentric sense of what it was like in America even only twenty-five years ago.

But we all probably benefit from reminders of what is possible here. There is for instance the lady on the train, a trite story perhaps, but true. It was Monday, the morning after the Oscars, about 9:30. The train was the No. 4 or 5 into Manhattan, full of commuters. A woman gets on with a friend, a man. They're both middle aged, both middle class, both on their way to work, both black. She is bubbling about what happened last night. She's saying—and she's really bubbling—". . . and she thanked Dorothy Dandridge and Lena Horne and oh I forget, she was thanking . . ." And I wanted to shout, "Diahann Carroll. Wasn't it great?" But the woman was ten feet away and I didn't want her to know we could all hear her.

Anyway, there was something lovely in it.

Mere sentiment you say. Maybe. But nations do run on many things, and sentiment is surely one of them.

It was nice that Halle Berry and Denzel Washington and Sidney Poitier won big awards. It's nice that there was a history-making breakthrough. It was nice that we noticed and thought about its meaning. It was nice that the progress of black artists in Hollywood highlighted a progress in our country that seems obvious to many of us but is not obvious to all of us. And it's nice that people paid attention. By the way, on the Oscars Web site, *God* was not capitalized in the transcripts of the speeches. Halle Berry was quoted as saying "Oh my god" and "My god." We are at the holiest time of the year, with Passover here, Good Friday today and Easter this Sunday, and I wonder if the good folk at Oscar.com couldn't give God a capital G. After all, he made the stars, every one of them.

29

Bush Makes the Right Move

FRIDAY, APRIL 5, 2002

Well that was one big, broad, bold statement from our president on the Mideast yesterday. His Rose Garden speech seemed to come late in the drama, but it may turn out that George W. Bush spoke at the right moment—when the action had reached its peak, with the Church of the Nativity surrounded, the tanks rolling through Nablus and on to Hebron, the watching world exhausted, and the rush of adrenaline that had sustained both sides the past week wearing off, leaving some combatants shaky and wondering no doubt if there wasn't a way back from the brink.

Mr. Bush's speech said there was. And he demonstrated it by seeming to take a step back himself from his own previous statements. Although his people will soon be calling it not a step back but an elaboration or extension of his previous position.

His announcement that he would send Secretary of State Colin Powell to Israel next week appears to be risky—certainly all the foreign-affairs professionals are calling it a big gamble—but it isn't, really. Things are so bad in the Mideast that if Mr. Powell makes any progress at all, sending him will seem a brilliant move. If Mr. Powell fails, who wouldn't have failed? It's the Mideast. And what would failure look like, anyway? Just more of the same.

As for how Mr. Powell's presence will be perceived, the Arab world, which understands him to be one Bush Cabinet member who is not reflexively pro-Israeli, will not complain; the Israelis understand him to be representing a president with a history of commitments to Israel; the Europeans see him as an American who has a detached view of the Mideast.

And Mr. Powell is a national and international hero. He has the power of the unhated man. His presence has force because his persona is dense with meaning: hero, leader, minority member who struggled to triumph in white institutions, a dove by nature who knows how to fight. He knows how to say tough things in a boring way, a great talent in diplomacy. He radiates warmth but is a reactor cool at the core. He can lower the temperature just by walking in. And the world press both admires and enjoys celebrating him.

So he's a good man to send at a time such as this. And just as Mr. Powell needs Mr. Bush in order to continue as secretary of state, Mr. Bush needs Mr. Powell for the signals his presence sends, and for the stature he lends. They need each other, know it, negotiate around it without acknowledging it, and work well together.

As for Mr. Bush's speech, it was impressive and, I suspect, clever. What was needed was a definitive statement of America's understanding of, and views on, what is happening in the Mideast, but a statement that didn't make things hotter or more passionate or encourage action that would not be helpful. Mr. Bush needed to give the world a sense of the context as he sees it. What was not needed was rhetorical flight, and he didn't take one. He needed words that weren't each of them little hand grenades but words that had a simple and definite meaning that became sentences that, strung together, built a suspension bridge of thought and well-meaning.

That's what he did. Neither the Palestinians nor the Israelis hold the immediate guilt; a fanaticism which "induces" an eighteen-year-old Palestinian girl to strap a bomb on her back and blow herself up, killing a seventeen-year-old Israeli girl, is the evildoer. "Suicide bombers are not martyrs," Mr. Bush said. "They're murderers, and they undermine the cause" for which they stand.

He said, essentially, that both sides in the struggle have a case, a plea that can be made to the world's conscience. He made it clear he remains a supporter of Israel's right to defend itself and to assert its right to nationhood and freedom. "I speak as a committed friend to Israel." But Israeli settlement activity must stop, and Israel should "lay the foundations of future peace" by halting its incursions into Palestinian areas, and in fact withdrawing from them. He asked Israel to show "a respect" for those who feel humiliated by the actions of its soldiers.

This was a step back from Mr. Bush's previous statements that Israel had a right to defend herself, period.

At the same time Mr. Bush made no bows to Yasser Arafat, saying he had "betrayed the hopes of his people" by failing to strongly or steadily oppose terrorism. Mr. Bush warned that terrorism could "blow up" the best chance for a Palestinian homeland. He challenged the leaders of Arab countries to play a constructive role, and warned Syria and Iran that they must "stay out" of the conflict.

At the end of remarks some bravado: He expects better leadership in the Mideast, and "I expect results."

The most surprising aspect of Mr. Bush's remarks was that they were so specific. They were not bland and vague as one might have expected from a diplomatic statement by a president to a world that fears a widening war. His remarks were highly specific and informational, full of citations on United Nations resolutions and support of past peace plans that could become a blueprint for progress. Which means his remarks gave everyone—the Palestinians, the Israelis, the Europeans, the foreign-policy community, the media, the Arab street, the Israeli street—something to think about, chew over. As most people can't think, chew and shoot at the same time, his specificity may turn out to have been a contribution.

But in general, at times like this, an American president simply has to speak. He must come forward with a voice that reflects the thinking of a great nation that is trying to be fair. It is good he finally spoke, good that he was comprehensive, good that he launched a new mission. To use the word *good* three times in a piece about the Mideast after the past six months feels . . . pretty good.

30

The Hard Way

FRIDAY, APRIL 12, 2002

We can all remember when the Mideast was not a crisis but rather an unanswered question: *How will they find peace?* It was a place that in our lifetimes had not achieved amity and accord but was not always at war, at least not always in full, hot war.

But now everyone—literally everyone you read, hear, speak to—has the sense that events are accelerating toward some unknown outcome. And no one—no one—believes the outcome will be good. We are out of optimists and optimism. The scenarios floated are dire. "Watch Lebanon," says the ahead-of-the-pack Charles Krauthammer. Hezbollah in southern Lebanon has 8,000 Katyusha rockets; they have already threatened to hit Haifa. If they do, Israel will answer, and not only in Lebanon but possibly in Syria, where the Hezbollah receives support. Syria would likely strike back with chemical weapons. Israel would answer unconventionally. And Armageddon is launched.

Tuesday night I bumped into a celebrated foreign-policy genius at a birthday party for a friend. He told me he thought that President Bush is doing well, has not yet made any serious mistakes. I said I agreed, and that I thought any effort that buys us time is good. By "us" I meant the world. He surprised me with his vehemence. "There is no 'land for peace,'" he said. "There is only land for time.

"This is not solvable," he added. And he had spent his life trying to solve international problems.

• • •

The Bush administration is passionately criticized from right and left. The right says he is shifting, unsure; that sending Colin Powell and calling for Israel to withdraw shows insufficient support for Israel and insufficient resolve in the face of terror. The left scores Mr. Bush for being reflexively pro-Israeli, as America always is. ABC News's daily political Internet report, "The Note," wonders if there's a method in Mr. Bush's madness. Perhaps he's crazy like a trapped fox, deliberately confusing everyone while he vamps up time and searches for options.

Mr. Bush stays in the kitchen and keeps stirring the broth, as Lee Atwater used to say. "Just keep stirring the pot, you never know what will come up." Thus Mr. Bush's statements, which haven't been so much contradictory as—well, let's say he chooses each day to emphasize a different truth. One senses the people at the White House hope they'll be able to look back on this as a strategy of creative ambiguity.

Mr. Bush criticizes Israel to buy time. He sends Mr. Powell to buy time. He criticizes Arafat to buy time. He has Ari Fleischer declare that Ariel Sharon wants peace to buy time. Why buy time? Because time is good. Because it's better than rushing hard and terrible events. Because the horse may laugh.

You remember the old English story. An angry king is about to put a disloyal servant to death. "My lord," the servant says, "give me only one year of life and I will do something amazing and unheard-of. I will make your horse rear back and laugh with happiness." The king says, "That's impossible, horses don't laugh." The servant answers, "I have the power to, in only one year, teach your horse to laugh at all your jokes. And when I succeed I will ask you, if your grace will, to spare me. And if I should fail I will peacefully lay down my life."

The king ponders and agrees. Later a friend asks the servant why he made such a stupid, impossible vow. The servant said, "Well, in a year the king may die, or I may die. Or the horse may laugh."

That's what I think Mr. Bush is thinking: The horse may laugh.

You think this way only when you have no other options.

But isn't it odd that in a world full of geniuses, no one has an answer? Isn't it amazing that the whole highly sophisticated, technologically evolved, psychologically and historically astute world feels so at the mercy of this drama, so unable to help it or end it?

This is the core of the world's pessimism: Everything you know of life tells you that if there are hundreds of thousands of Muslim fanatics who are shrewd, talented and capable, and if they live in the age of "obliterates," of weapons of mass destruction that can obliterate whole cities and countries, then some of them will get their hands on those weapons and slip through or over lines and borders. And everything you know of life and history tells you that Israel will not surrender; and that, as the writer Ron Rosenbaum, who normally speaks with a voice that is more cerebral than visceral, said this week in the *New York Observer*, "This is the way it is likely to happen: Sooner or later a nuclear weapon is detonated in Tel Aviv, and sooner, not later, there is nuclear retaliation—Baghdad, Damascus, Tehran, perhaps all three. . . . The unspoken corollary of the slogan 'Never again' is: 'And *if* again, not us alone.' "

Those are the emotions coming from both sides, aimed at and springing from the Mideast, which a Catholic writer has called the vortex, the portal through which God has talked to man since the very dawn of history. The Garden of Eden, Moses, the Ten Commandments, the prophets, the birth of Christ the Redeemer, the crucifixion, the fall of the temple, the return of Israel. The Mideast is the place where God talks to us. And where these days His message does not seem ambiguous. It's this: You're all in a heap of trouble.

So what are we to do? I was daydreaming about all this as I walked in my neighborhood on Pierrepont Street yesterday, and I found myself staring at a message someone had drawn onto newly poured concrete: "Smile. Today is what you have." It struck me, naturally, as sentimental street art. And then I thought no, it's both spiritual—"This is the day the Lord made / let us rejoice and be glad in it," wrote the Psalmist—and fatalistic. It made me think of Mother Teresa and the Catholic writer Henri Nouwen, who was a priest. He went to her once and poured out his problems—he wasn't appreciated, he was misunderstood, higher-ups weren't helping him in his good work. "You wouldn't be having these problems if you prayed more," she said. And that's all she said. At first Nouwen felt resentful—he had expected encouragement, sympathy, solidarity. Instead he got a blunt statement that he knew, in a moment, was true. He really wouldn't be having these problems if he prayed more. So he went home and prayed. And the problems became manageable, and life did not end.

Which got me thinking this: It is easier to fight than to pray. In fact it's much easier to fight than to pray. It's one of the reasons we do more of the former than the latter.

And fighting is hard. But it's not the hardest thing of all the things we could do. The hardest thing is this: I have been reading about Karol Wojtyla during World War II, long before he became Pope John Paul II. Mr. Wojtyla was in his late teens when the war started, and after the Nazis invaded Poland he worked manual labor, on the freezing overnight shift at a factory, outdoors, breaking and carrying rocks. He was ill fed, grew thin, suffered. He had only one pair of shoes, and they were wooden. What energy he had after work he gave to art, to help keep Polish drama alive, for he felt that art would help his nation live. He was unusually generous with others, shared what he had, was known for a particular kindness. He helped friends in the Resistance, but he did not join them. Why? Because, as he told a friend, the only resistance that would work was asking God's help. "The only thing that will be effective is prayer." So he quietly and constantly prayed, for the liberation of Poland and the end of Nazism and the safety of his jailed and abused Jewish and Christian friends.

Prayer is the hardest thing. And no one congratulates you for doing it because no one knows you're doing it, and if things turn out well they likely won't thank God in any case. But I have a feeling that the hardest thing is what we all better be doing now, and that it's not only the best answer but the only one.

31

The Pope Steps In

FRIDAY, APRIL 19, 2002

It has been said of Pope John Paul II that he has lived the great life of the twentieth century, a life utterly emblematic of its struggles.

The pope is an old man, gravely ill, exhausted by his asceticism. He is unable to show feeling or emotion through the Parkinsonian mask that freezes his features. When I saw him walk into a room two years ago—bent, moving slowly, his left eye drooping and rimmed red—his face seemed that of a half-submerged whale looking silently at the world, a great mammal risen from the deep.

In the midst of this suffering he is handed a great and final challenge. It is of a piece with his actions in resisting the third great "ism" of the twentieth century, a materialism that has brought what he calls "the culture of death." Next week, he meets the cardinals of the American church, to discuss the sex scandal that threatens in some ways the death of the church in this country.

In abruptly calling them to Rome, the pope declares the scandal a crisis. American Roman Catholics would agree. The problem within the church is systemic—in one of the grimmer cases, a serial-abuser priest explained that he in fact had been sexually abused by a now dead cardinal—and calamitous, with further calamity waiting down the road as trial lawyers line up for their spoils. But that is not the worst of it. There is no estimating the damage already done to the church's authority, its very respectability. And there are the abused children, who until the scandal had almost never received an apology.

The pope is dependent on those around him not only for factual information but for a truthful interpretation of the facts. He is not in America, and much of what he hears is filtered through the Vatican apparatus. One hopes he knows that the American church needs his leadership now, his authority, his standing as a great man who can be trusted. His American cardinals and bishops are losing that authority.

The pope has no doubt been told, repeatedly, that this is a media-driven scandal. Cardinal Theodore McCarrick this week told *The Washington Post,* his parish paper, that journalists are having "a heyday." The cardinal no doubt believes this to be true, but it is not.

Members of the media are leery of sex scandals and the church—for several reasons. They fear accusations of an anti-Catholic bias. They fear alienating 60 million readers and watchers. Moreover, American television news shows are not generally drawn to stories that are time- and labor-intensive, and that involve expensive legal proceedings to secure documents. TV air can be filled with easier, less inflammatory stories, with stories that are amusing and, as network producers love to say, poignant.

Only one newspaper, the *The Boston Globe,* had the persistence and courage to tackle this story by forcing the Boston archdiocese to release internal documents that finally revealed the scope of the scandal. The rest of the media, with some exceptions, such as *National Review,* had to be pushed. Often by ardent Catholics.

The pope should be told that sexual abuse by priests is the heart of the scandal, but only the start of the scandal. The rest is the racketeering dimension—the fact that a RICO suit has been brought, could be brought, against the church, charging that it acted as an institution to cover up criminal behavior by misleading, lying and withholding facts. The church has long attempted to keep priest-abuse cases quiet through the paying of hush money—estimated at a billion dollars so far—to families instructed to sign confidentiality agreements.

And it is a scandal in which not adults, not those able to care for themselves, but children—children—have knowingly and continually been put at risk. The church has deliberately allowed children to be put in close proximity to men it knew to be dangerous, if not deadly, to their safety and souls.

The pope should be told that some of the cardinals he will meet are, or have been, excusers or enablers of sex abusers. Some are so sympathetic to abusive priests that they have written touching letters to them. No one has yet unearthed such a letter to any of the victims. This week the bishop of Joliet, Illinois, Joseph Imesch, said that while priests who sexually abuse children should lose their jobs, priests who sexually abuse adolescents and teenagers have a "quirk" and can be treated and continue as priests. The leaders of the American church have acted, as one observer put it, as if compassion for victims is not part of their consciousness. Yet their compassion for colleagues is as florid as it is chilling.

Cardinal McCarrick has suggested that the church needs a declared policy. Perhaps. But the pope must know that, when he speaks of guidelines such as "It is wrong not to protect children from known sexual predators," he will be speaking not to men who have never heard such guidelines, but to men who have crossed them.

The pope chose, in his reign, not to govern the church strictly, trusting instead in local bishops. Cardinal McCarrick referred to this. "You can suggest, you can cajole," he said. "But if a bishop really thinks he has it under control in another way then it's hard to get him to change." He added, "If the Holy Father says, 'I think everybody should do this,' then we all tend to do it." The pope should know that that is the attitude of the American cardinals going in, that they tend to view his directives as suggestions.

The pope should know that many of the cardinals he will speak to have grown detached from life as it is suffered through by ordinary people. The princes of the church live as princes of the world. They live in great mansions in the heart of great cities, dine with senators and editors, and have grown worldly not in the best sense, in real sophistication and knowledge, but in the worst. They are surrounded by staff who serve them, drive them, answer their call. They are used to being obeyed. We all suffer from some degree of arrogance. But I have never seen star treatment ennoble the object of that treatment.

It would be wonderful, finally, if the pope spoke to the world about his recognition of the gravity of the situation, and his grief, and what hard steps he will take to save the soul of the American church.

He could begin with leaning toward a cardinal kneeling before him, thanking him for his long years of effort, and then removing and taking away his cardinal's hat and ring. Thus showing the cardinals and the world that he will not accept the continuance of the calamity.

He could start with Cardinal Bernard Law, whose actions have at least broken the spirit of the law. That would send a message to those in the church who need to hear it, that covering up, going along and paying off victims is over. That careerism is over, and Christianity is back.

32

Back to Life

The coming departure of Karen Hughes has been covered every which way but mostly as a story about a modern woman who, having it all, decided to relinquish some of it, at least for a while, so she could lead a more personally enjoyable life back home, in Texas, with her son in a local school with longtime friends and her husband, a lawyer, able to practice his profession free of the constraints necessarily placed on spouses of powerful Washington personages.

All of which is a long way of saying she wanted to return to life.

What is life? It is the nice big thing you enter each morning when the alarm goes off and you put your feet on the cool floor and then stand, with your hands on the bottom of your back, and look out the window.

Life is putting on coffee, picking up the newspaper and putting on the radio and listening for a few seconds to see if something huge and terrible happened last night. You can tell by the sound of the voices. Once you hear everyone sounds calm and nice and boring, you keep the station on but don't really listen.

The mist from the coffee in the mug is rising. The sun hits the newspaper you're reading as you stand at the kitchen counter and you feel it on your hand. You think: That's the feel of the sun on my hand.

You open the kitchen window and breathe in fresh air—grass, the man next door just mowed. It's fresh and cool. You hear birds. You leave the win-

179

dow open so you can keep hearing them. You think, I'll put a birdhouse back there.

You notice you do not have a hard little ball in your stomach. Your acid glands do not appear to have launched the morning's guerrilla attack on the bagel you're eating. Your heartbeat is not accelerating. You do not have the slight tremor you sometimes get when the phone rings so often it's come to seem like a constant alarm.

The rictus muscles around your mouth are not tightening. You are not frowning.

What's happening? Oh—you've returned to life.

You are standing there reading the front page. And the front page does not contain information you must respond to. It contains information other people must respond to—the mayor, say, or the head of the arts committee. You wish them well.

You have only one fear. For a long time you've had a hunch that fear keeps you slim. That anxiety creates a quicker metabolism. That happiness will make you fat.

You think: I'll worry about this next week. Or next month.

You dress in soft clothes. That's what cops and firemen and members of the armed services call not being in uniform. You wear soft old jeans and a thin cotton sweater. They smell of Tide and fabric softener. They feel warm from the dryer. They drape on you light as an oversized glove.

When Karen Hughes worked in the White House she wore hard clothes—wool blend suits and heels and jewelry and makeup; there were buttons and fasteners and flecks of mascara in the eye. She doesn't have to wear makeup now. She can have a soft face. She can wash her face in Dove foamy cleanser, pat it dry, put on a nice-smelling moisturizer and walk onward into the day.

In that day she can daydream. This is especially important for intelligent people; it's how they find out what they think.

She can walk and go for long drives. This is important for adults as it allows them unconsciously to absorb through their eyes a changing landscape while they think about things big and small, all of which relate to time going by, meaning to a changing of landscapes.

She can not answer the phone. Not answering the phone is a great gift in life. When you answer the phone, other humans very often bring you their need. "I need you to listen/know/react/advise." They get you on their agenda.

When you don't answer the phone you stay on your agenda. Which may or may not be clear but at least is yours.

She can shop. Shopping is a wonderful thing. It's more wonderful if you have money to buy what catches your eye if you want to own it, but it's also fun if you don't have money. It's really wonderful to just sort of walk along the mall and see what your country is selling, buying, offering. You get to see the other people look at and judge your country's products. You can buy a big soft pretzel at a stand and sit on a bench and watch the mothers and daughters buy shoes together. If you sit close enough to hear them you'll be hearing how mothers and daughters talk to each other these days. That's a good thing to know.

Then you can have lunch with friends and bring one another your agendas, which is a word you never use with friends because you don't have to. You know each other so well you don't have an agenda. Or you have one but it's unspoken, shared and simple: It is: We're friends, we help each other through life.

Then you can go home and read a book in a chair outside, or on your bed, with the sunlight streaming in on the comforter. It's good to read. When you read books by people who know things you don't know, or rather who know things you don't know and would benefit intellectually, spiritually or emotionally from knowing, you are giving your brain/soul good nutrients. No one ever got stupider, shallower or worse from doing this.

You can think of dinner. You can make it or order it. You can think of what everyone would enjoy and then try to make sure it'll be good for them too.

You can watch the news and be interested like a normal person by what's going on, as opposed to being interested like an abnormal person—a person who works for a president, say. You can watch TV shows with your son and husband and just enjoy them. You can daydream to them and have uninterrupted thoughts about what's happening in Hollywood and what's happening with people who are twenty-seven and secretly running the country. You can have these thoughts uninterrupted by bells that ring like alarms and agendas that are thrust on you and things you must attend to or the president may suffer.

You can become reacquainted with your country.

You can become reacquainted with the idea of normality.

You can find out how much—or how little—you miss The Great World. You can figure the difference between how much it needed you and how much you needed it.

You can find out how much you need the distractions you used to complain about. You can find out if you were right that you didn't need them.

You can find out what comes in to fill and take the place of the pressure, pleasure and importance you just left. You have to try and make sure that space is filled by better things. But you have to be open-minded, easy and welcoming about the word *better.* It can have broad meanings you didn't expect.

All of this sounds really nice to me. Does it sound nice to you? Then you may want to consider the Hughes Plan, if you can, if you're able to, if it's possible, if you're at a point in life where it's doable.

Let me tell you why I'm riffing along. I have a feeling the Hughes Plan is related to 9/11. The other day a writer friend e-mailed me and said quick, give me a quote on how 9/11 changed your life. She was writing an article and just needed another voice to jump in and give words she could put quote marks around.

I didn't know the answer, or rather I knew a bunch of answers but not one. My friend, however, needed one. So I sat and thought, and then I knew. I wrote back: "Let me tell you what 9/11 did to me. It made me hungrier for life. It made me feel more tenderly toward it and more grateful. It's all short, even in the worst life it's too short, and you want to really feel and experience it and smell it and touch it and thank God for it."

I realized, again, that 9/11 had given me a case of Judith Delouvrier. Judith Delouvrier was a wonderful woman who was my friend; our boys went to school together and she was a fine mother and a happy spirit and she loved her husband and they'd just left their apartment and bought a house in my neighborhood. She had a million plans. She jumped on a plane one summer day and never came back. It was TWA 800.

It was all so impossible, so jarring, so unnatural. And in the months and years after her death, if I was walking along and saw something nice—an especially cute dog, a sweet moment between humans, a pretty baby, a beautiful pair of shoes in the window—I'd feel my usual old mild pleasure. And then I would remember that Judith couldn't see this boring common unremarkable thing. And it made the boring common unremarkable thing seem to me more like a gift, more precious and worthy of attention and appreciation, and even love.

So 9/11 did to me what Judith's death did, only deeper and newer.

And Karen Hughes, who was with the president that day and the days after, maybe she got a case of 9/11 too. And maybe it made some part of her want to be more immersed in life. Or more urgently aware that life is not only what you're doing right this second at the desk, it's also going on out there beyond the desk, it's going by like the wind and if you want to you can step out and feel it.

To the extent her decision reminds us of the life outside the desk, it is a public service.

Not many public servants do things that you can immediately experience as a benefit. So thank you, Ms. Hughes. And now I'm going to go read Michael J. Fox's memoir. And then walk across the Brooklyn Bridge because it's fun.

33

Will Clinton Talk?

FRIDAY, MAY 3, 2002

"Former President Bill Clinton met with NBC executives Wednesday in Los Angeles to discuss hosting his own talk show, according to several television sources." —Los Angeles Times, *front page, May 2*

As befits our subject, I will begin this piece with an assertion of my brilliance. Years ago when asked what I thought Bill Clinton would do after his presidency, I began answering that he would probably have a TV talk show called *Here's Bill!* People would always laugh. I would explain that talking is what Bill Clinton does, that the subject matter of daytime chats would be congenial to him, and that he is a handsome, sunny-seeming and, as they used to say in the Clinton era, compelling figure. So why not?

His entire presidency seemed like a talk show. Or actually his entire presidency seemed like daytime TV—a talk show followed by a soap opera followed by a news bulletin followed by another talk show. Sometimes the last show of the day had the tone of *Washington Week in Review,* sometimes *Jerry Springer.* Looking back, one sees that at the end of his presidency Mr. Clinton was like Dave Attell in *Insomniac,* the Comedy Central show in which a charming and apparently aimless man stays up all night looking for company.

So: I was ahead of the curve in saying the talk show would happen. Now I wish to be ahead of the curve in telling you why it won't. And no, it doesn't have anything to do with the debate on whether he'd be sponsored by

184

Hanes underwear or the Gap. The primary reason Bill Clinton won't host a talk show is that Hillary won't let him. She won't let him because she is not a stupid woman. She doesn't want her husband in a job that would put him back on the media radar screen on a daily basis. She knows that if he had a TV show he'd wind up in the kind of trouble presidential spouses aren't supposed to get into. And she intends for him one day to be a president's spouse.

The Clintons are already wealthy. He is raking in tens of millions a year, including a record-breaking $12 million advance for his memoirs. More to the point, he is wealthy with little effort.

Talk shows take effort. A talk show is real work and not just talk. And Bill Clinton is a talker. Those who witnessed his presidency up close speak of its iconic moment: the endless bull session, with the president talking issues every which way and from every angle. Some suggested he did this to fill time while he avoided decisions; his labor secretary, Robert Reich, said he thought Mr. Clinton enjoyed talking so much because the sound of it made him feel like he had real beliefs.

At any rate he loves to talk but not necessarily to work—to decide, to carry through. Talk shows require discipline. You get up early, have conference calls, hold meetings, read every newspaper and magazine to stay current. You oversee the tone and topics of the show, prepare for and plan interviews, rehearse skits and bits. You meet with writers, you coddle, dominate, bond with and coolly fire producers. You meet with the network to discuss the focus-group data that say people think your hair is too thin, and then spend an hour insisting that you can't start wearing a toupee as you're a woman, or you can't start wearing black leather as you're a fifty-six-year-old man.

You make the hundreds of personal appearances that boost the show. You manage the charities you've created or agreed to head because how could you not—you're rich and famous in America. You take care of the bandleader going through a personal crisis and attend the drummer's debut with Paul McCartney's band. This allows you not only to show solidarity with your colleagues but to get to know Paul, which you must do in part because it will help to get the exclusive when Ringo dies.

You also do 128 more things, all the while getting the daily ratings that tell you if you're slipping or gaining, which information will be in the papers tomorrow with your producer's reaction, an amusing one-liner the two of you just made up on the phone. Talk shows are not for sissies. They are not for lazy people. Talk shows take actual leadership. And you have to do them without the power of the government of the United States behind you.

America is a great democratic meritocracy and an odd thing about it is that those at the very top of it, our media stars in New York and Los Angeles, who have more job security than political figures (Jimmy Carters come and go, but Tom Brokaw is forever) and are certainly better paid and more famous, actually work like slaves. They work like staff! Yes, they are wildly compensated, but they don't get enough sleep, they travel all the time, and half of them say on a semiregular basis, "I hate my life." Because they're always tired. Because they carry great responsibility. Because they have to prove they're good citizens and show up for the speech, the dinner, the fund-raiser, or else a gossip columnist will say they're not nice, and the bad publicity will hurt the show, whatever the show is.

Luckily for them they tend to love movement and action as it keeps them from having to think. But some of them really do think. And they suffer.

Which gets me back to Mr. Clinton. Not that he'd suffer, just that this would all be too much for him.

Also, Bill Clinton cannot do a talk show because he cannot do the monologue. He cannot do the monologue because to this day, seventeen months after his presidency, the most consistently reliable subject of mirth and merriment in monologues is Bill Clinton. (Indeed, Mr. Clinton's inability to do a monologue last night became the subject of a monologue, as Jay Leno joked that the former president "couldn't do a late-night show because he couldn't do Clinton jokes. You can't do a late-night show without Clinton jokes.")

And Bill Clinton cannot have a talk show because exactly half the guests on talk shows are young actresses who are beautiful and giggly or soulful and serious. And part of the long-standing talk show tradition is that the host, the Leno or Letterman, flirts with them, either eagerly or awkwardly or both.

Bill Clinton can't do that because . . . well, back to Hillary.

She knows her husband cannot have a talk show because it would give him a new alternate universe into which to bring his Billness. It would immediately be a success—early numbers at least would be wonderful. Mr. Clinton is and always will be a walking talking event. But success would give him the kind of pleasure that in his case is always the prelude to personal disaster.

He will be so happy he will get into trouble. It will be bad and public trouble. And if he gets into bad and public trouble, Mrs. Clinton may have to handle it. She would have to consider distancing herself from him even more than she does. She might have to divorce him to keep the scandal goo on him and not get it all over her. And one can imagine she does not want to divorce him for many reasons, including that there would be no clear political gain in it. There would be loss and a rehashing of old finger-waving film clips, and it would get in the way of her White House bid in 2004 or 2008.

I'll bet the talk show won't happen. Sometimes two people who've had a certain relationship for a long time experience something big and even painful: a power shift based on a status shift. With her election to the Senate and her slow subtle emergence as the country's leading Democrat, Mrs. Clinton's career is the dominant one in the Clinton family, and the one most promising of future dividends.

34

The Crying Room

How is George W. Bush doing? In Washington the past weekend everyone I spoke to answered that question by referring to the recent *USA Today* poll that said the president's popularity continues undiminished and, amazingly enough, for reasons apart from the war. People like him. They respect him. Almost eight in ten said they thought he was doing a good job as president.

Nor is the press fully immune, or so it seemed to me. After Mr. Bush gave his humorous speech at the White House Correspondents Association dinner, I mentioned to an acquaintance, a veteran journalist at a national newspaper and presumably not a reflexive Bush supporter, that I thought the president's speech all right but undistinguished. "Wasn't as good as Clinton," I said. Bill Clinton's material at dinners like this was top-notch.

"But Clinton was vulgar!" the journalist said. Mr. Clinton's very smoothness, the fact that he was at his best doing shtick for the media, was vulgar. Mr. Bush is more like a president: boring.

Presidents should be boring. We don't hire them to entertain us, we hire them to be stable, sane and sure-handed.

What is the key to Mr. Bush's popularity? I think the source of it is something that isn't new. He walked into the White House with it. But it has become more apparent with time and is, I think, more appreciated.

It is that he does not need the job. He did not lust for it and does not hunger for it. He does not need the presidency to fulfill a romantic sense of personal destiny. He does not have a neurotic fixation on the office. He does not love having or wielding its power. He views the presidency as a responsibility, and sometimes a burden. But he tries each day to meet it. Sometimes it is pleasurable for him, sometimes not.

There is with Mr. Bush an almost palpable sense that he would rather be at the ranch. He would rather be enjoying life and having fun with baseball teams, he would rather have privacy, he would rather go for a drive. He radiates a sense that he has given up a lot to be president. He radiates a sense that he will enjoy it when he gets back what he gave up. But right now he has work to do.

I do not mean to suggest that Mr. Bush is or seems ambivalent about the presidency. I don't think he is or does. He means to be a good president, that is obvious. He works hard, is committed, ambitious and serious. He means to win the war. He is capable of wielding the power he has to wield, and one senses he has enough vanity to believe he is as good a wielder of it as any, and maybe better than most.

But . . . he doesn't need it.

He doesn't love celebrity, doesn't gravitate to the glamorous, doesn't seem to think fame can bestow magic, gladness, personal contentment. I watched him sitting on the dais Saturday night; he looked like he was thinking about whether the jeep needs tires. He was not excited to be surrounded by the glittering prizewinners of Washington, who were arrayed in tuxedos and gowns before him. His wife, also on the dais, smiled pleasingly at everyone, but her smile is unvarying, almost inexpressive, and still seems to hide more than it reveals. She too radiates a sense that she'd be happy back home, kicking her shoes off with the girls and then falling asleep with a book.

When the Mideast was blowing up a few weekends ago, the president was at the ranch. When asked why he wasn't more involved in what was happening, he groused that he was; he'd spent half of Saturday morning on the phone. If he had been LBJ or Nixon or Bill Clinton he would have been a Toscanini of the telephone, talking to world leaders and attempting to bring some personal magic to the drama. Mr. Bush doesn't seem to believe in magic. Yesterday afternoon, talking in the White House to reporters about the struggle he has had getting his judicial nominees through Congress, he looked like someone who was indignant and frustrated but not loaded for bear. He looked like it was work.

Why does Mr. Bush's seeming not to need the presidency contribute to his popularity? Why would it be, in fact, a central reason for his high poll numbers?

Because when you know they don't need it, you know they won't do anything to keep it. And you can start to trust them.

When you know a man experiences an office not as a prize to which he is entitled but as a burden by which he is bound, you feel you can comfortably appreciate him and his efforts.

When a leader doesn't need the office he holds, the electorate feels free to have faith in him. They infer from his lack of need a simple thing: He will be less likely to sacrifice the country's interests to his own. He will not tend to put his own passing political interests over the needs of the nation in order to win. Because he doesn't have to win. When you know a man doesn't have to win, you know he probably won't do anything to win. And when you know he won't do anything to win, you feel more secure in letting him win.

In the Vatican after they have chosen a new pope, they lead him to a room off the Sistine Chapel where he is given the clothing of a pope. It is called the Crying Room. It is called that because it is there that the burdens and responsibilities of the papacy tend to come crashing down on the new pontiff. Many of them have wept. The best have wept.

That in a way is why people like Mr. Bush. They can tell he has been to the crying room. They respect him for it.

35

Dubya's New Deal

FRIDAY, MAY 17, 2002

Let me tell you what I think of the criticism that President Bush (a) reversed Republican philosophy on free trade and caved in on tariffs, and (b) endorsed a farm bill that was so pork-filled that if you held a match to its text, it would hiss, pop and sizzle like bacon in a skillet.

I think the criticisms are legitimate. I also think they miss the point.

Mr. Bush has been smacked by pundits, but the folks being polled don't seem to think much of, about or against it. Mr. Bush knows this and likes it. It means the gamble paid off. The base will forgive him, the nonbase hasn't noticed he did anything that needs forgiveness, and the opposition can hardly knock him for policy positions they've long supported.

Why will the base forgive Mr. Bush? Because they know it's all about the war. Which means it's all about the 2002 congressional elections. Mr. Bush caving in on tariffs helps the Republicans in Pennsylvania and elsewhere; his caving on the farm bill deprives the Democrats of an issue in the farm states.

Right now, Mr. Bush is taking a beating over charges that he was briefed before 9/11 with intelligence reports suggesting terrorists might be about to hijack airliners. We are at the beginning of a new Democratic foray. His political enemies will make as much of the story as they can. James Carville has said that the question is "What did the president know, when did he know it and what did he do about it?" He is echoing the Watergate question in hopes of replicating the Watergate disaster.

And why wouldn't he? Playing political games is what Mr. Carville does as a partisan. And the Democrats happen to be better at these games than the Republicans.

Democrats on talk shows tend not to be shy about hectoring, and murmuring sarcastic asides. They may not be courteous but they pound points home. Republicans, in part because they represent the tougher views of the tougher party, often try to be reasonable, or clever. They are no match.

Back to Mr. Bush and the criticisms he faces. I think the latest 9/11 story will be around for weeks, and he will have to address it. But he will silence his critics. He will also silence those who don't like the farm bill and his stance on trade.

The reason is Franklin D. Roosevelt. GWB is doing an FDR. And I think people know this.

FDR would sacrifice anything to win World War II. You can trace the end of his New Deal legislation to the beginning of the war. Yes, the court-packing scandal had something to do with it, and so did the Supreme Court finding aspects of the New Deal unconstitutional. But after Hitler moved on Poland, Roosevelt sacrificed almost all his liberal domestic plans, angering his supporters in order to mollify conservatives and refocus voters' attention onto the war. He knew he would need broadened support to execute a war. He disappointed much of his base to get it.

Mr. Bush is doing the same thing. He is accepting what he thinks he has to accept (pork, a bad trade bill) in order to keep or expand the power balance he has in Washington, and in order to keep from angering or offending your normal, politically nonobsessed citizen.

If Mr. Bush's popularity falls, his party's suffers. The congressional elections could produce a Democratic House and a more heavily Democratic Senate. Mr. Bush will do almost anything to keep that from happening, and I think people sense it. Because if it does happen, his ability to prosecute the war will be weakened. Power would shift and his opposition, no longer fearing his popularity, would go for his throat. The war effort would be compromised. He has to keep his popularity high. So Mr. Bush is doing an FDR, and angering only a base that will forgive him.

FDR too was dogged with the charge that he and his administration had been warned that the Japanese were about to move on Pearl Harbor.

Somehow FDR didn't hear the warnings, or heed them. Editorialists howled, Congress held hearings, Republicans tried to nail him. They didn't get anywhere. Not because there wasn't any evidence but because the public knew what Congress had forgotten: There was a war on.

There's one on now too. The thing to do is win the war, concentrate your efforts on it, focus, don't fritter away time and resources on a question we don't have to answer just this second. We have to enhance our defenses just this second.

The "when and how much did he know" question remains alive, but is muted. Whatever the truth, the people know that winning the war is more important than finding out what the president knew and when he knew it. FDR won his war, clear and clean. Mr. Bush will have to do that too.

36

Open Your Eyes

Every big speech has a text and a subtext. When Ronald Reagan spoke at Normandy on the fortieth anniversary of D-Day, in 1984, his text consisted of a remembrance of what had happened there on the beaches on that day in 1944. He spoke of the efforts of the English and Scots brigades, the Americans, the French; he lauded the U.S. Rangers who had clawed their way up to the top of the cliffs of Pointe du Hoc. "And in seizing back this soil," he said, as he stood on it, "they seized back the continent of Europe."

It is the text that is remembered: "These are the boys of Pointe du Hoc."

But it was the subtext of the speech that was most important, that contained the speech's true purpose. The subtext was a message aimed at the leaders of the West and the people of Europe. It was: Fellow NATO members, you must remember that just as our fathers beat back the totalitarian Nazis, we now must beat back the totalitarian Soviets—and we can do it, we can triumph if we hold fast, hold firm and stand together just as our fathers did forty years ago.

That message was important: In those days NATO seemed on the verge of breaking up over disagreements on how and even whether to resist the Soviet Union. Europe roiled with anti-American peace marches. The Pointe du Hoc speech was not a commemorative event but a speech intended to exhort, persuade and move history.

President Bush will go to Normandy this weekend, to speak at the

American cemetery there. Is he foolishly using a stage President Eisenhower used to such benign effect in 1964, that Mr. Reagan used to such famous effect in 1984, and that Bill Clinton also used? Isn't the stage already cluttered with presidential ghosts?

No. Mr. Bush and his people like the high wire when they think it promises to raise their standing. A presidential speech in Normandy is by definition an event; it ensures wide, broad and lengthy press coverage. The cameras can't resist the rows of white crosses, Normandy brings out the inner Spielberg-filming-Private Ryan in every network producer. So the Bush speech will receive big coverage.

Does Mr. Bush fear comparisons? If he did they wouldn't have scheduled it. Mr. Bush's people have a clever way of positioning things. They'll assume no one remembers what Ike said or Mr. Clinton said, and as for Ronald Reagan, Mr. Bush will probably take care of that problem by quoting him, lauding him and putting him away like a pretty Christmas ornament in an old brown box.

Mr. Bush always wants to bring big meaning to big events. He likes to say important things. This is not true of all politicians, and he does not always succeed. No one really remembers the meaning of his acceptance speech in the summer of 2000; no one remembers the meaning of the speech he gave when the election was resolved the following December. In both cases he said too many things, and they didn't seem like big things; at any rate, people left with a blurry sense of what had been said. But his speeches since 9/11 have mostly been clean, straight bullets. And that's probably what he'll do at Normandy, a clean, straight bullet.

I say that in part because that's what his speech was Wednesday, in Berlin—not only a bullet but a blast.

It was the big speech of the trip, the one I'd been told to watch for a few weeks ago when I asked the White House where the primary statements would be made. You can add Mr. Bush at the Bundestag to the list of speeches with a text and a subtext. I think you can also add it to your small list of great speeches of the twenty-first century. I think Mr. Bush at the Bundestag is going to be remembered for a long time.

The text: The American president, at a heightened and dramatic time in world history, travels to Europe to speak to its people of our continued friendship, ties and heritage, and to underscore our shared destiny; and to demonstrate in the process that Mr. Bush, though not a world traveler, is acquainted with the demands and disciplines of high diplomacy; that he is about to demonstrate the seriousness of his leadership by signing an arms agreement with the Russians that reflects the end of old enmity and the beginning of alliance; and that the signing itself shows his desire for and ability to achieve a safer world.

The subtext: Mr. Bush is trying to communicate to European elites that American actions, views and plans on Islamic terrorism are not a threat to Europe but its salvation. He is trying to tell Europe to open its eyes, see the threat, join the cause. He is trying to convince them that this is not America and Israel vs. the world but civilization vs. madmen. If he cannot convince the elites he may at least win new support from the people of Europe—he's talking to them too. And he is attempting to rally the American people again, using a European stage to drive home his worldview and display what he hopes will be perceived back home as growing personal stature.

A look at some of the speech.

"I am honored to visit this great city," Mr. Bush said of Berlin. "The history of our time is written in the life of Berlin. In this building, fires of hatred were set that swept across the world. To this city, Allied planes brought food and hope during 323 days and nights of siege. Across an infamous divide, men and women jumped from tenement buildings and crossed through razor wire to live in freedom or to die in the attempt. One American president came here to proudly call himself a citizen of Berlin. Another president dared the Soviets to 'tear down that wall.'"

Good stuff. It reminds the audience that America is Germany's longtime friend—the airlift, the war against communism. It contains an implicit reminder: Standing with you cost us plenty, but we paid the price because it was right. (Side message to America: Happy Memorial Day.)

Mr. Bush praises the new Germany "made whole"—an elegant reference to unification.

He then erects a generational platform from which to make his points, the same platform Mr. Reagan used in Normandy:

"On both sides of the Atlantic," says Mr. Bush, "the generation of our fathers was called to shape great events—and they built the great transatlantic alliance of democracies. They built the most successful alliance in history. After the Cold War, during the relative quiet of the 1990s, some questioned whether our transatlantic partnership still had a purpose. History has given its answer."

This got applause. Mr. Bush then jumps to today:

"Our generation faces new and grave threats to liberty, to the safety of our people, and to civilization, itself. We face an aggressive force that glorifies death, that targets the innocent, and seeks the means to murder on a massive scale."

Here we go. The subtext in full force: Europe, wake up!

"Those who despise human freedom will attack it on every continent. Those who seek missiles and terrible weapons are also familiar with the map of Europe."

"Are also familiar with the map of Europe" is a delicate but direct way of saying: Guess who's next?

Mr. Bush continues: "Like the threats of another era, this threat cannot be appeased or cannot be ignored. By being patient, relentless and resolute, we will defeat the enemies of freedom. . . . Together, Europe and the United States have the creative genius, the economic power, the moral heritage, and the democratic vision to protect our liberty and to advance our cause of peace."

Don't be pessimistic, he's saying, we can do it, we'll get through this. But only if you get serious and face the facts.

He reminds Europe that for all her pain she has been invincible. "From the Argonne Forest to the Anzio beachhead, conflicts in Europe have drawn the blood of millions, squandering and shattering lives across the earth. There are thousands, thousands of monuments in parks and squares across my country to young men of eighteen and nineteen and twenty whose lives ended in battle on this continent. Ours is the first generation in a hundred years that does not expect and does not fear the next European war. And that achievement—your achievement—is one of the greatest in modern times."

And so we know peace is winnable. We see this in the rise of the European Community, which is not seen by America as a rival but as living proof that "old hostilities" can be ended.

He asserts that NATO expansion will make Europe more secure; he commits American backing for membership for all European democracies; he asserts as a shared mission the encouraging of Russia to see its future "in Europe, and with America." This echoes Mr. Bush's statement in an interview with *The Wall Street Journal* last June, in which he said he had told President Putin in their first meeting that radical Islam was a threat to Russia, not the West. "Russia has its best chance since 1917 to become a part of Europe's family. Russia's transformation is not finished; the outcome is not yet determined. But for all the problems and challenges, Russia is moving toward freedom."

So: together, Europe and America have transformed the Soviet Union into free Russia. And let us now discuss more deeply what we must again do, together, to survive: "For the United States, September 11, 2001, cut a deep dividing line in our history—a change of eras as sharp and clear as Pearl Harbor, or the first day of the Berlin Blockade. There can be no lasting security in a world at the mercy of terrorists—for my nation, or for any nation. . . . Together, we oppose an enemy that thrives on violence and the grief of the innocent. The terrorists are defined by their hatreds: They hate democracy and tolerance and free expression and women and Jews and Christians and all Muslims who disagree with them."

He says that NATO's defining purpose now is facing down a threat as great as Europe has faced in the past. Like the Nazis, who threatened Europe by killing "in the name of racial purity," or the Soviets, who threatened Europe "in the name of class struggle," our new enemy kills "in the name of a false religious purity."

The answer is unity. "In this war we defend not just America or Europe; we are defending civilization itself."

Down to the nitty-gritty:

"The evil that has formed against us has been termed the 'new totalitarian threat.' The authors of terror are seeking nuclear, chemical and biological weapons. Regimes that sponsor terror are developing these weapons and the missiles to deliver them." If these regimes perfect their capabilities, he says, nothing will stop them. They will use them. "Wishful thinking might bring comfort, but not security. Call this a strategic challenge; call it, as I do, axis of evil; call it by any name you choose—but let us speak the truth."

This is deft. Those who have abjured the phrase "axis of evil" and made their unhappiness with it into a symbol of their opposition: Fine, make up your own phrase, what matters is the facts.

"If we ignore this threat, we invite certain blackmail, and place millions of our citizens in grave danger. Our response will be reasoned, and focused, and deliberate. We will use more than our military might. We will cut off terrorist finances, apply diplomatic pressure, and continue to share intelligence. . . . But make no mistake about it, we will and we must confront this conspiracy against our liberty and against our lives."

What Mr. Bush is saying is simple: We will not back down, we cannot back down, we cannot ignore this threat and survive.

He asks each nation of Europe to make "hard choices" about financial commitments to help the war on terror. He calls for the protection of Israel, the creation of a state for the Palestinian people; he insists peace in the Mideast is possible, points to old hatreds in Europe in which foes became partners and allies.

He says that "poverty doesn't create terror—yet terror takes root in failing nations that cannot police themselves or provide for their people." And so we must help—through trade expansion, and humanitarian aid. "We have a duty to share our wealth generously and wisely."

"Members of the Bundestag," he says, "we are joined in serious purpose . . . on which the safety of our people and the fate of our freedom now rest. We build a world of justice, or we will live in a world of coercion. The magnitude of our shared responsibilities makes our disagreements look so small. And those who exaggerate our differences play a shallow game, and hold a simplistic view of our relationship."

We are more than partners and allies, "we are heirs to the same civilization. The pledges of the Magna Carta, the learning of Athens, the creativity of Paris, the unbending conscience of Luther, the gentle faith of St. Francis—all of these are part of the American soul. The New World has succeeded by holding to the values of the Old."

This is not only liltingly fact-filled; it has, as Henry Kissinger is said to have said, the added benefit of being true. And while Mr. Bush is citing religio-cultural markers, he is also nodding to constituent groups back home.

"Our histories have diverged, yet we seek to live by the same ideals. We believe in free markets, tempered by compassion. We believe in open societies that reflect unchanging truths. We believe in the value and dignity of every life."

This is known as complimenting the other guy by suggesting he shares your best beliefs. It's not quite true, but it reminds him of what he ought to believe in. In any case, no one in the Bundestag is going to stand up and yell, "Hey, we don't believe in the dignity of life, buddy!"

"These convictions bind our civilization together and set our enemies against us," Mr. Bush ends. "These convictions are universally true and right. And they define our nations and our partnership in a unique way. And these beliefs lead us to fight tyranny and evil, as others have done before us."

We cannot afford ambivalence, Mr. Bush told Europe. We must not create or have faith in false equivalencies. We have to stay together to stay safe—but if we stay together we'll be safe.

Good stuff.

They will hear it in Europe. We'll see if they will absorb it, or come to agree with it, but they will certainly hear it.

And that's a good start. Watch for Mr. Bush to underscore his message in Normandy.

37

Weenies or Moles?

In October 2001, shortly after the attacks on the World Trade Center, an essayist who had worked in the U.S. government summed up the genesis of the tragedy this way:

> It was a catastrophic systems failure, a catastrophic top-to-bottom failure of the systems on which we rely for safety and peace. Another way to say it: The people of the West were, the past ten years or so, on an extended pleasure cruise, sailing blithely on smooth waters . . . through an iceberg field. We thought those in charge of the ship, commanding it and steering it and seeing to its supplies, would— could—handle any problems. We paid our fare (that is, our taxes) and assumed the crew would keep us safe. . . .
>
> The American people knew, or at least those paying attention knew, that something terrible might happen. But they knew the government had probably done what governments do to protect us. The people did not demand this; the government did not do it. . . . It was a catastrophic systems failure, top to bottom.

It is generally not good form to quote *yourself,* but I do it to make two points:

1. That a system failure occurred has been acknowledged almost since the tragedy took place. It was acknowledged because it was obvious to those

with eyes. The Democrats did not say it, nor did the Republicans, but citizens did, writers did, thinkers did, professionals did.

2. The depth and extent of the system failure, at least within the Federal Bureau of Investigation, was greater than citizens knew in the months after 9/11, and has only now become clear. FBI officials didn't fail to connect the dots; they refused to see a pattern. And this scandal is going to grow.

You know of the Rowley memo, the thirteen-page letter written last week by a twenty-one-year veteran of the FBI, the chief counsel to the Minneapolis field office, Coleen Rowley. She has joined the ranks of those women—these days, as others have noted, they are always women—who blow the whistle on sick and shameful actions within powerful organizations.

You can read an edited version of the *entire memo* on *Time* magazine's Web site. It is the story of what happened when FBI agents in Minneapolis discovered the presence of Zacarias Moussaoui's in their state taking lessons on how to fly planes. They quickly recognized him as a terrorist threat, and arrested him on immigration charges on August 15, four weeks before the World Trade Center became a burial ground. Moussaoui is now infamous as the "twentieth hijacker"—part of the cell or cells that planned and executed the attack on America.

Days after his August arrest, the Minneapolis FBI received information from French intelligence: Moussaoui was connected to Osama bin Laden's terror organization and other groups. The Minneapolis agents asked the FBI in Washington for a warrant to look at Moussaoui's computer and personal effects; they asked too for a wiretap.

The FBI in Washington already had in its hands the Phoenix memo—the one that warned that Middle Eastern males in great numbers were taking flying lessons in Arizona. The FBI also had in its hands the French intelligence report on Moussaoui. Yesterday we found they had in their hands a report from the FBI's chief pilot in Oklahoma warning that "large numbers of Middle Eastern males" were receiving flight training in the Sooner State. It was happening "all over the state," said the Oklahoma agent who wrote the memo. He suggested this might be connected to future terrorist attacks.

The FBI may also have had in hand other clues, tips, warnings and data that have not yet been made public.

• • •

How did FBI headquarters in Washington respond to the Minneapolis request for a warrant? It refused. It said no—"no probable cause."

The days ticked by. Ms. Rowley: "FBIHQ personnel whose job it was to assist and coordinate with field division agents on terrorism . . . continued to, almost inexplicably, throw up roadblocks and undermine Minneapolis' by-now desperate efforts" to obtain a search warrant.

The Minneapolis FBI agents finally, frantic to move forward, took an act that required some courage. They went around FBI headquarters to the CIA's counterterrorist unit. The FBI found out; Ms. Rowley doesn't say how. The FBI then "chastised" the Minneapolis agents.

And continued to refuse a warrant.

You know when the FBI finally okayed a search? On 9/11—after the attacks. Even then, it wasn't without a fight. Ms. Rowley writes that FBI supervisory agent in Washington who had been making the decisions on Minneapolis's requests seemed to have been "consistently, almost deliberately thwarting the Minneapolis FBI agents' efforts." On 9/11, just minutes after the attacks began, the supervisory agent in Washington headquarters phoned Minneapolis, and Ms. Rowley took the call. In that call, she says, he "was still attempting to block the search of Moussaoui's computer." Ms. Rowley recounts the conversation this way: "I said something to the effect that, in light of what had just happened in New York, it would have to be the 'hugest coincidence' at this point if Moussaoui was not involved with the terrorists. The [supervisory agent] stated something to the effect that I had used the right term, 'coincidence' and that this was probably all just a coincidence and we were to do nothing in Minneapolis until we got their [FBI headquarters'] permission." He added, she says, that he didn't want Minneapolis to "screw up" investigations "elsewhere in the country." Ms. Rowley adds another chilling detail. In the early aftermath of 9/11, whenever she told the story of the Moussaoui investigation to FBI personnel, "almost everyone's first question was: 'Why? Why would an FBI agent(s) deliberately sabotage a case?' " She adds that "jokes were actually made that the key FBIHQ personnel had to be spies or moles, like Robert Hansen [actually Hanssen], who were actually working for Osama bin Laden."

This is no laughing matter. When an FBI field operative who is the chief legal counsel of her office tells the head of the FBI in Washington that they've been wondering, out in the field, if spies or moles made the fateful decisions, she is saying something huge. She is saying she thinks it is possible that spies within the FBI thwarted attempts to stop or diminish the attacks of 9/11. And she wants the FBI director to know this. She uses the word *joke,* but she knows what she's doing. She's saying: *This may be true.* When she put this information in a memo that she knows she herself will soon hand-deliver to the Senate Intelligence Committee, she is telling Congress, the press and the people to consider the possibility that spies or moles had some part in the attack on America.

Ms. Rowley asserts that a terrible problem within the FBI in Washington, a problem that likely affected the handling of this case, is "careerism." The FBI is staffed by "short term careerists" who "only must serve an eighteen month-just-time-to-get-your-ticket-punched minimum." The FBI supervisory agent who thwarted the Moussaoui search was one of them. He and his kind are a reason FBI headquarters is "mired in mediocrity." She made it a point to look up and share with the director the dictionary definition of *careerism:* "the policy and practice of advancing one's career often at the cost of one's integrity." Ms. Rowley said she would not use the term *cover-up* to characterize the FBI's official statements since 9/11. She said she will "carefully" use, instead, these words: "Certain facts . . . have . . . been omitted, downplayed, glossed over and/or mischaracterized in an effort to avoid or minimize personal and/or institutional embarrassment on the part of the FBI and/or perhaps even for improper political reasons."

What improper political reasons? She does not say. But throughout her memo she demonstrates a seriousness about words, a carefulness as to meaning. It will be interesting when she is asked by Congress or the press what she meant exactly.

Which is where our media come in. Tim Russert, *60 Minutes:* This is the story you've lived for. Were there spies in the FBI helping out the other side? What political influences may have dictated or affected their decisions? Why did the FBI ignore all the information coming in from French intelligence, from Phoenix, from Minneapolis, from Oklahoma?

There are those who say sure, the picture is always clear in hindsight. But that itself now sounds like the language of cover-up. Bin Laden made his plans clear enough over the years. The World Trade Center had been bombed in 1993, two U.S. embassies in 1998, the U.S.S. *Cole* in 2000. U.S. and Western intelligence had every reason in the world to think something terrible was coming. Anyone who read a Tom Clancy novel knew what was possible, and anyone who read a Tom Clancy novel and had a higher than average IQ knew the possible becomes the probable becomes a tragedy. Senator Dianne Feinstein had a sense of foreboding about U.S. security; so did many of us. And the FBI is supposed to know more than we do.

It is true, as Slate's Mickey Kaus and the columnist Ann Coulter have pointed out in different ways, that the long political-media campaign against "ethnic profiling" had an impact on this case and a bad effect on the FBI. It is true that many Democrats and Republicans who now criticize President Bush and Attorney General John Ashcroft for not combing the flight schools for possible Arab terrorists were previously complaining about profiling.

But it is also true—and here I display what is perhaps naïveté—that a lot of us think the FBI is supposed to be full of people with the sense and toughness to work around irresponsible demands and limitations, and not just fold in the face of potential heat. They're not supposed to be complete weenies in the FBI. They're supposed to have some guts and common sense.

If this were a dark Hollywood thriller, Ms. Rowley would feel it necessary to request whistle-blower protection.

She did.

The supervisory agent in FBI headquarters who thwarted and insulted the responsible men and women of the Minneapolis FBI would get a promotion.

He did.

And the attorney general would announce, just days after the Rowley memo became public, that FBI field offices will now be given expanded authority to move independently on terror threats without going through headquarters.

Two hundred sixty-one days after the attack on America, he did.

38

The Other Shoe

We have come to quite a pass. The nation continues on high alert as our teenagers gulp antidepressants and Osama's spokesman tells us to fasten our seat belt. The attorney general asks if his agents could please be allowed to surf the Internet; we debate that, and whether or not it would be insensitive to fingerprint young Mideastern males trying to enter America. Palestinian terrorists kill another seventeen people in another suicide bombing on another Israeli road, and Israel hits back, with Yasser Arafat under siege for a few hours. The biggest newspaper in India thinks to make vivid for its readers the likely human toll of a nuclear war over Kashmir, a patch on the map that contains nothing that India and Pakistan cannot happily, fruitfully and prosperously live without. *The New York Times* puts a plain recounting of New York's vulnerabilities to nuclear attack on the cover of its Sunday magazine, and as I write on Thursday the director of the FBI, Robert Mueller, is squabbling with Senator Arlen Specter over the agency's failure to give flowcharts to its oversight committee.

As I watch I think of the comment of a friend whose sister lives in an ashram in Washington state. Her swami, a follower of an Indian form of astrology, has announced that June 10 and 11 will be cataclysmic for the world. She called her brother, my friend, to tell him that she loved him. My friend tells me all this and we look at each other and know what the other is thinking: I don't believe in swamis and I don't believe in Indian astrology, but June 11 is nine months after 9/11, and the enemy seems to like nines.

206

We both sort of breathed in and out again. Should we avoid cities on those dates? We live in a time in which we constantly have to try to find the line between paranoia and prudence, between superstition and sensitivity to the weirdness that reigns.

One has a sense of a quickening of history, of a gathering of its forces, of things hurtling toward some unknown end.

At the same time the institutions that keep us up and humming, or at least help keep us mutually invested in and respectful of one another and our way of life, continue to wobble and groan from the weight of their misconduct. The American Catholic Church is a victim of self-inflicted wounds, its corruptions as towering as its cathedrals. Big business—Enronned. Wall Street—stock-tipped, finagled and fooled by a bubble. Big accounting, by which we judge how our business investments are doing, is a joke. The FBI and the CIA are more joke fodder. Our serious journalists are focused on today's testimony, tonight's game and the 2004 Democratic presidential primaries. The others do shark attacks and entertainment awards. Our intellectuals are off on various toots, most of them either irrelevant—the latest edition of the *New York Review of Books* leads with stories on David Brock, Clarence Thomas, sexy Puritans, Peggy Guggenheim and Noël Coward—or all too relevant and wrong.

Congress doesn't seem any more damaged than it was last year or the year before, but then we haven't gotten to the part of the 9/11 investigations where we find out exactly what the intelligence committees knew and when they knew it. The Senate this week was talking. That's what the Senate does, and God bless it. But in its investigation of the FBI and 9/11 it is talking too much. We could dispatch all questions quickly if the senators didn't have to have their airtime. Each senator must be seen on TV grilling the FBI director. This slows things, but it is assumed it will play well back home.

I live back home, and it doesn't play well with me. This is what we need to do: Reveal everything now and fire those who failed us. Take a long hard day and do it. Swift bureaucratic brutality is what we need, not a time-consuming drone.

But back to my theme: At a time of unprecedented national peril the institutions on which we rely for relief, inspiration, guidance and succor are fallen or falling, or at least failing. Really, what a moment in history.

Here is a great irony: We are distracting ourselves from our predicament by obsessing on our tragedy. We are investigating the systems failure of 9/11, and while we investigate it we are contributing to the next systems failure. Every minute, every bit of energy and focus we give to 9/11 is stolen from the amount of time we have to concentrate on how to avoid the next 9/11—and what to do if we fail and it happens. What should we be giving our attention to? What should we be passionate about, dedicated to, focused on? Here is one of many things: making sure our children are inoculated against smallpox. We know bioterrorism is more than possible, and we know few Americans under thirty have been vaccinated; we wiped out world smallpox, and stopped vaccinating in 1972. My son was born in 1987. When were your kids born? Here is another thing. Why isn't our government telling people, through television and pamphlets and speeches and announcements, what they need to do to survive a potential nuclear attack? Why aren't they launching a great campaign now to tell us what we can do in case of one? Is the government getting together the medicines and protections necessary to help the poor of the cities who, in a moment of terrorism, would have nothing to protect them? If not, why not? What should Mom and Dad in the suburbs do if they see a flash of light and a two-mile-high cloud in the city twenty-two miles away?

Why aren't we addressing these things? In part I think because humans just aren't good at facing terrible things that are future things. They face today and think of yesterday. And in part because we are distracting our officials with the demand that they make their lame explanations for how they failed last time. Yesterday Mr. Mueller testified most of the day. I would rather he had spent the day concentrating on finding terrorists. Wouldn't you?

As you read this I want you to do something. If you think that another bigger, more terrible shoe will not drop in our time, stand up right now.

You're still sitting. Because just about every sane and sentient adult knows that more shoes will drop, some with a deadening thud.

If you think New York City will not be a target, or the target, of the next big shoe or shoes, stand up.

You're still sitting. Me too. I don't know many people in my beloved city who don't think we're still targeted, we're a top target, and the madmen who mean to harm us won't be happy until the skyscrapers are cinders.

If you think Washington will not be a target, or the target, of the next big shoe or shoes, stand up.

You're still sitting. Me too. Which has the benefit of giving us something in common with, say, the Senate. They're kind of sitting around too.

Think dark. There is nothing the madmen would rather do than take out or disable two of the biggest, most central entities that unite us in America, the seat of our financial institutions and power and the seat of our government.

Be dire. Imagine: On the same day, New York and Washington are, say, dirty-nuked. This will cause chaos, pain and horror of almost unimaginable proportions. And yet we must imagine.

We are living in a time when it is one's patriotic duty to be imaginative. And then to imagine what we can do, now, to keep The Second Terrible Thing from happening, or to help us all survive and struggle through The Second Terrible Thing.

We are not doing this.

We are in the middle of another systems failure.

We are busy for instance debating absurdities. Such as: In an era in which certain Arab and Muslim males roughly eighteen to forty years old are taking active steps to severely damage the United States and kill Americans, is it wrong to give added scrutiny to Arab and Muslim males eighteen to forty years old as they attempt to enter America, board planes, rent charter planes and ask for maps to the nearest nuclear power plant?

How absurd and clueless do you have to be to be having this debate? You have to have surrendered all common sense.

Here is my emblematic moment for the systems failure we are currently in—not the one that caused 9/11 but the one that continues, that we're in now. I was in an American airport a few months ago. I was in line with thirty or so people waiting to board a plane. I watched—we all watched—as an elderly couple, a man and woman in their seventies or eighties, were ordered out of line to be searched. They were old, frail, embarrassed. They stood forty feet away from us, their shaky arms held wide as they were wanded by a low-wage worker not endowed with enough human grace to show them sympathy or respect. The old man and the old woman were forced to take their shoes off when everyone knew—we could see it—that it was hard for them.

It is a great regret of my life, and I am ashamed of it, that I did not attempt to intervene. I knew that if I did I, dangerous middle-aged American female terror threat that I am, would cause myself the kind of trouble that would mean missing the plane and disappointing my son, who was at home waiting.

So I did nothing, and in the end we were all allowed to board. But I will never forget that couple being searched, thanks to the heightened compassion of Norm Mineta.

Norm Mineta, our transportation secretary, has a searing memory, and that memory determines U.S. airport security policy in 2002. When he was a little boy at the start of World War II, Mr. Mineta and his Japanese-American family were sent to an interment camp. It was unjust and wrong. The Japanese of America in 1942 were American citizens, not illegal aliens or visitors newly arrived; moreover, they had never, not one of them, launched an attack on the United States. What FDR did to them was wrong.

But the facts of Japanese-Americans in 1942 do not parallel the facts of our enemies today. Our enemies have already killed civilians and announced they will kill more. We know who the enemy is—we know many names, and we certainly know the general profile—and we have every right, or rather duty, to give those who fit the profile extra scrutiny. Instead we play games and waste time wanding people we know to be innocent, and searching their tired old shoes. We do this to show we're being fair. But we really know otherwise, all of us.

We are being irresponsible and careless in the hope that history will call us tolerant and compassionate. It is vanity that drives us, not the thirst for justice and a safer world. Mr. Mineta has received many awards for his sensitivity to ethnic profiling. Good for him, but I'd personally give him an award if he'd begin to act like a grownup and recognize that his childhood trauma shouldn't determine modern American security policy.

We are acting as if we don't know what time it is.

This is an unprecedented moment in human history. It is an unprecedented moment in the history of the United States of America. We face the threat of bit-by-bit, piece-by-piece attempts to undo our country through weapons of mass destruction that are carried and created by the delusional, the malformed, the mad.

The longer we obsess on the systems failure that contributed to 9/11, the more we contribute to the next systems failure. The more we indulge our vanity, our petty concerns and our bureaucratic gamesmanship, the more we contribute to the next 9/11, and its systems failures.

My government is very busy with a conversation about how it failed to protect us on 9/11. Too bad it isn't busy protecting us from the next one. That's where we should direct our energy, our focus, our time.

Or we can just let the next shoe drop, and then hold congressional hearings about that systems failure.

39

Rudy's Duty

Will President Bush get his proposed Department of Homeland Security through Congress? Yes. Should he? Yes. Why? Because what preceded it didn't work; because it is what we have at a moment when time is of the essence; because an administration that has the responsibility of keeping the nation safe from terrorists must be given the authority, power and structure to do so; because no one—no one—knows if moving boxes on a federal flowchart makes complete sense, but giving the administration what it asks for leaves them fully accountable for its success or failure, and that does make sense; because if defending our nation against the terror threat is the great necessity of the age and the government's number one job—and it is—then a single department dedicated to that function is in order.

We think labor is important and we have a Labor Department, ditto transportation and a Transportation Department. When you have a huge and crucial task being shared by a half dozen departments it doesn't work. Sometimes you have to tear down and rebuild. A friend of mine, as part of his living, helps big companies merge; he finds the bureaucratic pressure points, the likely weak points, the overlapping, the pending personality conflicts. When I asked him sometime back what the government should do about the FBI/CIA mess, he said: "Start over. Make it new."

Or as Napoleon said and generals quote, "Never reinforce failure."

· · ·

President Bush should do two things to get the department he wants and to increase its chance of ultimate success.

The first and more important is to name Rudy Giuliani now as his nominee for head of the new department.

It is absurd even to consider anyone else. Mr. Giuliani may in fact be the only person who could do it. He has the standing for the job. He is the symbol of 9/11 leadership and 9/11 suffering, of 9/11 success and American toughness. He is a galvanizing, dramatic figure who comes with his own klieg lights. People on the ground admire him, and people in the bureaucracy will fear him. This is good.

Tom Ridge, through little fault of his own, is a symbol of failure, a symbol of a governmental response that so far has not worked. He is Mr. Yellow Alert.

Mr. Giuliani's unique standing gives him the one thing the new director must have: pull and sway with Congress and the public to do what needs to be done, from profiling to a national ID card to fingerprinting to taking on Norm Mineta's Transportation Department for its security rules, which at once betray a frightened timorousness and an unwillingness to respect others (e.g., pilots can't be armed because they can't be trusted not to run around shooting people). Unlike Mr. Mineta, Mr. Giuliani knows what time it is. And he loves to tell people what he knows.

Just as important, the national press is invested in his excellence. The media have been celebrating Mr. Giuliani for nine months as *the best we have*. (Or, as David Letterman put it, "This, ladies and gentlemen, is a man.") Because they are invested in Mr. Giuliani's excellence, they will be invested in his success as homeland security secretary. The story line will go this way: 9/11 champion becomes terrorism savior. When reporters are invested in a story line like that they help it come true. They can't help themselves.

Tom Ridge's story line will be: The guy who didn't do it right is given new authority to not do it right. And reporters will help that story line come true, too.

The new department will be a bureaucratic nightmare—a new agency that is the third largest in the government, employing 169,000 people. It will need an experienced tough guy to run it. Mr. Giuliani has the right background—eight years in New York's fractious political and bureaucratic fields, eight years in the Justice Department as a killer prosecutor. Remember when he had U.S. agents drag some Wall Street guys off the trading floor in shackles and chains? That's the kind of overkill that bureaucrats never forget, and that would not, frankly, be utterly and totally unwelcome in the new role.

Moreover, the announcement that it would be Rudy will help get the new department through Congress in one piece. Mr. Bush can't afford to let it bog down or be torn apart. The White House could send Mr. Giuliani up to the Hill to give testimony on how he envisions the new agency, which would no doubt be riveting, increasing public support and putting new pressure on Congress to move.

None of the other rumored potential nominees carry Rudy's standing, his ability to rally, to lead, to command respect. Which makes him such an obvious choice you have to wonder why Mr. Bush hasn't chosen him.

Mr. Bush is often accused of preferring to be around family retainers and what a former colleague of his calls "ethical cronies." I never completely bought this. Mr. Bush likes to be around talent, but yes, he prefers men and women who, as they say in Hollywood, play well with others. Mr. Bush likes Dick Cheney, for instance, because he's solid as a rock—but some of his solidity comes from the fact that he is smooth, cool, and doesn't ruffle feathers that don't need ruffling.

I think it's true that Mr. Bush likes those who add to his luster more than those who might outshine him. This in general is true of political figures. But it is something Mr. Bush should get over—especially now and especially in this case. Right now Mr. Bush needs someone on his team to outshine him. He needs someone who is known to be independent, known as his own persona. Mr. Bush needs a star.

Mr. Bush is not the only problem, not the only one reluctant to pick Mr. Giuliani. Democrats aren't keen to give a historic new platform to a Republican who might run for the presidency in 2008.

But the Democrats should, on this one, be wily. Knowing Mr. Bush doesn't want him, they should push for Mr. Giuliani. The public will love it, Democrats will get credit for backing the right guy, they will be able to claim it's for the good of the country and partisanship be damned, and their efforts will make Mr. Bush look smaller. That's a four-fer. In addition, if Mr. Giuliani gets it and fails they can say he's a Republican—he's Mr. Bush's, it's his fault. If Mr. Giuliani gets it and succeeds, the Democrats did it. Mr. Giuliani is a half-Democrat anyway; he supported Mario Cuomo over George Pataki in 1994. The Dems owe him.

Of course another problem may be Mr. Giuliani himself. He is enjoying being a hero, making money, speaking, being adored. He has not run out of ambition, but he might think he can move forward politically while unattached to office. Just float, goes this thinking, and see what raft comes by. Keep the options open.

But this almost never works. Ask Dan Quayle, Bill Bradley, Bob Kerrey, Colin Powell. If you want to rise in the game, you better be in the game.

And at any rate, Mr. Giuliani owes it to the country. He knows he's the best for this too. Personality and temperament mean a lot in the making of a career. Mr. Giuliani illustrated this when he was mayor of New York. He was both very successful and truly high-maintenance. He led a great city to new heights, and then when the city faced its greatest crisis since Black Friday of 1929 on the black Tuesday of 2001, he led us the way a genius would if he had a big heart.

That day Mr. Giuliani finally found a foe big enough for his aggression. Before then he had brought his own dramas with him, entering each room with a sack of dysfunction on his back, creating new spats and fights when things got slow. His temperament was at odds with peace. He flourishes in war. When there wasn't a war he created battles just for fun and out of need.

Now we have a war, and it is big enough for him. In this war, as a bureaucratic leader and policy setter, his flaws—impatience, combativeness—will be virtues. If Mr. Bush is serious about security—and he is—he should pick Mr. Giuliani. Who even comes with an easy nickname—"The Jewel." Give the Jewel the crown.

The second thing Mr. Bush should do is change the name. The name Homeland Security grates on a lot of people, understandably. *Homeland* isn't really an American word, it's not something we used to say or say now. It has a vaguely Teutonic ring—*Ve must help ze Fuehrer protect ze Homeland!*—and Republicans must always be on guard against sounding Teutonic.

As a brilliant friend who is also actually an intellectual says, "I think it's creepy, in a Nazi-resonating way, any time this sort of home-and-hearth language is used by people who are essentially police. When police honestly call themselves police, or 'domestic security,' I salute and say 'Yes, officer.' When they call themselves 'Protectors of the Hearth,' I get the creeps." He adds, "I'd argue we want to feel we're pursuing our old values in a new more dangerous world" and suggests "trusty, familiar-sounding words as our touchstones."

Who could argue? Not me.

My own imperfect nominee is Heartland Security, which unfortunately sounds like an Omaha-based insurance company, though maybe that's not all bad. But it's hokey. Brilliant readers of this site will likely think of a better name. You are invited to jump in. We'll send your ideas to Karen Hughes who when she is not beating swords into plowshares is said to read this site, and would I'm sure, as she readies to leave the White House, enjoy giving a new name to the new department as her parting gift.

40

Failures of Imagination

FRIDAY, JUNE 21, 2002

Dear Karen Hughes,

The results are in, a consensus is forming, we want you onboard.

It appears we hit a nerve last week when we asserted that *Homeland* isn't really an American sort of word but a European, or rather Teutonic, sort of word, and should be retired as the name of the government's new antiterrorism agency. In the past year no one has wanted to make an issue of this when other things, such as whether terrorists planned to blow up the Brooklyn Bridge, seemed more pressing. But if we wait for a perfect time to stop *Homeland* we'll never do it. And it must be done, because words matter.

Last week I outlined the arguments against *Homeland*. Let me add two more. First, the essence of American patriotism is a felt and spoken love for and fidelity to the ideas and ideals our country represents and was invented to advance—freedom, equality, pluralism. "We hold these truths . . ." The word *Homeland* suggests another kind of patriotism—a vaguely European sort. "We have the best Alps, the most elegant language; we make the best cheese, had the bravest generals." It summons images of men in spiked helmets lobbing pitchers of beer at outsiders during Oktoberfest.

When you say you love America, you're not saying our mud is better than the other guy's mud. And the name of the newest and most important agency in recent history, charged with the crucial task of thwarting terrorism and protecting our nation from weapons of mass destruction be they chemical, biological or nuclear, should reflect this.

Second, the Homeland Security Agency headed by Tom Ridge was not a conspicuous success, and was in fact nightly monologue fodder on Leno and Letterman. So it makes sense, as we create a new agency, to give it a new name. *Homeland* failed. Start over, make it new, change the title.

To what? The redoubtable Mickey Kaus of Kausfiles.com, shoulder to shoulder in this battle (even National Public Radio has joined us, making it either bipartisan, nonpartisan or multipartisan), has been collecting names. So have I. Brilliant readers of this column sent brilliant ideas. (I hope you looked at their letters. We got a lot. Almost none supported the use of *Homeland*.)

As you ready to leave Washington for Texas, Karen, please give the president and his advisers, as your parting gift, three or four of the following suggested names from the Kaus/Noonan list:

- Department of Domestic Defense, or 3-D
- Department of Domestic Security, or DDS
- Department of Interior Security, DIS
- Department of Federal Safety, DFS
- Department of Civilian Security, DCS
- Mainland Defense, MD
- Department of Mainland Security, DMS
- Federal Security and Intelligence, FSI
- Department of American Protection, DAP
- Homefront Security, HS
- Department of Security, DS
- Civil Security, CS
- Department of Civil Defense, DCD

Any one of these would be an improvement on Homeland. As an NPR commentary said last week, "We do live in a world where real enemies mean us real harm. We do have to fight them. We have to defeat them. But in every battle we've fought and won our most powerful weapons have always been words. We ought to use the best ones we can find now, which means the ones that sound most like us."

One cannot improve on such wisdom.

A final reason the administration should change the name. If the Republicans don't do it the Democrats likely will. It is hard to imagine the literate and savvy Senator Joseph Lieberman or the tactful and shrewd Senator Diane Feinstein, both involved in congressional efforts to shape the new agency, being linguistically numb to the name of an agency whose creation will figure in their legacies.

They'll change it. So beat 'em to it.

My best to you. Go write a book on what it means to return to life.

Peggy

Now on to other elements in the issue of our physical security. One senses that slowly but hopefully surely, federal and state governments are finally moving forward on actions to make our people safer in the age of weapons of mass destruction. Your basic citizen, busy living his own life, is still inclined, amazingly enough, to think "the government" is taking care of business. But governments are run by politicians, and politicians respond to pressure. No pressure, no progress.

Here is an example of a political figure making progress. In New Jersey, Governor Jim McGreevey has decided the state will distribute potassium iodide pills—that is, radiation-protection pills—to residents who live anywhere near a nuclear power plant. The pills will be free. They are being given to the state itself, appropriately so, by the federal Nuclear Regulatory Commission. If the pills are taken either just before or just after exposure to radiation they hinder the thyroid gland's ability to absorb radioactive iodine.

This is good. A cheer for Governor McGreevey. A cheer too, perhaps, for his focus groups. He may have consulted one or two; perhaps they made it clear that they do not disapprove of state leaders making decisions and announcements that are by their nature unpleasant and anxiety-inducing. As focus groups move, so moves the nation.

Here I will repeat what a Democratic official told me in the late 1990s when I asked him, in a private conversation, why Bill Clinton wasn't moving to make civil defense and defense against terrorism a great issue of his final term. People will thank him, I said, and if he's so worried about his legacy this is how to get one. The Democratic official, a charming and intelligent man, shook his head. He agreed with me, he said, but Clinton is driven by the polls, he'll never do anything that isn't high in the polls.

Well, Mr. Clinton got his legacy. But politics is full of Little Clintons, and if our leaders are not pressed to make our population safer they will not do it. It's up to us.

It has occurred to me recently that civil defense in America is like being a cancer patient. If you have any friends with cancer, you know they have been forced to become experts on their illness. With so much experimentation going on, with so many swirling changes in the field of cancer research, every protocol, every treatment is debatable. There's no one sure way to arrest this cancer or that; there are a myriad of possibilities—scores of schools, regimens, theories. More and more, cancer patients are forced to seize the initiative, make the big decisions, study, oversee treatment.

This, in a way, is where we are on civil defense. We have to do it. We have to think and study on our own. And then we have to push the "doctors," our political leaders. If we don't do it, it won't get done.

Which gets us to smallpox. Smallpox as you know is a potent biological weapon that could be used against our country by those who wish us ill. We have known this for a long time. We know also that this virus has the potential to kill thousands, tens of thousands, millions. (When Cortez's men brought it to Mexico it killed more than three million Aztecs.)

Why would it be so effective now as a weapon against America? Because, as you know, almost no Americans have been vaccinated against smallpox since 1972. We stopped our national vaccination program because it was thought that smallpox had been eradicated throughout the world. The last known case was reported in Somalia in 1977.

It happens that I am lucky. One day in grade school I noticed I didn't have the scar on my arm that everyone else had. When I was in college and hoping to travel abroad, I went to Dr. Miller's office in Rutherford, New Jersey, and asked to be vaccinated. He pulled out a needle and gave me the shot.

I was probably one of the last people vaccinated in America. Lucky me. But my son, born in 1987, was never vaccinated. Were your children? Were you? Not if you're under thirty you weren't.

Unless you're a medical professional. We'll get to that later.

. . .

Last summer, shortly before the attack on America, the Centers for Disease Control's Advisory Committee on Immunization Practices came out with its study of and recommendations on the smallpox threat. It makes for fascinating reading. It said use of the smallpox virus as a biological weapon would have "substantial public health consequences" but asserted it was "unlikely." Why unlikely? Because of its "restricted availability." How did they know terrorists couldn't get their hands on it? They didn't say.

Which was odd. We knew then and know now that there are stores of the smallpox virus in Russia; we don't know exactly how secure they are, and we have reason to suspect that other nations, including North Korea and Iraq, may have illegal supplies. We know smallpox is highly lethal, and we know it can be spread different ways, including aerosol spray.

But the CDC panel spoke with the kind of authority doctors seem to get the day they receive their degrees, and they had recommendations. They were: If smallpox happens, we should "declare an emergency." If you see smallpox, you should call the CDC. As to those who become sick, we must "isolate" and "observe" them. "Medical care of more seriously ill smallpox patients would include supportive measures only." Why? Because currently, "specific therapies with proven treatment effectiveness for clinical smallpox are unavailable."

Oh.

Should we look into that? They didn't say.

What they did say, in short, is that there's no real reason to inoculate the public, and if smallpox is introduced by terrorists, we should make the sick as comfortable as possible and watch them closely as they expire.

That's what I call a plan. An idiotic one, but a plan.

This week the CDC is again studying smallpox, and one hopes this time their report will get a lot of attention. The panel—it's the CDC's Advisory Committee on Immunization Practices again—has been charged with advising on whether Americans should be allowed to get the smallpox vaccine if they want it. *The New York Times* reported Wednesday that the leader of the study, Dr. John Modlin of Dartmouth Medical School, is approaching his work with great concern. What is he concerned about? The *Times* reports he's not sure the threat of a biological attack using smallpox is real, or real enough, or likely enough.

Odd. Just last summer the committee "knew" terrorists probably couldn't get their hands on smallpox. So they didn't move forward with a national vaccination program. Now they can't move forward because they don't "know" the actual risk of a bioterror attack. It makes me shake my head. Does it make you shake yours?

No one "knew" a year ago that people shouldn't work above the fiftieth floor of the World Trade Center. It was "unlikely" terrorists would slam a jumbo jet into the Pentagon—if indeed anyone thought of the possibility at all. That is the essence of our problem: No one knows.

No one knows if smallpox will ever be released into America. But if we have the vaccine (and we do; the CDC once announced we don't, but in March 2002 a drug company found 70 million to 90 million doses of vaccine that had been forgotten in some freezers in Pennsylvania, and since then the Bush administration has bought more) and people want to be vaccinated, and they are told of the dangers—smallpox vaccinations can make some people sick, and historically, as Senator Bill Frist, a physician, has noted, the vaccine has caused one death for every million people who receive a first-time vaccination—and they agree to sign a waiver saying they will not sue if the vaccination's outcome is unfortunate, then why not make it available?

Why not let people choose? Why not give them the freedom to protect themselves? It seems odd that we're even debating it. The worst that could happen is that in the next twenty years we are never faced with a smallpox epidemic and so didn't need to be vaccinated. That's a pretty good worst case.

Right now virtually the only Americans who receive vaccinations against smallpox are medical professionals such as the CDC's own first-response units. This week the National Academy of Sciences met to discuss smallpox, and asked that local doctors and their staffs be given the vaccine too.

When I read this I thought, God bless doctors, I love them, and they certainly, as professionals who would be exposed by sick patients, need to be vaccinated. But—there's a very rude thought coming—when medical professionals band together to press for protection for medical professionals, one thinks of the very human tendency for people to take care of their own. And take care of themselves. It makes me wonder if the members of the CDC immunization advisory group have been vaccinated. Somehow I can't help but think yes. After all, they're essential.

People have a funny way of protecting themselves while they undertake the strenuous task of debating whether other people, common people, nonessential people, ought to be protected.

People in positions of authority sometimes get like CEOs who complain about the high cost of the company's medical coverage while seeing to it that the board okays payment for the very best and most expensive coverage for the company's officers and their families.

I hope the CDC's advisory board isn't consciously or unconsciously thinking this way. One hopes they're being serious, respectful, and thinking imaginatively.

The astronaut Frank Borman once said a brilliant thing. He was testifying before Congress on the deaths of the three American astronauts who, in 1967, were incinerated when a fire broke out in the space capsule in which they were training. Congress, rightly concerned, called hearings. When Colonel Borman was asked how such a terrible accident could have happened, he could have given many truthful answers. But he chose a broad one of great clarity and meaning. He said, "It was a failure of imagination." NASA had planned for so many things that could have gone wrong. But they never sat back one night and brainstormed about what would happen in an enclosed, oxygen-drenched environment if a short circuit created one spark. Which is what started the conflagration.

"A failure of imagination." One hopes the CDC is not undergoing such a failure. Their immunization panel seems to be asking for certainties—*Yes doctors, we are certain Al Qaeda operatives will introduce smallpox into America on November 13, 2003, delivering it by five "suicide bio spreaders" who will arrive in five geographically equidistant airports*—in the midst of a crisis that derives its very shape and definition from one fact: uncertainty. The unknown. The merely possible.

We don't know what will happen. We must be imaginative, take chances, do our best, protect people. And if that means giving a vaccination to those who want it, give it. Period.

41

Capitalism Betrayed

Three scenes.

It is a spring day in the early 1990s and I am talking with the head of a mighty American corporation. We're in his window-lined office, high in midtown Manhattan, the view—silver skyscrapers stacked one against another, dense, fine-lined, sparkling in the sun—so perfect, so theatrical it's like a scrim, like a fake backdrop for a 1930s movie about people in tuxes and tails. Edward Everett Horton could shake his cocktail shaker here; Fred and Ginger could banter on the phone.

The CEO tells me it is "annual report" time, and he is looking forward to reading the reports of his competitors.

Why? I asked him. I wondered what specifically he looks for when he reads the reports of the competition.

He said he always flipped to the back to see what the other CEOs got as part of their deal—corporate jets, private helicopters, whatever. "We all do that," he said. "We all want to see who has what."

Second scene: It is the midnineties, a soft summer day, and I am crossing a broad Manhattan avenue, I think it was Third or Lexington. I am doing errands. I cross the avenue with the light but halfway across I see the switch to yellow. I pick up my pace. From the corner of my eye I see, then hear, the car. Bright black Mercedes, high gloss, brand-new. The man at the wheel, dark haired, in his thirties, is gunning the motor. *Vroom vroom!* He drums his fingers on the steering wheel impatiently. The light turns. He vrooms forward. I sprint the last few steps toward the sidewalk. He speeds by so close the wind makes my cotton skirt move. I realize: If I hadn't sprinted that guy would have hit me. I think: *Young Wall Street Titan. Bonus bum.*

Third scene, just the other night. I am talking to a shrewd and celebrated veteran of Wall Street and Big Business. The WorldCom story has just broken; he tells me of it. He has a look I see more and more, a kind of face-lift look only it doesn't involve a face-lift. It's like this: The face goes blanched and blank and the eyes go up slightly as if the hairline had been yanked back. He looked scalped by history.

For years, he said, he had given speeches in Europe on why they should invest in America. We have the great unrigged game, he'd tell them, we have oversight and regulation, we're the stable democracy with reliable responsible capitalism. "I can't give that speech anymore," he said.

Something is wrong with—what shall we call it? Wall Street, Big Business. We'll call it Big Money. Something has been wrong with it for a long time, at least a decade, maybe more. Probably more. I don't fully understand it. I can't imagine that it's this simple: A new generation of moral and ethical zeroes rose to run Big Money over the past decade, and nobody quite noticed but they were genuinely bad people who were running the system into the ground. I am not sure it's this simple, either: A friend tells me it all stems from the easy money of the 1990s, piles and piles of funny money that Wall Street learned to play with. That would be a description of the scandal, perhaps, but not the reason for it.

At any rate it no longer seems like a scandal. *Scandal* seems quaint. It is starting to feel like a tragedy. Not for Wall Street and for corporations—it's a setback for them—but for our country. For a way of living and being.

Those who invested in and placed faith in Global Crossing, Enron, Tyco or WorldCom have been cheated and fooled by individuals whose selfishness seems so outsized, so huge, that it seems less human and flawed than weird and puzzling. Did they think they would get away with accounting scams forever? Did they think they'd never get caught? Do they think they're operating in the end times and they better grab what they can now and go hide? What were they thinking?

We should study who these men are—they are still all men, and still being turned in by women—and try to learn how they rationalized their actions, how they excused their decisions or ignored the consequences, how they thought about the people they were cheating. I mention this because I've been wondering if we are witnessing the emergence of a new pathology: White Collar Big Money Psychopath.

I have been reading Michael Novak, the philosopher and social thinker and, to my mind, great man. Twenty years ago this summer he published what may be his masterpiece, *The Spirit of Democratic Capitalism*. It was a stunning book marked by great clarity of expression and originality of thought. He spoke movingly of the meaning and morality of capitalism. He asked why capitalism is good, and answered that there is one great reason: Of all the systems devised by man it is the one most likely to lift the poor out of poverty. But, he asserted unassailably, capitalism cannot exist in a void. Capitalism requires an underlying moral edifice. Without it nothing works; with it all is possible. That edifice includes people who have an appreciation for and understanding of the human person; it requires a knowledge that business can contribute to community and family; it requires "a sense of sin," a sense of right and wrong, and an appreciation that the unexpected happens, that things take surprising turns in life.

Mr. Novak was speaking, he knew, to an international intellectual community that felt toward capitalism a generalized contempt. Capitalism was selfish, exploitative, unequal, imperialistic, warlike. He himself had been a socialist and knew the critiques. But he had come to see capitalism in a new way.

Capitalism, like nature, wants to increase itself, wants to grow and create, and as it does it produces more: more goods, more services, more "liberation," more creativity, more opportunity, more possibilities, more unanticipated ferment, movement, action.

So capitalism was to Mr. Novak a public good, and he addressed its subtler critics. What of "the corruption of affluence," the idea that while it is moral discipline that builds and creates success, success itself tends to corrupt and corrode moral discipline? Dad made money with his guts, you spend it at your leisure. The result, an ethos of self-indulgence, greed and narcissism. The system works, goes this argument, but too well, and in the end it corrodes.

Mr. Novak answered by quoting the philosopher Jacques Maritain, who once observed that affluence in fact inspires us to look beyond the material for meaning in our lives. "It's exactly because people have bread that they realize you can't live by bread alone." In a paradoxical way, said Mr. Novak, the more materially comfortable a society becomes, the more spiritual it is likely to become, "its hungers more markedly transcendent."

Right now Mr. Novak certainly seems right about American society. We have not become worse people with the affluence of the past twenty years, and have arguably in some interesting ways become better. (Forty years ago men in the New York City borough of Queens ignored the screams of a waitress named Kitty Genovese as she was stabbed to death in an apartment building parking lot. Today men of Queens are famous for strapping sixty pounds of gear on their back and charging into the Towers.)

But it appears that the leaders of business, of Wall Street, of big accounting have, many of them, become worse with affluence. Or maybe it's just worse with time. I think of a man of celebrated rectitude who, if he returned to the Wall Street of his youth, would no doubt be welcomed back with cheers and derided behind his back as a sissy. He wouldn't dream of cooking the books. He wouldn't dream of calling costs profits. He would never fit in.

Mr. Novak famously sees business as a vocation, and a deeply serious one. Business to him is a stage, a platform on which men and women can each day take actions that are either moral or immoral, helpful or not. When their actions are marked by high moral principle, they heighten their calling—they are suddenly not just "in business" but part of a noble endeavor that adds to the sum total of human joy and progress. The work they do builds things—makes connections between people, forges community, spreads wealth, sets example, creates a template, offers inspiration. The work they do changes the world. And in doing this work they strengthen the ground on which democracy and economic freedom stand.

They are, that is, patriots.

"The calling of business is to support the reality and reputation of capitalism," says Mr. Novak, "and not undermine [it]."

But undermining it is precisely what the men of WorldCom et al. have done. It is their single most destructive act.

Edward Younkins of the Acton Institute distills Mr. Novak's philosophy into "Seven Great Responsibilities for Corporations": satisfy customers with good services of real value; make a reasonable return to investors; create new wealth; create new jobs; defeat cynicism and envy by demonstrating internally that talent and hard work will and can be rewarded; promote inventiveness, ingenuity and creativity; diversify the interests of the republic.

As for business leaders, their responsibility is to shape a corporate culture that fosters virtue; to exemplify respect for the rule of law; to act in practical ways to improve society; to communicate often and openly with investors, pensioners, customers and employees; to contribute toward improved civil society; and to protect—lovely phrase coming—"the moral ecology of freedom."

To look at the current Big Money crisis armed with Mr. Novak's views on and love of capitalism is to understand the crisis more deeply.

Businessmen are not just businessmen. They are not just moneymakers. Businessmen and -women are representatives of, leaders of, exemplars of an ethos and a way of life. They are the face and daily reality of free-market capitalism.

And when they undermine it with their actions they damage more than their reputations, more than the portfolios of investors. They damage and deal a great blow to our country. They make a great and decent edifice look dishonest and low because they are dishonest and low.

When we call them "thieves" or "con men" we are not, with these tough words, quite capturing the essence of the damage they do and have done.

It would be good if some great man or woman of business in America would rise and speak of that damage, and its meaning, and how to heal it. It would be good if the Securities and Exchange Commission held open hearings in New York on what has been done and why and by whom, and how they got away with it until they didn't anymore. It would be good if the business leaders of our country shunned those businessmen who did such damage to the very freedoms they used to make themselves wealthy. And it just might be good if some companies, on the next casual Friday, gave everyone in their employ the day off, with just one assignment: Go read a book in the park. They could start with *The Spirit of Democratic Capitalism,* and go from there.

42

The Lights That Didn't Fail

WEDNESDAY, JULY 3, 2002

I mark the coming holiday remembering the words of a friend of Samuel Johnson, who said, "I meant to be a philosopher, but happiness kept breaking through."

Tomorrow is the Fourth of July, and we must celebrate. Let us hold high a single sparkler to honor those American institutions that, in this interesting year, did not flounder or fail. Much has been said of those that did— Wall Street, big business, big accounting, the Catholic Church, the FBI and CIA. But most didn't. Some stayed good and some improved and some seem to summon a metaphor: While the towers of the institution tottered, the men and women who worked within them took the stairs two at a time, hauling eighty pounds of gear to save the structure.

So: Let us hold a single sparkler to the lights that didn't fail.

The U.S. military. Honored more than ever across the country and the world. They're not just tough, they're smart and brave, and to the extent we dig our way out of the current crisis they'll be the ones with the shovels and pails.

Cops and firemen. Once patronized, now poster boys, and rightly so. They're exemplars of courage and sacrifice, especially the firemen. What they did at the Towers last September was like what was done at Omaha Beach on D-Day: They raced to fight a battle and proved we'd win a war.

Airline pilots and stewards. Under incredible stress, in a fearful time, without combat pay, they get us seated, settled and flying safely and in style. They have tons of guts. They do their jobs in spite of terror threats, pressure from family and friends to get out, and Department of Transportation rulings and methods that seem almost deliberately designed to encourage the bad guys and discourage the responsible.

The men and women of newspapers. We forget until history reminds us. But there are times when the lengthy, detailed, independent coverage of the great newspapers, and the gutsy work of reporters and editors, is irreplaceable. The past year reminded us of what Thomas Jefferson said: Given the choice between government and a free press, he'd take the free press.

American television. More news shows, more stations, more networks means more voices, more views. Only twenty years ago Big Media still had a monopoly on information, greatly pleasing those who found stimulation in bland, gray-suited corporate liberalism. It's changed. Now more than ever we need options, now more than ever we have them. And: On 9/11, reporters and crews on the ground in New York literally risked their lives to get the story and the pictures.

Television entertainment. Once MGM had "more stars than there are in heaven," but now the great studio of our time is a cable outfit. HBO will be studied by future social historians who'll ponder the cultural impact of groundbreaking drama from *The Sopranos* to *Six Feet Under* to *Oz.* No network has reached such a consistently high level of product excellence since William Paley's CBS, in the first golden age of television, when his shop was called the Tiffany Network.

American wit. From Conan to Dave to Jay to Comedy Central. It more than thrives, it keeps the country together each night as comics and writers tear apart What Isn't Working Now.

Science and medicine. Research labs, new treatments, technologies, medicines. All continue as the best in the world. Some day someone really will cure cancer. It will happen here.

The Internet. On 9/11, it was the light that didn't fail. Phones in New York and Washington went down but the Internet kept humming. Separated parents, children and friends instant-messaged news of their safety, or wrote last words. And within the Internet this year the rise of a new institution:

Blogging. The 24/7 opinion sites that offer free speech at its straightest, truest, wildest, most uncensored, most thoughtful, most strange. Thousands of independent information entrepreneurs are informing, arguing, adding information. Imagine if we'd had them in 1776: "As I wrote in yesterday's lead item on SamAdams.com, my well-meaning cousin John continues his grammatical nitpicking with Jefferson (link requires registration) 'Inalienable,' 'unalienable,' whatever. Boys, let's fight. Start the war." Blogs may one hard day become clearinghouses for civil support and information when other lines, under new pressure, break down.

Local government. The federal government tends to flail about at the beginning of national crises but local governments continue doing what they do: seeing that traffic lights work, garbage is hauled, libraries stocked. Local governments provide the basic services of protection of person and property. They did their job this year.

The local church. Whatever is happening in the higher structure, chances are the ministers, priests, nuns, rabbis and brothers on the ground in your hometown are doing the work of God. They're like airline pilots and stewardesses: They're saving the institutions they represent by doing their daily work with professionalism and love.

American abundance. From the farm fields to your table it all still worked, and shows no signs of weakening. A friend wrote the other day: "Have you tasted the peaches this year? So sweet they'll make you cry, the best in years. Tomatoes too."

The American Dream. Our greatest institution. Our greatest tradition. It proceeds apace. Individual dreams continue to flourish, and we chase them with a freedom of movement, an encouraged creativity and a sense of possibility that remain unparalleled.

The other day I went to the oath-taking ceremony for new citizens at the U.S. District Court in Brooklyn. There were hundreds of people in saris, in skullcaps, in suits made in Romania. There was a hugely pregnant woman from Nigeria, dressed in a red-and-white plaid cotton dress; there were young Eastern European women in too-tight pants from the Gap; there were young men in gym clothes. The usual mix from all over the world. They were so happy to be joining what others of us were lucky enough to be born into. They knew they were in the right place doing the right thing, and changing their lives for the better.

New Americans. We hold high this sparkler for you.

43

Privileged to Serve

FRIDAY, JULY 12, 2002

Maybe he was thinking, "Ask not what your country can do for you, ask what you can do for your country." Maybe it was visceral, not so much thought as felt and acted upon. We don't know because he won't say, at least not in public. Which is itself unusual. Silence is the refuge of celebrities caught in scandal, not the usual response of those caught red-handed doing good.

All we know is that twenty-five-year-old Pat Tillman, a rising pro football player (224 tackles in 2000 as a defensive back for the Arizona Cardinals, a team record) came back from his honeymoon seven weeks ago and told his coaches he would turn down a three-year, $3.6 million contract and instead join the U.S. Army. For a pay cut of roughly $3.54 million over three years.

A week ago, Pat Tillman "came in like everyone else, on a bus from a processing station," according to a spokesman at Fort Benning, and received the outward signs of the leveling anonymity of the armed forces: a bad haircut, a good uniform and physical testing to see if he is up to the rigors of being a soldier. Soon he begins basic training. And whatever else happened last week, nothing seems bigger, and more suggestive of change than what Pat Tillman did.

Those who know him say it's typical Tillman. In college, he sometimes climbed to the top of a light tower to think and meditate. After his great 2000 season, he was offered a $9 million, five-year contract with the

234

St. Louis Rams and said thanks but no, he was happy with the Cardinals.

But it was clear to those who knew Mr. Tillman that after 9/11 something changed. Len Pasquarelli of ESPN reported that the "free-spirited but consummately disciplined" starting strong safety told friends that "his conscience would not allow him to tackle opposition fullbacks where there is still a bigger enemy that needs to be stopped in its tracks."

"I'm sorry, but he is not taking inquiries," said the spokesman at Fort Benning. She laughed when I pressed to speak to someone who might have seen Mr. Tillman or talked to him. Men entering basic training don't break for interviews. Besides, "he has asked not to have any coverage. We've been respecting his wishes. And kinda hoping he'd change his mind." Mr. Tillman would, of course, be a mighty recruiting device. The army might have enjoyed inviting TV cameras to record his haircut, as they did with Elvis. But Mr. Tillman, "wants to be anonymous like everyone else."

Right now he has thirteen weeks of basic training, then three weeks of Airborne School, and then, if he makes it, Ranger School. "It's a long row," said the spokesman, who seemed to suggest it would be all right to call again around Christmas. Until then he'll be working hard trying to become what he wants to become.

Which I guess says it all.

Except for this. We are making a lot of Tillmans in America, and one wonders if this has been sufficiently noted. The other day friends, a conservative intellectual and his activist wife, sent a picture of their son Gabe, a proud and newly minted Marine. And there is Abe, son of a former aide to Al Gore, who is a lieutenant junior grade in the Navy, flying SH-60 Seahawks. The son of a noted historian has joined up; the son of a conservative columnist has just finished his hitch in the Marines; and the son of a bureau chief of a famous magazine was commissioned a second lieutenant in the army last month, on the day he graduated from Princeton.

As the Vietnam-era song said, "Something's happening here." And what it is may be exactly clear. Some very talented young men, and women, are joining the armed forces to help their country because, apparently, they love it. After what our society and culture have become the past thirty years, you wouldn't be sure that we'd still be making their kind, but we are. As for their spirit, Abe's mother reports, "Last New Year's, Abe and his roommate were home and the topic came up about how little they're paid compared to the kids who graduated at the same time they did and went into business.

"Without missing a beat the two of them said, 'Yeah—but we get to get shot at!' and raised their beer bottles. No resentment. No anger. Just pure . . . testosterone-laden bravado."

The Abes and Gabes join a long old line of elders dressed in green, blue, gray, white, gold and black. Pat Tillman joins a similar line, of stars who decided they had work to do, and must leave their careers to do it. They include Jimmy Stewart, Clark Gable and Tyrone Power in World War II; Ted Williams and Joe DiMaggio in the same war; and quarterback Roger Staubach in Vietnam. It is good to see their style return, and be considered noble again.

And good to see what appears to be the beginning of a change in armed forces volunteering. In the Vietnam era of my youth it was poor and working-class boys whom I saw drafted or eagerly volunteering. Now more and more I see the sons and daughters of the privileged joining up.

That is a bigger and better story than usually makes the front page. Markets rise and fall, politicians come and go, but that we still make Tillmans is headline news.

44

The Nightmare and the Dreams

FRIDAY, JULY 19, 2002

It is hot in New York. It is so hot that once when I had a fever a friend called and asked me how I felt and I said, "You know how dry and hot paper feels when it's been faxed? That's how I feel." And how I felt all day yesterday. It is hot. We feel as if we've been faxed.

I found myself fully awake at 5 A.M. yesterday and went for a walk on the Brooklyn Bridge. Now more than ever the bridge, with its silver-corded cables and dense stone casements, seems like a great gift to my city. It *spans*. In the changed landscape of downtown it is our undisturbed beauty, grown ever more stately each year. People seem to love it more now, or at least mention it more or notice it more. So do I. It's always full of tourists but always full of New Yorkers, too.

I am struck, as I always am when I'm on it, that I am walking on one of the engineering wonders of the world. And I was struck yesterday that I was looking at one of the greatest views in the history of man's creation, Manhattan at sunrise. The casements were like medieval arches; the businessmen with umbrellas like knights without horses, storming the city walls; and the walls were silver, blue and marble in the light.

And all of it was free. A billionaire would pay billions to own this bridge and keep this view, but I and my jogging, biking and hiking confreres have it for nothing. We inherited it. Now all we do is pay maintenance, in the form of taxes. We are lucky.

The sun rose in haze, its edges indistinct, but even at 6:30 A.M. you could feel it heavy on your arms and shoulders. When I looked at it I thought of what Robert Bolt called the desert sun in his screenplay of David Lean's *Lawrence of Arabia*. He called it the Anvil.

As I rounded the entrance to the bridge on the Brooklyn side, a small moment added to my happiness. It was dawn, traffic was light, I passed a black van with smoked windows. In the driver's seat with the window down was a black man of thirty or so, a cap low on his brow, wearing thick black sunglasses. I was on the walkway that leads to the bridge; he was less than two feet away; we were the only people there. We made eye contact. "Good morning!" he said. "Good morning to you," I answered, and for no reason at all we started to laugh, and moved on into the day. Nothing significant in it except it may or may not have happened that way thirty or forty years ago. I'm not sure the full charge of friendliness would have been assumed or answered.

It made me think of something I saw Monday night on local TV and thought to point out somewhere along the way. They were showing the 1967 movie *Guess Who's Coming to Dinner?* with Katharine Hepburn, Sidney Poitier and Spencer Tracy, the slightly creaking old drama—it was slightly creaking when it first came out—about a young white woman and a young black man who fall in love, hope to marry and must contend with disapproving parents on both sides. It's held up well, and parts of it seemed moving in a way I didn't remember, and pertinent. Sidney Poitier, who has always brought his own natural standing to whatever part he's playing, had a lovely kind of sweet intelligence, and everyone in the movie was physically beautiful, in the way of the old productions of the old Hollywood.

There was a bit of dialogue that packed a wallop. Spencer Tracy as the father of the would-be bride is pressing Mr. Poitier on whether he has considered the sufferings their mixed-race children might have to endure in America. Has he thought about this? Has his fiancée? "She is optimistic," says Mr. Poitier. "She thinks every one of them will grow up to become president of the United States. I on the other hand would settle for secretary of state." Those words, written thirty-five years ago by the screenwriter William Rose, may have seemed dreamy then. But in its audience when the movie came out would likely have been a young, film-loving army lieutenant named Colin Powell who, that year, was preparing for a second tour of duty in Vietnam. And now he is secretary of state. This is the land dreams are made of. Does that strike you as a corny thing to say and talk about? It is. That's another great thing.

Late Tuesday, on a subway ride from Brooklyn to the north of Manhattan, I resaw something I'd noticed and forgotten about. It is that more and more, on the streets and on the train, I see people wearing ID tags. We all wear IDs now. We didn't use to. They hang from thick cotton string or an aluminum chain; they're encased in a plastic sleeve or laminated; they're worn one at a time or three at a time, but they're there.

I ponder the existential implications. What does it mean that we wear IDs? What are we saying, or do we think we're saying? I mean aside from the obvious.

I imagined yesterday the row of people across from me on the train, looking up all of a sudden from their newspaper, their paperback, their crossword puzzle book, and answering one after another:

"It means I know who I am," says the man in blue shirt and suspenders.

"It means I can get into the building," says the woman in gray.

"It means I am a solid citizen with a job."

"I am known to others in my workplace."

"I'm not just blowing through life, I'm integrated into it. I belong to something. I receive a regular paycheck."

"I have had a background check done by security and have been found to be a Safe Person. Have you?"

I wonder if unemployed people on the train look at the tags around the other peoples' necks and think, *Soon I hope I'll have one too.* I wonder if kids just getting their first job at seventeen will ever know that in America we didn't all used to be ID'd. Used to be only for people who worked in nuclear power plants or great halls of government. Otherwise you could be pretty obscure. Which isn't a bad way to be.

I work at home on my own and do not have an ID. But I am considering issuing myself one and having it laminated at the local Hallmark shop. It will have a nice picture and a title—President, CEO & CFO. I will wear it on the subway and when I get home I will hold it up in front of my doorbell, which

I'll rig so when I swipe the tag my front door pops open. Then I'll turn to the friends I'm with and wink. "I know people here. I can get you in."

A month ago there were news reports of a post-9/11 baby boom. Everyone was so rocked by news of their mortality that they realized there will never be a perfect time to have kids but we're here now so let's have a family. I believed the baby boom story and waited for the babies.

Then came the stories saying: Nah, there is no baby boom, it's all anecdotal, there's no statistical evidence to back it up. And I believed that too. But I've been noticing something for weeks now. In my neighborhood there is a baby boom. There are babies all over in Brooklyn. It is full of newborns, of pink soft-limbed infants in cotton carriers on daddy's chest. It is full of strollers, not only regular strollers but the kind that carry two children—double-wides. And triple-wides. In the stores and on the streets there are babies cooing, dribbling, staring, sleeping. I see them and feel a rush of tenderness. I want to kiss their feet, I want to make them laugh. Kids are always looking for someone to make them laugh. The sight of any dog can do it. The sight of another baby can do it. The sight of an idiotic adult covering her eyes with her hands and moving her hands away quickly can do it. I would know.

I don't care what anyone says, there have got to be data that back up what I'm seeing: that after 9/11, there was at least a Brooklyn baby boom.

A dream boom, too. The other day I spoke with a friend I hadn't seen since the world changed. He was two blocks away when the Towers fell, and he saw everything. We have all seen the extraordinary footage of that day, seen it over and over, but few of us have seen what my friend described: how in the office buildings near the World Trade Center they stood at the windows and suddenly darkness enveloped them as the Towers collapsed and the demonic cloud swept through. "It was total darkness," he told me. But the lights were on. They stood in his office wearing wet surgical masks. They couldn't go out, but inside their building the smoke worked its way into the air conditioning. So they turned it off and stood there sweating and watching on TV what was happening two blocks away.

Did you see those forced to jump? I asked.

"Yes," he said, and looked away. No descriptions forthcoming.

Have you had bad dreams?

"Yes," he said, and looked away. No descriptions forthcoming.

I thought about this for a few days. My friend is brilliant and by nature a describer of things felt and seen. But not this time. I spoke to a friend who is a therapist. Are your patients getting extraordinary dreams? I asked.

"Always," he laughs.

September 11-related?

"Yes," he says, mostly among adolescents.

I asked if he was saving them, writing them down. He shook his head no.

So: The 9/11 Dream Project. We should begin it. I want to, though I'm not sure why. I think maybe down the road I will try to write about them. Maybe not. I am certain, however, that dreams can be an expression of a nation's unconscious, if there can be said to be such a thing, and deserve respect. (Carl Jung thought so.)

To respect is to record. There is a response function at the end of this column, and you can use it to send in your 9/11-related dream—recurring, unusual, striking, whatever. (If you are a psychiatrist, send as many as you like—without identifying your patients, of course.) I will read them, and appreciate them and possibly weave them into a piece on what 9/11 has done to our dream lives and to our imaginations, when our imaginations are operating on their own, unfettered, unstopped, spanning.

45

A Time of Lore

I am thinking about the moment in history in which we are immersed, and as usual my mind turns to the words of a great writer of the movies. In Robert Bolt's screenplay of *Doctor Zhivago,* Lara and Zhivago, near the end of their drama, are huddled at his family's old estate in the Ural Mountains, waiting for the local Bolsheviks to descend. All seems lost, all exits blocked. The wolves of the forest howl with foreboding. Lara comes awake in the night and begins to weep. "This is a terrible time to be alive," she says. "Oh no, no," says Zhivago in all his innocence and belief. "It is a wonderful time to be alive." Life itself, whatever the circumstances, is good; it is a miracle no matter what.

He is right. She is right. It is a terrible time to be alive, it is a wonderful time to be alive. It is wonderful right now. And not terrible but deeply, almost dazzlingly, strange. And we must take note.

You are perhaps reading this at the beach, or after a day at the pool, or at home in your den near midnight as you sneak a bowl of Häagen-Dazs frozen yogurt with fresh strawberries. You are comfortable, well fed, well clothed; the air conditioner hums. Everything feels normal. Everything is! Which is why you haven't gotten your brain fully around the fact that we are living through abnormal times.

We are living Days of Lore. Days of big history. We are living through an epoch scholars fifty years hence will ask about and study. (Yes, I think there will be scholars fifty years hence.) They will see us, you and me, as grizzled veterans of something big. Which is funny since we don't even see ourselves as soldiers.

This is the lore I grew up with, the folklore of an earlier era that brought with it pictures we still carry in our heads: The Great Depression came (bankers jumped from windows, men sold apples on the street). Then came the Dust Bowl (dark and whipping winds leave farms and families uprooted; John Steinbeck's Joads' move to California). Then the war, World War II, the big one (a million newsreels, films and pictures from Henry Luce's *Life* magazine).

But we are living through an era just as big. Bigger, perhaps, or so ultimately I fear. And we haven't fully noticed. The collapse of the bubble, the fall of the market, the sinking of the AOL Time Warner empire (once known as the great house of Luce), the emptying of retirement accounts, the declarations of the biggest bankruptcies in U.S. history—this is the stuff of Lore.

A picture to put in your head: The founder and former CEO of the sixth-largest cable company in America, which is the great cable country, is hauled away in handcuffs, charged with looting his company of hundreds of millions of dollars and bilking investors of billions. John Rigas of Adelphia Communications, seventy-eight years old, does the perp walk in Manhattan surrounded by photographers. His thick white hair stands up uncombed, his eyes seem perplexed, dulled by enormity. He looks like a defrocked priest.

That perp walk, that look, are as much a picture of our times as bankers jumping from windows and Okies selling apples on the street.

All this financial woe, all these economic headlines, take place against a backdrop of a Pentagon attacked, of falling towers and America at war.

Sort of. We know it's going on, but unlike World War II few of us feel it. Do you know anyone who has died or been wounded in it since 9/12? Most of us experience the war as an abstraction, a background against which pundits occasionally explain that an event is occurring.

But it is an abstraction taking place within a new time, the Era of Weapons of Mass Destruction. An era in which the nature of war and warfare has changed utterly, an era that promises, truly promises, bad pain ahead.

•   •   •

The sitting president, our leader, was nine months into a new presidency when history's assault began. He is friendly, intelligent, funny, not deeply experienced in terms of his personal experience but deeply experienced in terms of watching up close the experiences of his father and of the president before his father.

He was elected legally but with fewer votes than his opponent, a new-age whack job who, upon his loss, grew a beard and came to look like a portly Gilded Age banker. This man will have his rematch.

And there is the current president's predecessor, who seems more and more like Warren Harding, president as the Roaring Twenties came to a screeching halt—handsome, gray-haired, wayward, blame-deflecting and, as Alice Roosevelt Longworth memorably said, "a slob."

The Mideast pot boils high, the Gaza front heats up, Osama remains un-caught or is dead. There is strange weather: forest fires historic in their size and destruction, weird temperatures—134 degrees, according to news reports, in a California town two weeks ago—earthquakes, landslides, floods, hail, melting glaciers, weird thunder, weird darkness, everything but locusts . . . and then the Chinese report locusts. Signs, portents of signs, wars and rumor of war.

Time magazine does a cover on Christians who are wondering, for the 2,014th time in history, if we are in the end times, and Christian Web sites buzz with this question: Is God taking the institutions on which we normally lean away from us one by one in order that we might learn to lean more completely on him?

The great man of the age, a giant, the old pope, comes to our continent, to Canada, and arouses now a thing he never inspired, pity. Well, pity and awe. The *Toronto Sun* called the trip "a stubborn act of courage" and said his arrival was "magnificent." On Wednesday when a little girl was pushed forward to greet him on behalf of the children of Canada, she seemed to flinch, accepted his kiss and fled in tears. Her mother later said she was so moved she wept. But she seemed frightened to me, and understandably. Why would God allow the slow public withering of the man who fills the shoes of the Fisherman just as the Church rocks with crisis? Is God allowing the beauty and gallantry of

John Paul's soul to be obscured and hidden from us by the now rough outer shell? Why? Is the pope bearing the woe of the world outwardly, for all of us to see? What does his suffering mean? What are we to learn from it?

Meantime in the church the pope leads, a gathering of American lay Catholics is held in Boston. They seek to wrest some control from the hands of the bishops, and good luck to them. They call themselves "Keep the Faith, Change the Church." The group is only five months old but it draws 4,000 Catholics to its first conference. They gave an award to a priest who has for years acknowledged and uncovered sex abuse within the church. The priest told them that the clergy sex scandals are equaled in their horror "only by the bloodshed of the Inquisition."

Equaled only by the Inquisition! There's a man who isn't afraid to define.

A congressman who regularly fills the Capitol with his deranged banter and whose head looks like the last sanctuary of tree squirrels is expelled this week from the House, the second man to be so removed since the Civil War. The vote was 420–1, the holdout being the congressman famous for being assumed to have murdered his young lover.

And Wednesday came reports that an asteroid hurtling toward earth could hit us in 2019. Which gave me cause for optimism. Think of all our warring parties. We'd come together to battle the asteroid, pooling our best talent and sharing our genius, wouldn't we? And then once we blew the asteroid up, and had a party, and felt safe, we'd get back to fighting again.

It is amazing that all of this is happening, isn't it? This rush of history. Amazing that we are aware of it, see it, shake our heads over it as we eat the Häagen-Dazs, and don't see it. Maybe we are living in a perceptual warp, in a time when so many stray images and thoughts are coming at us that none of them successfully and completely come to us. Five hundred years ago there was Agincourt, a battle that changed Europe's history. And yet most of Europe slept through Agincourt, far from its fields. Most of Europe continued in peaceful oblivion to the fact its life had changed. Word spread but slowly. By the time an old lady living in a hut in Winchelsea heard the news, the news was old, which meant she already knew how the story ended: The world did not end. Her tree hadn't shook. She absorbed the new information by imagining what it was like, and by picking up reports from the gossip of travelers over fires in homesteads acres away. Months away. Years away.

Now we hear of an Agincourt a day. And we don't know what the outcome will be. We don't know how the story will end. We don't know if we'll be able to say: *Yes, but the world did not end.*

This is big stuff, isn't it? I don't know where to go with it. Do you? I have a sense of our initial and surface duty to the facts at least as I've presented them. That we know, first, that we are living in a time of Lore. That we pay attention. That we see the oddness of our time. That we recognize its majesty and bigness, and assume that we were made as big as the time we were born in. That we plow ahead. That we do our best. That we keep our head, talk to God, say our prayers, set an example. That we take notes. And not only park them under a heading that we won't remember but print them out, too, and paste them in a book. That we remember that each day, every day, we go into the world and either make it a little bit better or a little bit worse. And maybe you're in a time of life now that you're making it better. And maybe that's good.

46

John Paul the Great

The pope's trip to the Americas has ended in Mexico with the canonization of the fabled Juan Diego of Guadalupe, the 464th saint recognized by the church since John Paul's papacy began. The pontiff has now recognized more saints than all his predecessors combined. His readiness to canonize is in service of an eagerness to evangelize. This is John Paul's desire: To raise up from as many nationalities, ethnic groups and indigenous peoples as possible a saint who is of them, from them and yet an exemplar of the universal church.

Keep the base and build the base.

Twelve million people lined the streets of Mexico City to greet John Paul the day he arrived—twelve million! The church may have suffered in the field this year, but the troops apparently remain.

What did his trip accomplish? Something big. He proved that no matter how healthy or capable-seeming the pope is or is not, he is here, he is loved, he has power, he is a presence. The trip was a reply to those within and without the church who have called for the pope's resignation or retirement. John Paul said, through his actions, *God decides when a pope "resigns"; God will take the pope from the earth, and as long as God keeps the pope here, the pope will fill the shoes of the Fisherman and do the work of the Lord.*

I don't think we'll be hearing any more calls for the pontiff's departure any time soon. By presenting the fact of his presence, the pope demonstrated not his personal power but the enduring power of the papacy itself, and of the church, too, come hell or high water, come scandal or shame.

On the streets of Mexico City they sobbed as he went by. Did you see it on the news? The pope was in the glass-enclosed popemobile, and as he passed, the people who jammed the streets and sidewalks reached out to him with their hands and burst into tears and sobs. The pope they were reaching for, of course, was not the sturdy, charismatic man in white who had wowed the crowds on his first trip to Mexico as pope, twenty-three years ago.

This man is old, a caged lion bent and spent.

And still they sobbed and reached for him.

Why?

"The force of his presence was like a blow to the heart." That's how the actor Richard Burton described meeting Winston Churchill. I thought of that after I met the pope. It was late June 2000, and I was visiting Rome to speak to a business group. When I was invited to speak I called a friend of a friend in the New York Archdiocese and asked if I could get a ticket to an audience with the pope. She took down the number I'd be staying at and told me to stand by.

I was to be in Rome for five days, and each day I hoped a call would come. The day before I left, the phone rang in my room, and a young woman with perfectly enunciated English told me that the next morning I would see the pope. "Go to the big bronze doors of the Vatican," she said, "and wait."

That's what I wrote in my notes. No address, just big bronze doors, Vatican. The next morning at sunrise I hailed a taxi and said in English: "The big bronze doors of the Vatican," and the driver said, "Okay!," as if he'd been told that destination before. We drove through silent streets. I was excited. You're supposed to get less enthusiastic about people as you get older, or at least less moved by them, and be less impressed by them, but that hasn't happened to me. And the pope was the person I most admired in the world— John Paul the Great. Writer, poet, evangelist, lover of children, comforter of the pained, inspirer of the caged and controlled, resister of fascism, defeater of communism, definer and denouncer of materialism, great foe of the culture of death. A great man of the ages, a man for all seasons and times.

We got to the big bronze doors, and I stood in front of them in the thin morning sun. I knocked. The sound of my knocking seemed tinny, almost comic against the weight of the doors. No one answered.

Soon a young man came by—early twenties, tight black jeans, tight black T-shirt, pierced earrings up and down his ears, pierced earring in his eyebrow, black spiky hair, sideburns shaved to points on the curve of his jaw. We waited silently, looked at each other and looked away. Finally I looked at my watch. "Guess they're not open yet," I said.

He nodded and said, "I'm early."

"Do you have an appointment here?"

"Yes," he said. "I'm going to see the pope."

He was from Canada, he said. He writes rock music and is an aspiring musician. He was in Rome for work and asked his bishop back home if he could see the pope.

I told him I had done the same.

Little by little they came, our motley crew. A hearty, high-colored middle-aged man with an Australian accent, in a sober black suit, his wife and teenage children. They looked like the richest Catholics in Sydney. Then a Polish family in full native costume—dirndls, braided hair, pleated white dresses and blue cotton bows. Soon there were more than a dozen of us.

Suddenly, silently the great bronze doors opened, and we were gestured in by a man in a janitor's clothes. He hustled us up the stairs, past Swiss Guards in their black-and-red uniforms. Up a series of marble stairs, to the right and up some more, then a landing from which one looked down great marble halls. Then up another floor until we were ushered into a huge and stately room of white-gray marble.

Here waiting were more people. There were about thirty of us in all now, and we lined the room standing against the walls. The room filled with excited chatter. I had stuck with my heavy-metal Canadian, and the Australians had stuck with us.

My Canadian looked at me and said, with some urgency, "What do we do when we meet him? How do you meet the pope?"

It hadn't occurred to me to think about this. I shrugged and said, like a happy American idiot, "I think you shake his hand."

"You do?" he said. "I thought you, like, kiss it, or bow."

"I don't know," I said, and turned to the Australian burgher to ask him when suddenly there was silence. Like a blanket of silence had fallen on us. And we all looked in the same direction and suddenly two great doors were opening soundlessly, and then there was a rustling noise, and we stood straight up.

And he entered. John Paul the Great. Massive and frail, full and bent—a man like frail marble. He was dressed in white robes, a white beanie on his white hair. He walked slowly, a cane in his right hand, his head tilting forward. The face expressionless—the Parkinsonian mask.

He stepped into the room and the room burst into applause. And suddenly there was singing. It was a group of dark-haired young nuns dressed in blue. They almost levitated at the sight of him and they had burst into song. He stopped in front of them and his head went back and his chest filled. Then he took his cane and shook it at them merrily and said in a baritone that filled the room, "Philippines!" Feel-ah-PEENZ.

And the nuns exploded with applause because they were indeed from the Philippines and he had known. They one after another knelt on the floor as he walked past.

Now he looked at another little group and he shook his cane comically as he passed them and said, "Brah-SILL!"

And the Brazilians cheered and started to cry.

And the pope moved on, shuffling now, and he walked by an extraordinary-looking young man—coal-black hair, thick and cut so that it was standing straight up. It looked like Pentecost hair. He was slim, Asian, in the dress of a seminarian. He had been watching things dreamily, happily, his hands in the attitude of prayer, and then the pope stopped, turned and held his cane toward him.

"China!" he said.

And the young man slid to his knees, bent toward the floor and moved to kiss the pope's shoe.

And the pope caught him in an embrace as if to say *No, I am not your hero, you are my hero.*

And from nowhere came to me the electric charge of an intuition. I felt with certainty that I had just witnessed a future saint embrace a future cardinal of Beijing.

And my eyes filled with tears.

The pope proceeded down the line, nodding and patting, and when he got to me I jerked into a kind of curtsy-bow and touched his right hand with my hands. Then I bent and covered his thick old knuckles with Chanel No. 23 Red Raspberry lipstick.

I couldn't help it. I think I said, "Papa." He nodded. He was probably thinking, "Oh Lord, another lipstick leaver." And then he pressed into my hand a soft brown plastic envelope bearing an imprint of the papal seal. When I opened it later I saw light and inexpensive rosary beads, the crucifix of which carried an aluminum Christ on the cross, his broken body ungainly and without grace. It is this depiction of Christ that the pope carries at the top of his crozier, the long silver staff he uses when he walks into the world.

I still have the picture of our meeting. I never saw anyone take it and was surprised to receive it in the mail. I look gooney. Like a happy gooney woman transported by bliss.

The last person in line was the Canadian rocker. When the pope came to him, he bowed and kissed John Paul's hand. "I have written music for you," he said. He showed the pope a sheet of music, beautifully done by hand and laminated. It had a title like "A Song for John Paul II."

The pope looked at it and said, "You wrote?"

And the rocker, rocking, said, "Yes, for you."

The pope took it, walked ten feet away to where there was a big brown table, and signed it in a big flourish—Johannes Paulus II. And came and handed it back.

And then he walked on, and out of the room.

There was silence again until it was broken softly by my rocker. "This is the greatest day of my life," he said to me. And my eyes filled with tears again because I knew it was true and because it is a privilege to be there on the best day of another human being's life.

We were ushered out and I went into the streets of Rome and in time hailed a cab and told the cabdriver all about it. I was so excited I left my eyeglasses on the seat. But I still had the rosary beads, and they're here with me right now, right in front of me on my desk.

So when I saw those sobbing, reaching Mexicans I knew what they knew. When you see the pope something happens. You expect to be moved but it's bigger than that and more surprising. It feels like a gaiety brought by goodness. It feels like a bubbling up. I think some people feel humbled by some unseen gravity and others lifted by some unknown lightness.

It's like some great white dove flutters from your chest, emerges and flies upward. And you didn't even know it was there. And all this leaves you reaching outward, toward one who is broken, ungainly, without grace. And it fills you with tears. Or so it seems to me. At least that was my experience.

47

The Fighter vs. the Lover

FRIDAY, AUGUST 9, 2002

The Gore-Lieberman feud is a minor political classic, something to read the newspaper for in this so-far-quiet August. The Republicans are enjoying it because it's Democrats fighting. Al Gore and Joseph Lieberman are enjoying it because everyone's watching them, which underscores their view that they're the two most interesting men in the party. And the other Democrats who are thinking of getting in the ring like it because Mr. Gore may bloody Mr. Lieberman and Mr. Lieberman may bruise Mr. Gore but no one's hurting them.

To recap: Messrs. Gore and Lieberman have been sparring—feinting and jabbing—as they circle each other in the ring.

Mr. Lieberman says Mr. Gore's populist strategy in the 2000 elections was "ineffective"—smack! Mr. Gore says this is no time to "stop telling the truth" to the American people—pow! Mr. Lieberman says Americans reject "us versus them" rhetoric—take that! Mr. Gore says centrism is "bad politics and bad principle"—there's more where that came from, buddy!

Why are the former allies now foes? You know why. Joe Lieberman thinks Joe Lieberman's a winner and Al Gore's a loser. He shares the views of most of the leaders and funders of his party: Mr. Gore is damaged goods, a bad campaigner who wasted the precious patrimony of peace and prosperity, a charm-free zone who took a weird turn in his acceptance speech two years ago this week, abandoning centrist sophistication and embracing Huey Long populism. In the debates with George W. Bush, Mr. Gore seemed like a cross between Frankenstein and Carrot Top. Also journalists, always more important to Democrats than Republicans, do not and never will warm to him.

Mr. Lieberman has a point. Mr. Gore, on the other hand, feels he
plucked Lieberman from the Senate gaggle, got him past the vetting of the
left, made him a person in history, the first Jewish vice presidential nominee, and on top of it all he brought the ticket 500,000 votes more than the
winners (Messrs. Bush and Cheney) got.

Mr. Gore has a point too. Mr. Lieberman has vowed that he will not run
for the Democratic presidential nomination if Mr. Gore does. He has also
told Godfrey Sperling of the *Christian Science Monitor* that he is "meditating and activating" on whether to run. Sounding a lot like Al Gore, he
defined activating as "moving around the country meeting with many leaders, speaking out on issues." He said he will make a final decision after the
midterm elections and before the end of the year.

He says he has no opinion on whether Mr. Gore should run. But everyone knows Mr. Gore is running. So what exactly is Mr. Lieberman doing?

He's having fun and being serious at the same time. He's keeping the
spotlight, he's investigating Enron and helping to fashion a Homeland
Security Department, and he's demonstrating to party leaders that he isn't a
cream puff, he knows how to be aggressive on the issues. By taking on Mr.
Gore, he elevates himself from Beta Man to possible Alpha Man. Good
work for a slow summer.

Mr. Lieberman made it as a moderate. He feels the future of the Democratic Party lies in sympathetic centrism. He sees the vast, vote-rich American
middle class as the true potential home of the party. And again he has a point.
This is how two-term winner Bill Clinton read the playing field, and if Mr.
Clinton knew anything it was popular politics. But while centrism may be
the future of the Democratic Party, it isn't the future of Al Gore.

Politics, as they say, is a game of addition. Middle-class appeals expand the
party, and unite the country. Populism pierces: Its message is often rousing
but inherently divisive. It attempts to divide the electorate between the bad
people who think of nothing but themselves, and the good people who seek
to help the working class. What of those who seek to help working people
through conservative policies? According to left-wing populists, they don't
exist, or don't really mean it, or are unwitting pawns of economic royalists.

In the 2000 campaign, Mr. Gore figured that he would have to rouse his left-wing base to win. And the way to do that, he judged, was to play to the presumed passions and resentments of the little guy. He can argue now that he was right: He did bring out his base.

Still, when Mr. Gore, whose career had been one of self-proclaimed centrism, went left two years ago, many political observers were surprised, including me. I wondered if perhaps Mr. Gore judged himself to be a rather chilly character, a man who could not approach the electorate with a Clintonesque warmth because . . . he doesn't have much warmth.

If you don't have warmth maybe heat is the next best thing. And maybe that's what Mr. Gore's turn to populism was all about.

But his populist stance was never a perfect fit. Mr. Gore never made the old rhetoric new. He never made it something alive and pertinent to the moment. He sounded stale, and merely rhetorical. He was like a bright Ivy League student who had gone to a revival of a Clifford Odets play and thought he'd bring the rhetoric home to upset Dad. Mr. Gore's populism seemed cynical, a mere strategy chosen for the maximum gain of the candidate.

The Gore-Lieberman feud also raises the question of whether, in national politics, it's better to be a Lover or a Fighter. Lovers seem to voters to be driven by a desire to help and protect. The most successful conservatives (George W. Bush, Ronald Reagan) have been Lovers. They may carry the sterner message, but they put it forward with a certain joy and moral confidence. Fighting conservatives don't last so long or do so well. (Ask Fox News analyst Newt Gingrich.)

But there's a downside to Lovers. They can get too soft. A few months ago I asked a Republican senator what President Bush should do next. He said, "Veto something." I asked, what? He said, "Anything!" Meaning: Loverboy ought to show some muscle, jab someone, show 'em who's the man.

With Democrats, too, it's probably true that Lovers flourish and Fighters don't, at least long term. Mr. Lieberman seems to see himself as a Lover, embracing the middle class. He's painting Mr. Gore as a Fighter. And Mr. Gore is helping him. Because he likes the pose of the pugilist. His aggression may be joyless but it's interesting to watch, and makes its own heat. And it can be intimidating. It's just not inspiring. Unless you're the left wing of his party.

<h1 style="text-align: center">48</h1>

The Fall After 9/11

This is written for you to read when you come back from vacation, either this weekend or next week if that applies. So just park it if you like, and come back.

I want only to say: Welcome back.

Maybe you are tired, and need a vacation from your vacation. Or maybe you're a little sad that vacation is over—it was so wonderful, like a gift. Or maybe you feel a little disheartened—you planned for months and arrived at the hotel and it rained and the kids fussed and work called and nothing was really . . . peaceful. And that's what you wanted, peace, harmony and love.

But: Welcome back. Put down your bags. Uncrick your neck. Wonderful things are about to happen.

I have no particular standing to welcome you but someone should, and I have nominated me.

I have been home in Brooklyn the past few weeks. I have been keeping the city safe for you. So has Tomas, who works in the Garden of Eden food shop in Brooklyn Heights. He is from Mexico. He did not have a vacation this summer. He worked, stocking produce and removing products that approached their expiration date. When I talked to him he was spraying the lettuce with water so it would look fresh and bright. He was in a happy mood, and so was I. We have been preparing the city for your return and

256

have had a good time doing it. Everything has been slow and nonintense. Now, as you return, everything will pick up. We're glad. We missed you.

So: You just got home from the beach, or the lake, or your aunt's guest house outside Knoxville, Tennessee.

You unlock the front door, walk into the living room and put down your stuff, your gear—dirty clothes, boogie boards, portable CD players, a backpack full of books, a bag of corn. You open the windows, put on the air conditioner, get the air moving. The house smells unlived in. It smells the way empty houses smell when the real estate agent unlocks the door.

You'll cook something soon and the house will get back its people-live-here smell. You pick up the mail. Bills, circulars, a postcard from Paris. Sale day at JC Penney. School supplies at *Tarjay*.

Realize: It is the beginning of the year. Not the end, but the beginning. This is when school starts. It's when college begins. It's when the new secretary begins work, and when the new vice president at the bank takes over Gil's old office.

It's when you return to a new year.

It's when the latest first impressions you get to make will be made. It's when the government returns, the network anchors return. They will need news. The government will supply it.

It's when the new leather of shoes smells fresh. You'll shop for loafers for the kids tomorrow and pick up one and smell it and every autumn of your life will come back—every autumn. You will half swoon.

Autumn is the beginning of everything.

Are you ready to begin again? It takes a bit of courage on some level, doesn't it? Don't worry. No one else is ready either. You don't have to be. Autumn just comes one night at 3:11 A.M., and you step into it in the morning and are in it and running. This year the thought of autumn fills me with some kind of longing. On the days now that it's cooler than 80 degrees in New York I walk with a spring in my step. I miss autumn, my favorite time of year, and the tenderest time in New York. The parks, never more beautiful than they have been the past few years, are at their most beautiful. The Museum of Natural History and the Metropolitan Museum hang big color-

ful sheets with the names of upcoming shows from their façades. They billow like sails. They move in the breeze. When the wind is high you can
stand under them and hear them snap. All the outdoor vegetable and fruit
stands have new bounty and color. All the kids are rushing to school in
their very newest faded jeans and distressed cotton shirts.

We haven't had an autumn in New York in two years. We lost last
September last year. It was the summer of '01, and then before the leaves
could turn it was the trauma of '01, and we woke up six months later, in
the spring. So all those tender leaves—they didn't register. I would walk
along the streets and think of the old song from *The Fantasticks:* "Try to
remember the kind of September when life was an ember about to billow."
It was sad here as summer elided into winter.

But this year we will have autumn, and we will notice it. This is good.

We will of course mark 9/11. A big question people here ask is: Will the
nonstop all-network 9/11 memorials on TV do harm or good? Is it wallow-
ing? Do we need closure? I think for those fully mature, fully stable people
who have successfully absorbed the past year, the TV stuff won't hurt. And
for those feeling deep wounds and damage, for those who have not so far
successfully absorbed, the memorials may help. In any case they'll happen,
and we'll watch them.

The other day I walked by St. Vincent's Hospital in downtown Manhattan
and thought, as I always do when I walk by: This is where they waited for
the wounded. The interns and nurses waited outside right here with gur-
neys for patients who didn't come. Because so few people were "wounded."
The three thousand were dead. What happened to them?

They were exploded into air. They became a cloud. We breathed them in.

None of us here in New York will ever "get over it," as they say. But
most of us have gotten over it. We continued our lives and enjoy them, and
if you go to any restaurant in the five boroughs there will be laughing and
flirting and people joking and being intelligent and enjoying the food.

The other day I had lunch with two men who run a company that lost
sixty-one people on 9/11. Sixty-one out of fewer than three hundred! They

suffered. They were on the eighty-fourth floor of Tower Two. A wing from the second plane probably tore into their floor. They're having a memorial on 9/11 and they asked me to speak. I don't know what I'll say. No one, really, knows what to say that day. That's why the politicians and governmental leaders will be reading the Gettysburg Address.

We talked at lunch about what that day had been for them. One, Brian, who had been an office fire marshal, had helped a man trapped under debris and then, he still doesn't know why, walked down and out of the tower instead of up. He lived. So did the man he helped from the debris. The only person Brian saw walking up in the tower as he was walking down from the eighty-fourth floor was a coworker named José. José worked in plant management and security. He had a walkie-talkie in his hand. He was going up the stairs because he'd heard from another coworker who was trapped above. He went up to find and help the trapped coworker. José died, and so did the man he was going to help.

A week later Brian had a dream. He dreamt that he was sleeping soundly in his bed when he woke and saw José standing at the foot of the bed, dressed in a kind of billowing white shirt, or gown, and he was fine, and he wanted Brian to know it was all all right. Brian was astonished in the dream, and blinked his eyes wide. Then he awoke for real, blinking his eyes wide, with his head off the pillow and tilted forward, as it would have been if he had really been looking at a man standing at the foot of his bed.

Classic wish fulfillment. Or something else.

I asked him what he thought it meant.

"That José is all right," Brian said. "That they're all fine, all those who died. And that we'll be fine too."

People here keep asking each other if they've changed since 9/11. I say I think I've just become more so. Everything is provisional and tentative. Everything is infused with grace. Life can turn on a dime. There are levels of mystery we don't understand. Life is good in and of itself. These to me are facts that, once you have absorbed them, leave you moving on, and appreciating the moment you're in, and looking forward to steak and merlot and the brightness of friends.

. . .

Life is here.

It is a new year.

Breathe in that new shoe leather, get those new school supplies, make that pie, rearrange those clothes, get out those suits, retire those sandals, line up those pencils, make that appointment, call that meeting, start that diet, gas up the car. It is good to be alive. Sleep good tonight, and deep. Tomorrow you just might step into autumn, which is the beginning of everything.

49

A Heart, a Cross, a Flag

Everyone here now asks, "Where will you be?" They don't say "on September 11." They don't have to. Everyone knows. Most everyone has a plan. Some people are leaving town. They just don't want to go through it again, through the nonstop TV and the weeping families and the memory of the smoke and the sound and the sight of it all.

A lot of people are staying, of course. Those who are working, or going to school; those who can't leave, or won't. I'm one of the latter. I feel a kind of loyalty to that day, and those who suffered through it, and I'm not leaving.

So on Wednesday, on September 11, 2002, I plan to walk across the Brooklyn Bridge before dawn. I will, as I pass under its two heavy stone towers—the original twin towers of downtown Manhattan, and still the most beautiful—reach out my hand and touch them lightly, as you would the arm of an old friend.

On the Manhattan side of the bridge I will make my way to Ground Zero, and watch the sun come up at dawn. I don't know why. I just want to see the new beginning of a new day at the place that was the World Trade Center. I want to see the sun rise and light the skyscrapers all around it.

I will carry in my pocket a little metal cross about two inches high, and a little metal heart the same size. They're twisted and bear burn marks, like pots left too long on the stove.

. . .

One night after 9/11, I went to a church near the site. I poured coffee for construction workers and Con Ed guys on the overnight shift. A construction worker who'd been at the site since 9/11, first trying to find and save people, then trying to clean up, walked up to me. He was a big man in work clothes with a hard hat. He looked beat. He told me he had read my columns, and he told me he'd heard I was here, pouring coffee. He said, "I have something for you." And he pulled from a soft brown paper bag the little cross and the little heart. He had cut them from a beam that held up one of the Towers.

To me they were like an old bullet pulled from the ground of Gettysburg, a treasure of history. When people come to my house and see them on the wall, they're always silent after I tell the story.

I'm going to bring them with me, back to where they came from, on 9/11. I'll probably look at where the Towers used to be and think, The buildings were here. A year ago today they were here. And then they became the cross and the heart.

A year ago on 9/11 it was so beautiful, just the most beautiful day. The school year had just started, and kids downtown were being walked to class. They heard the first plane. They were walking on the sidewalk when the shadow of the plane passed over them.

Where would we be if the shadow hadn't come, if 8:46 A.M. that day had not happened? Where would we be if the whole day had been as peaceful as its start?

We'd be where we were on September 10, 2001.

On September 10, 2001 we were, a lot of us, immersed in a national culture—a big, vivid, full-network, broadband, opens-soon-at-a-theater-near-you culture—that allowed us to live knee deep in distraction. *What's on tonight, who's pitching, when are* The Sopranos *back, who won, when does the sale start?* There was nothing inherently wrong in this—fun is part of life, or should be, and entertainment, art and sports are worthy endeavors. But for a lot of us our emphasis was off. We weren't paying attention to core things, essential things, first things. We were staring at the peripheral, missing the big picture.

And then 9/11 came. The demonic cloud chased modernity down the street. It chased businessmen down the tall and narrow pathways of downtown Manhattan, a city that lives on the periphery of the continent but is at the core of its commercial life, its art, its hedonism and hipness, its focused and full-throttled pursuit of the tangential.

Thousands died. The buildings disappeared. And were transmuted into the cross and the heart.

The heart, to me, stands for the explosion of human sympathy, kindness, forgivingness and generosity that came from the people of our city starting at 8:46 A.M. on September 11, 2001. It's been—and here I think, oddly, not of an American word but of the highest accolade used by an old friend from New Zealand—brilliant. Brilliant and shining. You all know the stories—the friendliness on the streets, the helpfulness to strangers, the millions of volunteers, the money given, the hands held.

The cross stands for a renewed sense of the centrality of the spiritual in our lives. People say it was fleeting, but I don't think so, and I base this simply on my interactions with friends, family and acquaintances who are New Yorkers. Something big happened here. The spiritual was reborn. It started with the spontaneous shrines that filled the city sidewalks last September and it has continued with a greater sense of individual pondering. People are thinking about God. I believe I have witnessed from so many people an enhanced sense of the sacredness of ordinary things, and a greater ability to see grace at work in the lives of others, and ourselves. This week *Newsweek* had the story of the boy in the red bandana. He was a young man in the north tower who didn't think first of his own safety after the planes hit, but tried to help strangers. He pointed them to exits in the smoky corridors, led them down the stairs, carried a woman on his back. He was last seen going up the stairs as others walked down. They found out later who he was, a twenty-four-year-old equities trader. Life is rich and unknowable: You don't know when you'll accidentally bump into hell, you don't know what angel you might meet there.

"He was last seen going up the stairs." Those are famous words here now. Usually we say it about the firemen. It's going to be a long time before we get used to the idea that 343 of them lost their lives that day. Or rather gave them.

Those 343—they were mostly tough Catholic men with soft hearts from the outer boroughs. They were Italians and Irish and Poles and Puerto Ricans, and they lined up for absolution, received a blessing and ran into the buildings lugging their gear. Their funerals were at Our Lady Queen of Peace, and St. Rose of Lima Church. And sometimes at the funerals they played an old 1970s song whose title you'll never hear the same way again: "Stairway to Heaven."

The other day I got a letter from the mother of Michael Dermott Mullan, Ladder 12, Engine 3, 19th Chelsea. He was a graduate of Holy Cross High School, a registered nurse attending Hunter College School of Nursing, a captain in the U.S. Army Reserves stationed at Fort Totten, and a New York City fireman. He must have been some guy, Michael Mullan. His mother wanted all of us to know who he was. She wrote, "He was dedicated to the well-being and protection of his fellow man." She wrote, "He was second-generation Irish by way of County Tipperary, County Down and County Kerry." She wrote, "He loved his God, his Country, his family and his city."

Michael Mullan called from his truck on the way to the Trade Center the morning of the attacks. "He called to tell us, 'I love you. Good-bye, good-bye, good-bye.' Michael never said good-bye—it wasn't a part of him to think good-bye, he would always say, 'See you later,' or 'Take care.' But that fateful day he said good-bye to his family." His body was found on October 7. Then the Mullan family found out about his last hours. After Michael called home he bowed his head and, with a friend on the rig, prayed. Michael and his crew went to the Marriott Hotel, next to the Trade Center. It had been badly damaged, and later collapsed. They made their way to the upper floors and then were ordered out by their lieutenant. The way was blocked, but they found a path down. Then word came there were two firemen on a higher floor who couldn't find a way down. "Michael's last spoken words," his mother said, "were, 'I'll go back and get them.'"

He was probably last seen going up the stairs. He was a man of the heart and the cross.

And the flag. For that was the other thing that reemerged, the explosion of America-love.

We had been losing it as a society, and for a long time.

The immigrants of a century ago arrived to a flag-flying culture. They were told that they were investing their lives, their futures, their unseen grandchildren in something high and good and decent. Free speech was here, the free practice of religion, democracy, the ballot, free markets—everyone, from the brilliant and altruistic to the bright and merely greedy, could get in on the great bazaar, and make his way. What a country—all that freedom and the streets were paved with gold.

They were taught to love America by the culture all around them—the penny newspapers, George M. Cohan, John Philip Sousa, the nascent movie industry, the stage, the schools—taught a burly America-love.

Which was good. Because when you don't love something you lose it.

We were losing it. But now the flags are out again, and loving America isn't considered a faux pas, or evidence of limited intellect. The thing now is to see it doesn't degenerate into mere conceit: "We're number one, we have the best tanks." That's triumphalism.

Patriotism is solid and grounded; it holds up the ideal of a nation founded on the equality of men; it has to do with founding documents, guaranteed freedoms, clear rights, stated responsibilities. That's what the flag stands for.

It's certainly how Michael Mullan must have seen it. And the boy in the red bandanna, too. And that in the end is my 9/11, a trauma that was transmuted into a heart and a cross and a flag. Each expressing a facet of a great and fabled people who are still, one year after, the hope of the world.

50

Time to Put the Emotions Aside

Rudy Giuliani said the other day that he wasn't absolutely sure the next morning, on September 12, that the sun would actually come up. When it did, he was grateful. And so we are today, as we mark the anniversary of the day that changed our lives.

We are all busy remembering. A friend in Washington e-mails in the middle of the night yesterday: She cannot sleep because jets are roaring overhead, and because this is the anniversary of the last time she talked to Barbara Olson. Another e-mail, from an acquaintance: "Last year this time we were comforting each other in instant messages." Most everyone is getting and sending these messages.

I thought it would be flatter, this formal time of remembering, and not so authentic. Days that are supposed to be rich in meaning often aren't. But people seem to be vividly refeeling what they experienced a year ago, and being caught unaware, mugged by a memory. Last week a friend was telling me where he was, and in the middle of the telling a sob rose from nowhere and cut off his words. Yesterday on CNN Rosalynn Carter seemed taken aback by welling tears when she was asked how she had explained terrible events to her children when they were young. She told them, she said, that bad times didn't mean God wasn't there. Bad times meant God was weeping too.

Washington is marking this day with patriotism and a certain martial dignity. New York is approaching the anniversary with solemnity and respect. We are immersing ourselves in the trauma to free ourselves of the preoccupation. The great words of great presidents will be read, and some schoolchildren will hear the Gettysburg Address and the preamble to the Constitution for the first time.

A company of bagpipers will cross the Brooklyn Bridge, retracing the route of the hardy firemen of Brooklyn who roared across the bridge toward Manhattan a year ago this morning. Sirens blaring, they craned their necks to see the smoking ruins of the place where they would make their stand. For six months after that day, bagpipes were the sound of New York in mourning. They were played at all the funerals. None of us in New York will ever hear their rich and lonely wail in the same way again.

What we are doing is taking a last hard and heartbreaking look at what happened last year. In time we will put the memories away, pack them away in a box with a pair of old gloves, and a citation and a badge, and some clippings and pictures. This is what Emily Dickinson called "the sweeping up the heart." She said it was the "solemnest of industries enacted upon earth."

But before we put it all away, there is a story to remember. There was a glittering city, the greatest in the history of man, a place of wild creativity, of getting, grabbing and selling, of bustle and yearning and greed. It was brutally attacked by a band of primitives. The city reeled. We knew what to expect: The selfish, heartless city dwellers would trample children in their path as they raced for safety, they'd fight for the lifeboats like the wealthy on the *Titanic.*

It didn't happen. It wasn't that way at all. They were better than they knew! They saved one another—they ran to each other's aid, they died comforting strangers.

Then the capital city was attacked, and there too goodness broke out. And sleeping boomers on planes came awake and charged the cockpit to keep the plane from hitting the home of the American president.

And then the mighty nation hit back at the primitives, and hit again.

This is, truly, some story. This is not a terrible thing to have to tell our children. It is a warm story. But now a certain coldness is in order.

The sun rises tomorrow on the new era, the post–9/11-trauma era. We will make our way through the next year without the wild emotional force of 9/11 pushing us forward. We can be cool now, and deadly if need be.

This can be the year when we find Osama bin Laden. This, the next twelve months, can be when we deal the death blow to the Taliban, for this drama will not even begin to end until we have laid Osama and Osama-ism low. This is one case in which justice and vengeance are intertwined.

This is the year when the president and his advisers will or will not make the case, as they say, on Iraq. The president thinks a key part of the war on terror will be moving against Saddam Hussein and liberating Iraq from his heavy hand. But if Mr. Bush is to make the case it will not be with emotional rhetoric, with singing phrases, with high oratory. It will not, in this coming cooler time, be made with references to evil ones. All of that was good, excellent and Bushian the past passionate year. But now Mr. Bush should think in terms of Sergeant Joe Friday, "Just the facts, ma'am."

"Saddam is evil" is not enough. A number of people are evil, and some are even our friends. "Saddam has weapons of mass destruction" is not enough. A number of countries do. What the people need now is hard data that demonstrate conclusively that Saddam has weapons of mass destruction which he is readying to use on the people of the United States or the people of the West.

If Mr. Bush has a good case, he will make it and the people will back him. If he does not, he will not convince the American people that blood and treasure must go to this endeavor. The people must believe, as Mr. Bush does, that their children are endangered. There was a time—I think it was September 10, 2001—that Americans may not have been able to accept such an assertion. That time has passed.

There's another area where coldness is called for. The folly of what is happening to our airline industry is due to a wet and weepy conception of what is fair. People are afraid to fly because they see what a politically correct joke our airline security is. Searching for every last toenail clipper, forcing eighty-five-year-old people with walkers to stand spread-eagled as some oafish wand-wielder in a blue jacket humiliates them—this is absurd and cowardly.

Let's get coldly serious: Arm the pilots, fortify cockpits, man flights with marshals and profile passengers. We don't have a transportation secretary who is willing to do these things. Someday when something terrible happens we'll wish we did. Why not coldly remove Norman Mineta now?

Warm tears, honest remembrances, passionate tributes, giving credit where it's due, absorbing 9/11, teaching our children what it meant and means: These are good things. And a little coldness starting at sunrise tomorrow: That will be good too.

Acknowledgments

These pieces were edited patiently and sometimes late at night by James Taranto, Max Boot and Brendan Miniter of *The Wall Street Journal*. They worked hard to make them better. I'm grateful to them, and to everyone at the *Journal*, especially Bob Bartley, great man of journalism, who first asked me, in the spring of 2000, to write regularly. The *Journal*'s Steve Adler approached the publication of these pieces with enthusiasm, charm and encouragement. At Simon & Schuster I am grateful to my low-key, high-producing and talented editor, Dominick V. Anfuso, and to the intrepid and excellent Wylie O'Sullivan, who has one of the great names in publishing. I thank also Martha Levin, Michele Jacob and Isolde Sauer for their assistance and professionalism.

I was working on a book as I worked on a number of these columns, and I thank my friends at Viking Penguin, especially the patient and persistent Pam Dorman, and Susan Kennedy Peterson, who is like a warm and charming general.

As always I want to thank Joni Evans, who in the course of helping me organize myself over the years has become a dear, admired and irreplaceable friend. Thanks also to the tireless, fearless Andy McNicol. I am grateful to a whole troupe of inspiring friends. And I am most grateful to my son, who allowed me to borrow some of his perceptions. I don't imagine it's easy to be the child of a writer, especially an occasionally controversial one, but he acts as if it is.

About the Author

Peggy Noonan is a columnist and contributing editor at *The Wall Street Journal*. Her articles and essays have also appeared in *Time, Newsweek, The Washington Post, Forbes,* and many other publications, and she is a contributor to the award-winning television show *The West Wing*. Noonan is the author of five previous books, including the bestselling *What I Saw at the Revolution* and *When Character Was King*. She was a special assistant to President Ronald Reagan from 1984 to 1986. Noonan currently lives in her native New York City.